B U N T Y

Remembering a Gentleman of Noble Scottish-Irish Descent

Halwart Schrader

Foreword by Gregor Fisken

Translated by Nick Fox

More biographies from Veloce ...

A Chequered Life – Graham Warner and the Chequered Flag (Hesletine)
A Life Awheel – The 'auto' biography of W de Forte (Skelton)
Amédée Gordini ... a true racing legend (Smith)
André Lefebvre, and the cars he created at Voisin and Citroën (Beck)
Chris Carter at Large – Stories from a lifetime in motorcycle racing
(Carter & Skelton)
Cliff Allison, The Official Biography of – From the Fells to Ferrari (Gauld)
Edward Turner – The Man Behind the Motorcycles (Clew)
Driven by Desire – The Desiré Wilson Story
First Principles – The Official Biography of Keith Duckworth (Burr)
Inspired to Design – F1 cars, Indycars & racing tyres: the autobiography of Nigel
Bennett (Bennett)
Jack Sears, The Official Biography of – Gentleman Jack (Gauld)
Jim Redman – 6 Times World Motorcycle Champion: The Autobiography (Redman)
John Chatham – 'Mr Big Healey' – The Official Biography (Burr)
The Lee Noble Story (Wilkins)
Mason's Motoring Mayhem – Tony Mason's hectic life in motorsport and television
(Mason)
Raymond Mays' Magnificent Obsession (Apps)
Pat Moss Carlsson Story, The – Harnessing Horsepower (Turner)
'Sox' – Gary Hocking – the forgotten World Motorcycle Champion (Hughes)
Tony Robinson – The biography of a race mechanic (Wagstaff)
Virgil Exner – Visioneer: The Official Biography of Virgil M Exner Designer
Extraordinaire (Grist)

You can find many more books at:

www.veloce.co.uk

First published in February 2019 by Veloce Publishing Limited, Veloce House, Parkway Farm Business Park, Middle Farm Way, Poundbury, Dorchester DT1 3AR, England. Tel +44 (0)1305 260068 / Fax 01305 250479 / e-mail info@veloce.co.uk / web www.veloce.co.uk or www.velocebooks.com. ISBN: 978-1-787113-48-0 UPC: 6-36847-01348-6

BUNTY

Remembering a Gentleman of Noble Scottish-Irish Descent

Halwart Schrader

Foreword by Gregor Fisken

Translated by Nick Fox

VELOCE PUBLISHING
THE PUBLISHER OF FINE AUTOMOTIVE BOOKS

Contents

I dedicate this book to Hazel Robinson, who spent a great deal of her lifetime joining Bunty as an ever-indulgent and trustworthy assistant. Without her I would not have been able to master this job.

"Nature hath framed strange fellows in her time!"
Salerino in William Shakespeare: The Merchant of Venice, 1.1

PARTICULARLY IN SCOTLAND, BEARERS of the double-barrelled surname 'Scott-Moncrieff' are numerous, they are also found elsewhere in the United Kingdom as well as in Australia, Canada, and in the United States. Amongst these Scott-Moncrieffs there are doctors, lawyers, scientists and authors. Readers spending a little time on internet research will discover that many Scott-Moncrieffs have achieved high reputations in their fields of expertise.

Apart from the late David "Bunty" Scott-Moncrieff, his wife Averil (née Sneyd), and their sons Humphrey and Ambrose, I never had contact with any other bearer of this name, so the only persons I am referring to in this book are those of that family, and to whom my feelings are tied with affectionate sympathy.

By the way, adult Britons will remember "Bunty" as the title of an 8-penny weekly comic magazine, born in the late 'fifties and featuring a courageous little girl as the central character. The contents consisted of a collection of many small strips, the stories typically being three to five pages long. "Bunty" published 2,249 issues and went monthly in 2001 before ceasing publication after a further five months. The magazine was aimed at readers under the age of 14. The matching of the name Bunty with this publication is purely incidental.

Halwart Schrader

Foreword

WHEN HALWART SCHRADER ASKED if I would contribute a foreword for his book, firstly, I was honoured to be asked, and secondly, curious as to how good the English translation would be of his originally German book. Frankly, I was amazed at how well Nick Fox's translation read, how much Hazel Robinson remembered, and what a great story Halwart has written about Bunty's life and adventures. He has done remarkably well in understanding and capturing in print Bunty's remarkable character.

I first met Bunty as an impressionable teenager when he and Averil were staying at 'Idvies House' near Forfar in Scotland, a time capsule of a Victorian country house which Averil had inherited. My mother and father were great friends of Humphrey and Ambrose, and the Scott-Moncrieff's weekend visits were always accompanied with wonderful motor cars, many of them bought and sold between Humphrey and my father. Upon meeting Bunty, my brother and I were captivated by his many incredible stories, his ability to bring the fun of the past to the present with endless anecdotes, and his huge knowledge and many opinions on the greatest automobiles.

Finding myself, on one occasion, unexpectedly at home during school time, following an incident which left me unsure if the headmaster would let me return, Bunty threw me a lifeline with the offer: "Send the dear boy down to me if the school won't have him back." Thereafter, I spent over two years, the happiest of my life, living at Rock Cottage, with rent sent to Averil in the form of a bottle of gin a week, and my daytimes were spent working as an apprentice for Hazel and the boys at the Scott-Moncrieffs' learning the mechanical side of Rolls-Royces, Bentleys and wonderful prewar sports cars. No day, nor especially evening, at Rock Cottage was ever dull; fascinating characters from all around the world would turn up to stay, undeterred by the Scott-Moncrieffs' limited culinary repertoire, which mostly consisted of sausages and boil-in-the-bag rice, with fascinating conversation and fun never in short supply.

Bunty and Averil introduced me to the Vintage Sports Car Club, and in my first year with them I would drive him in his famous Vauxhall 30/98 Special AOA2 all around the UK. He absolutely thrilled me by allowing me to have my first motor race in the AOA2, just short of my 18th birthday, which started my career in motorsport, and led to me driving the 24 Hours of Le Mans four times now. Poignantly, life has come full circle, with me taking custody of the AOA2 from Humphrey and racing the Vauxhall again, unaltered from Bunty's time. When

Bunty decided that he wanted to make a European tour in his beloved Derby Bentley, Bunty, the Bentley and I drove some 9000 miles through Europe taking in a Fiva World Rally on Corfu, staying (or rather *overstaying*) our welcome with various aristocratic and automotive friends of his throughout most of Europe; it's an adventure I will never forget, nor Bunty's fabulous stories and filthy limericks along the way. And, talking of stories, as Humphrey remarked after reading Halwart's book, "My father was never one to let the details get in the way of a good story!"

Halwart's book really encapsulates all of Bunty. He was certainly a character from another age. He could be a rascal, he could be naughty, but as you read the book you will see he was easy to forgive and, along with his incredible thirst and passion for life and a knowledge he freely passed on, he gave me an apprenticeship in life beyond any I could have dreamt of, and for that I shall always be personally grateful. I hope you will enjoy reading about Bunty and all the fun this remarkable man had with his life.

Gregor Fisken

Visitors from England. O Tannenbaum!

THE END OF OCTOBER, 1970. On one of those glisteningly sunny, breezy yet warm, golden autumn days – one which had brought an unexpected upturn for the Munich beer gardens, yet at the same time undoubtedly marked the end of the season. I was sitting at my desk, when the telephone ringing grabbed my attention. Barely a word had begun to enter my ear before I knew exactly who was ringing: Bunty. You could tell from his first breath.

Unusually, he wasn't being put through via a connection from his secretary Hazel, nor asking for a call back; for whatever reason, he had obviously decided to ring me himself. This had to be important.

"My dear friend, this is old Bunty speaking. Can you hear me?"

"Of course, Bunty! What can I do for you? Were you not planning to come to Munich in Autumn?"

"Yes indeed. How lovely of you to have remembered that. Yes, I will be making my journey to Italy, passing through Munich, and thought of stopping-over ... I should take this opportunity to visit Oktoberfest with Averil, so we'll be needing a room for two nights. But bear in mind that we really must be frugal so please find the cheapest hotel room in Munich. We'll meet at some point in the day on Saturday."

"Bunty ... the festival finishes on the first weekend of October ... that was about three weeks ago already. Sorry, no Oktoberfest!"

It seemed as though he hadn't been listening. "I really am looking forward to this, you know, I can still recall the first Oktoberfest in Munich which I experienced, must have been 1938, but the beer must surely be just as good these days I reckon! Are you quite sure you won't have any problems in sorting this room out? Back then I stayed in a hotel called Zum Tannenbaum, that one was really cheap. Give them a call, will you, see if it's still going. Tell the folks there that the strange Englishman from 1938 will be coming back to Munich for a second visit, they'll certainly remember him, and that he'd be delighted to get his hands on that cheap little room again ..."

I tried to interrupt Bunty several times but to no avail. Above all, I wanted to share with him that, in theory, he and his wife Averil would always be welcome to stay at ours, but that we currently had lodgers staying with us and thus unfortunately the timing wouldn't work out. "Well, see you on Saturday then, I'll head over to Tannenbaum first and then we'll pop straight down to enjoy Walpurgisnacht at Oktoberfest, ha-ha-ha ..."

Walpurgisnacht. One of Bunty's favourite German words, one which he could pronounce at near-native level and which he used in general to denote an evening of pub crawling in German-friendly circles. The word Walpurgisnacht normally stands for a bonfire and dancing festival held on April 30/May 1.

Bunty rarely rang, he preferred writing letters. When we communicated by phone, I would typically have the pleasure of speaking to the Churnetside 300 (connecting from abroad was pie in the sky), or I would receive a friendly albeit brief response from Hazel, asking if I would call back at tea-time. 'Bunty would love to chat, but he's unfortunately unavailable at the moment.' Upon hearing this, I could ascertain that Bunty was perched next to her, passing on the message.

Bunty's ancestors came from Scotland. And the Scots are well known for their frugality. Even before the invention of the telephone, they were frugal. Bunty was certainly not one to renounce his heritage or change his ways (take Hotel Tannenbaum for example).

Fortunately, the Hotel Zum Tannenbaum did indeed still exist. I reserved the small room at the front for the two of them and discovered that it was in fact possible to book a room in the centre of Munich in 1970 for just 24 marks (without breakfast, but nevertheless!), equivalent to two pounds ten shillings.

Bunty and Averil's journey over took place in a car built in 1926. It was the most natural thing in the world for the pair of them to chauffeur themselves around Europe in a car such as this one. Their Italian OM offered so little room for baggage that their two average-sized suitcases, held together with a leather strap, had to be fastened to the tail of the two-seater, whilst a reserve petrol jerry can was rigged to the left-hand side of the car.

Bunty was disappointed to discover that one of his chief reasons for making the journey from Rock Cottage in Staffordshire to Santa Margherita, Italy, via Munich was no longer valid. "You should have told me that Oktoberfest was already over my dear boy! Oh my, it wasn't as a result of the Suez Crisis, was it? The Americans have been reacting very pettishly lately. They ought to have kept you out of it really. Well, my personal experiences with Americans have been very varied, there was the time we had that brief visit from the Mafia boss of Chicago, that is a story I really ought to tell you about …"

"Oktoberfest hasn't been abandoned, Bunty, it always finishes at the end of the first weekend in October, and as far as the Suez Crisis is concerned, that event has long since passed …"

Bunty was off again. "I almost forgot, my dear, I really must head to the petrol station today. I must confess I haven't heard about any supposed end to the Suez Crisis, and frankly, if it's supposed to be coming soon, petrol certainly won't be getting any cheaper. I have already enquired about the cheapest petrol station in Munich. It's situated in a district of the city known as Germering. You must know where this is, my dear boy. Would you be so kind as to accompany me there?"

He had pronounced Germering as something akin to 'Germany.' At first, I was understandably baffled as to where exactly in Germany he was hoping I would take him. Aha! Germering! "No, on this rare occasion I'll actually have to politely refuse the offer of your company, as today I have urgent business to attend to – namely that the lodgers at home have requested my presence for something. Besides, Germering is such a very long way from the Hotel Zum Tannenbaum that I must warn you it may hardly be worth your calculated potential savings, driving to a petrol station many kilometres away." I'd made the fatal mistake of offering Bunty advice, which unfortunately only strengthened his intentions. And he indeed successfully managed to persuade me to accompany him on the ride, despite my initial protestations. He always knew exactly how to back me into a corner. "Obviously you'll be driving the car, you realise, so you do understand the deal here, don't you?" Bunty was well aware that I was the owner of a 1933 Audi, a 1931 Lagonda and a 1929 Riley, and that I had just as soft a spot for driving cars of this class as he himself.

Bunty's regretful admittance that he'd seemingly left his wallet in the hotel room was a similar masterstroke on his part. The petrol attendant had little tolerance for Bunty's muddled apologies and had no intention of trying to understand his German, so simply turned to me instead: "42.35 – want a receipt, Sir?"

"You'll have to be a dear and explain to the friendly gentleman why you're covering the bill for me and getting the petrol, my good man, for it is dreadfully awkward, particularly since I am also searching for the cigar shop in Perusastrasse, they had the most wonderful Havanas there in 1933, back then I had to park my Mercedes outside every shop to let the engine cool down ..." Bunty's eyes were glowing expectantly, his shaggy handlebar moustache twitching from side to side.

It was perfectly clear to me. Bunty fully believed (even if he wouldn't admit it) that the responsibility of filling up the tank and considerably voluminous reserve canisters lay with the host. This wasn't my first time with Bunty by any means. We'd known each other a good five years by this point. But until now, I had never been allowed to pay his petrol bill – fortunately too, since if he were travelling in his Rolls-Royce classic, his big Vauxhall 30/98 or 'Charlotte,' his coffee-brown 3.5-litre Bentley, then frankly it'd be goodnight from me: the petrol capacity in each of those would be at least twice the size of his OM tourer. All in all, I got off lightly.

Perusastrasse. Six Havanas at 4.50 marks a pop and a further six at 2.20 marks. It was Bunty's Walpurgisnacht!

"The shop is exactly as I remembered it," began Bunty's commentary the moment we got outside. "Except back then they didn't have such queer salespeople, ha-ha-ha." We'd left the OM in a no-stop zone, (where else ...), and a parking warden was already stood waiting next to it as Bunty and I approached. Bunty appeared not to notice her at all, or perhaps simply not wishing to acknowledge her, whilst I strained to look elsewhere, so as to give the impression that I had mistaken her for a postman or someone else in uniform, particularly since the woman hadn't yet addressed us. I made a concerted effort to speak my most convincing Queen's English, as I heaved the old, limping and sighing gentleman in the threadbare brown corduroy suit into the passenger seat of this antique-looking, grubby, Staffordshire-registered automobile – are you alright, Sir? Ooouh, we will manage it, won't we, Sir? Of course we will, here we gooouh! I clambered in behind the steering wheel, and, through activating the starter button on the dashboard, coaxed the engine to spluttering life, which not only caused the poor meter girl with the chic uniform cap to jump two steps backwards, but also seemed to dissuade her from writing out a ticket.

"Did you see her? The sweet little sugar doll with the pen? Ha-ha-ha!" Bunty cackled all the way until we stopped – legally this time – in front of the Tannenbaum, wiggling his moustache with enjoyment.

"You've got to point-blank ignore the meter maids, particularly the cute ones. I've never once had to pay a ticket in my life. Although I did pinch a bottom once, ha-ha-ha. And even then, it didn't cost me a penny. But don't tell Averil, please ..."

Parking a rather valuable classic car on the roadside in Munich city centre overnight is the sort of decision that could give you a rather nasty surprise the next morning. Yet Bunty seemed to have a degree of faith in the Bavarian criminals, if there were any such poking around. "They'd sooner snap the aerial off an expensive Porsche than be so impolite as to steal the spare wheel of a rickety old OM," he explained, "we're taking pretty much everything else up into the room!" He would have been wholly against paying ten marks or more for a parking spot in the underground car park, which is what I would have advised him to do. He was much happier dragging his and Averil's conjoined travel bag all the way up to the room. Mrs. Tannenbaum was luckily able to avoid having to help take up the extra jerry cans.

The following day, we met shortly after twelve at the Augustiner Brewery beer hall near the Main Station. We didn't speak about the money lent for petrol and cigars. Whilst Averil frequented department store after department store from top to bottom, I treated Bunty to a pint and a dumpling-heavy lunch, followed by a piece of gateau with cocoa for dessert and then after all that another half-litre, accompanied by a nice schnapps, before we dragged ourselves to two car accessories stores on Schwanthaler Strasse, in which Bunty enquired about cheap headlight bulbs, fan belts and sparkplugs, things which, unbeknown to me, could be acquired the same day for petty cash. Unfortunately, the pieces on offer here were apparently not suitable for what the OM needed but might perhaps be useful for one or other of his motors back home.

To Bunty's amazement, of the two shops we visited, neither the Südmotor GmbH, nor Altmeister Fahnebrock premises, offered original Rolls-Royce replacement parts from the pre-war period. "I could have bought them so cheaply, because who needs soiled goods like those here ..." As quirkily as ever, Bunty trailed off and then promptly back onto a politely phrased follow-up question, to which the attendant mustered up his best English in response:

"The loo is after the office, and the waschbecken can you there also benutzen." Two pints of Augustiner beer are indeed rather a lot of liquid after all.

Chips but no fish

FEBRUARY, 1971. I'D HAD an appointment in London with the celeb photographer Charles Wilp; we were scouting out locations for Gauloises cigarette scenic motifs and had discussed a thousand and one details. A perfectionist like Wilp left nothing to chance. In those days, I was employed and sent over by the Munich-based F W Heye advertising agency.

During my three-day stay, I'd also had the chance to visit a veteran and vintage car auction. I was hardly surprised to encounter Bunty there. For Britain's most prominent Rolls-Royce used car dealers, an auction of such relevance is more a duty than a choice.

"Oh, how nice to see you again! Bernard has successfully opted for the green Silver Wraith over there and that black Bentley R-Type at my request. You know Bernard surely?"

"Yes, Bunty, you had introduced me to Bernard."

"I almost certainly paid too much for both sets of wheels, because the auctioneer brought everything out again ... but it's an excellent investment, you know, I'll sell both these wonderful cars in the States ..." What followed was a long foray into the interesting, highly receptive Rolls-Royce markets in California, Texas, Oklahoma, Illinois, Louisiana, and above all in Arizona: "My boy, there's people just sat there waiting for my goods!"

The auction was over, and Bernard had agreed to driving the cars to wherever Bunty had requested. "Ladies and Gentlemen, the house of Christie's will accept no responsibility for goods left uncollected!" announced auctioneer The Right Hon Patrick Lindsay, after the last fall of the hammer. Patrick was a whizz when it came to his job, he himself owned several classic Bentleys, and now and then would arrive and depart in one of his aeroplanes – ex-Royal Air Force reconnaissance aircraft from the second world war. Patrick was almost as infamous as Bunty on the old-car stage, and, as a result of this, they tried to keep clear of one another as much as possible.

My time was pressing, I had to get to Victoria Station as I didn't want to miss my train to Dover. "Frank Dale will take you there, I know him very well, and Victoria is on his way. Frank's shop is on Sloane Square, you know! If that will allow us to have just another hour's time ..."

"All right, but really just an hour, I cannot allow any more, the 8pm train is my last chance!" I made this very clear to Bunty. I needed to be in Ostend to catch the midnight train to Brussels.

"Oh, how wonderful indeed, then let's go and get something to eat right away ... Frank knows a good pub nearby. The only problem is I can't see him anywhere, where is the chap hiding ..."

I figured Frank Dale was also securing one of his purchased cars, so suggested a taxi. After what seemed like an eternity, one finally stopped. There was no longer time for lunch, as the traffic was solid and the last few yards to Victoria took an age. Bunty wasn't up to walking far but insisted upon accompanying me to the platform. And then suddenly, the unexpected happened.

"My good man, I owe you so very much, you were ever so generous in Munich recently. I would have liked more than anything to treat you to lunch. I'm sad, it distresses me deeply that we no longer have the time, you have to understand."

The tears which formed in his eyes were definitely not caused by emotion, rather by the draft on the platform, just as the blobs on his nose weren't always an indicator of a cold.

I boarded the train, there was still another five or so minutes until the departure. Bunty's speeches – if a little interspersed with many a drawn out hmm and ahh – always flowed with wonderful continuity, but he was particularly talkative on this day, even for him. Granted, he probably was able to land the deal of a lifetime at the auction, and had already correctly calculated the dollars he was set to make upon resale in the US. "You're hungry, I'm sure of that, and I wasn't able to treat you to lunch! But I know what's proper, you know me well enough to know that, don't you? So, wait just a second, my boy, so that I don't just let you head back to Germany!"

He turned around and hobbled away, before returning seconds before departure with a paper carrier bag to hand up to me. "At last, I can make up for what I owe you! And don't forget to ring me when you get home, but not before five o'clock please, oh I have ever so much to tell you! Were you aware, for example, that Frank got his hands on the Phantom II Continental, which has gone for twenty thousand in the past, for just seven thousand five hundred? Should I reveal what I'd have offered? Not even twelve! That was namely Lady Ashcroft's car, you must have heard that her two chauffeurs were killed, both poisoned! Or is that news to you? I'd never have offered twelve. Ahh, hmm, perhaps thirteen actually. She poisoned the pair of them, one after the other! She'll never admit that though, the prosecutor didn't have any concrete evidence, but the car bears a curse in any case! Hopefully good old Frank doesn't experience any bad luck as a result, he still owes me £20 after all ... oh yes and do please have another go at chasing down two dozen sparkplugs if you can. They'll have to give you a discount. Just give them my name! And when you ring me, please don't forget to ask me about my proposed trip down the Danube. I need your expert technical advice, I'm now actually the owner of a boat, – ahh – and my nephew in the Royal Geographic Society ..."

It was the first time that Bunty had mentioned his boat to me. What sort of boat? Had he acquired it in exchange for one of his vintage Rolls-Royces?

I had once been the owner of a wooden lifeboat (albeit one without an engine) for a while, and was interested in this topic. Had I been aware beforehand that Bunty and I shared a second passion, I would have been prepared to extend my stay a little longer in order to inspect his boat. I kept my curiosity under control for once and decided to write a prompt letter to Bunty, particularly since he seemed to be intending to take it down Europe's inland waterways. It was too late at this time, and, based on experience, I could be sure that Bunty would be all set to speak verbosely about the story of the boat. For this ship was also by no means his first, as I would later discover.

Even before I had the chance to sort through everything that Bunty had thrust upon me on the platform edge, the train set off – "don't forget those sparkplugs and ask for a decent discount!" I could hear Bunty calling. I shut the compartment window, winked at him one last time and opened up the contents of the lukewarm, heavily salted contents of the little paper bag. It was supposed to be fish and chips, but unfortunately the fish was missing. Sticky, stale chips. I was lucky enough to have the time and the opportunity to dine on something a little more substantial aboard the train. I emptied a half bottle of St. Emilion as an accompaniment – three glasses to the wellbeing of ship captain Bunty – and looked forward to a speedy reunion with the quirky old gentleman from Rock Cottage, the old miser who we all loved so dearly.

But why? Because of his charm? Because of his wittiness and flair for telling funny stories, his so lovingly presented insolence, his well provoked situational comedy, his ability to play-act and always fool the unsuspecting so convincingly?

"Call me Bunty"

MY FIRST ENCOUNTER WITH Bunty had occurred in seemingly similar circumstances to those later described to me by other visitors of his, including my friend Albert Leonhard. With the exception that they had all set out en route to Rock Cottage firstly in the daylight and secondly by car. I had arrived at night and on foot.

I could have rented a car at Manchester airport, but I decided against it; preferring the adventure of getting to know England as a bus passenger on this occasion. It's possible that I had wanted to write a story about this, but I cannot remember anymore. Most likely as a result of the many details of my visit to Rock Cottage.

My flight had taken off an hour late and therefore arrived an hour late too, funnily enough. It was a cold and wet autumn evening, frightful, chilling, rife with swear words; it couldn't have been any more quintessentially English. Before I knew it, I was stood by a bus stop somewhere in the country, the green intercity coach having left me to my fate at Basford Hall station, and this was coming back to haunt me in several ways.

Not only was it cold and wet and windy and dark, but I was also hungry and thirsty, and had a heavy camera bag in my hand. I couldn't ask anyone for directions, because every normal English person was already back at home, with their feet stretched out in front of their dimly lit electric fireplace, and because, so far as I could tell in the gloominess, Basford Hall appeared to be neither a village, nor any other sort of settlement for that matter; but rather merely a geographical but otherwise insignificant landmark on the regional map of Staffordshire county.

What on earth was I playing at. I could have spent the night at the airport, in a hotel, and then the following morning, or at least at a sensible time of day when even the English November could be expected to provide a hint of daylight, making my way to Basford Hall in order to find the so-called Rock Cottage of a certain Mr Scott-Moncrieff.

I'd taken the last bus. There was nothing in sight. No traditional red telephone box, from which I could have at least successfully connected to Churnetside 300, no petrol station, no pub. Nothing. I had genuinely intended to reach this part of Britain by day, to ask locals for the way to Rock Cottage in order to pay Mr Scott-Moncrieff my respects. As a journalist from Germany, who had grown curious about meeting the man who was supposedly the largest Rolls-Royce used car dealer in the world. Why was this legendary figure living out here in no man's land, why not London, Birmingham, Liverpool, Manchester ...?

Forty to fifty old and not-so-old Rolls-Royces, starting from the 1912 Silver Ghost right up to the most modern Silver Wraith. What a story! My Hasselblad camera could hardly wait for the chance to go 'clickcack' however, at this moment in time, I had no idea whether I would ever actually get the chance to meet the man whom I had arranged to see via letters. Much more likely was that I would be devoured by wild English animals within the next hour, wild animals like the infamous hounds of the Baskervilles, or that I would trip and plunge into a ditch from the period of the Roman occupation of Britain. In fact, I remembered reading about the great train robbery in the country in August, in which the perpetrator had escaped with £2.63 million without a trace. How dangerous life in England really is! Ronald Biggs and his companions had halted a Royal Mail train heading between Glasgow and London by manipulating the line signals, attacking the poor, oblivious driver before proceeding to take the train further to Bridego Bridge, where they could load the cases filled with banknotes into an escape car standing by.

According to Conan Doyle, they would have escaped with much more money, had it not been for a number of severe crimes already committed in this region ...

I could have waited until a car came past, tried to stop it and asked the driver for directions. Surely everyone in these parts would be familiar with the world's greatest Rolls-Royce car dealer. The magazine to which I was intending to sell the story was called 'twen' and was, despite the slightly misleading name, aimed at people over thirty, over forty even. The topic of the Rolls-Royce had appealed to them instantly when I proposed the idea. Hardcore twens could really dig a snazzy Alfa Romeo or a funny story about the Citroën 2CV.

However, I still hadn't resolved how I was going to obtain this story; and simply standing by the roadside, freezing until I was in need of hospital treatment come dawn was not in the script. Colds always kick in, too, when dealing with an unpleasant situation, which was the last thing I needed.

Churnetside, incidentally: similarly to Basford Hall, I was completely unable to locate any landmark bearing this name on the map. But even if I had discovered that there was a village of this name, unlike the certainly non-existent Basford Hall, it would have been just as hopeless – and even a comforting sign such as '3 miles' on white laminated cast-iron would still have resulted in a cold, wet march for an hour. At least.

After this long period of self-pity, I was pleased to note that the rain eventually stopped after all, and the wind brought about movement in the cloud layers – which I was especially relieved about, because a shimmer of moonlight began to light up this part of the county of Staffordshire as if it were a heavenly corner. The phrase 'light up' is perhaps an exaggeration here, but I was at least able to begin making out the topography of the surrounding land on which I had been dumped. The clouds continued to move, blocking my source of light at periods before drifting on to reveal its glow.

I began to walk, hoping that the direction I was taking would somehow bring me closer to my destination. Indeed, I had some fortune; after just a few steps, I came to a turning with a road sign indicating that the unsurfaced road to my left led to Rock Cottage. It was a sort of forest trail, with tracks such as those made by tractors, or possibly Land Rovers. I couldn't tell whether they were also marked by Rolls Royce tyres – for one it was far too dark out, with the rain also rendering the mud tracks rather silty. Not to mention that I was rather inexperienced when it came to the field of tyre track analysis. One piece of fairly vital information had been lacking from the signpost; nevertheless, I set off down the muddy pathway, unsure if I'd be walking one, five or even ten miles down it.

A suitcase-wielding youngster from Germany, hungry and shivering, in a sodden rain coat and shoes poorly suited to a muddy track, trudging his way slowly through a forest in West England in an attempt to interview an eccentric car dealer, with no idea what would await him on the other side. An arrogant nobleman with a butler? A drunken ruffian, sprawled out in front of the fireplace? A nervous Mrs Scott-Moncrieff, refusing to open the door to any strangers after dark, whilst her consort was away on a business trip in Australia? I hadn't awaited a response to my proposed visit, I had just set off on a whim eight days later.

Where was I planning to sleep? I surely couldn't be expecting Mr Scott-Moncrieff to ready a guest bed for an unknown and potentially even unwanted visitor.

The tractor tracks buried into the muddy path actually led me straight to my destination. I had no idea of the time as my watch had no backlight. As I neared Rock Cottage, I was able to make out the silhouette of three or four oversized car bodies, exaggerated to a colossal size in the fragmented moonlight. They were hollow, without windows, rather cubic. Not exactly befitting my preconceptions of the mythical Rolls-Royce; in truth they looked more like hearses, waiting to be laid to rest six feet under themselves.

Some distance ahead, behind these grim monuments, a shimmer of light could be made out. I wanted to hasten my pace, but I was stuck up to my ankles in a sludge of mud and cowpat and then had to negotiate a family of stinging nettles, causing me to stumble over various odd-shaped objects lying in the overgrowth. As I struggled to keep my balance, I began to make out what they were: cylinder heads, rear axles, steering wheels … of course.

The outline of a house slowly appeared before me. It had the eerie and unmistakable shape of a haunted castle, with two small spires and giant chimneys coming out from the gables. One of the windows on the first floor was illuminated.

Rock Cottage! I'd done it!

An iron garden door stood ajar, flanked by further scrap metal and odd components of cars here and there. Directly in front of the entrance stood an out of use goldfish pond, decorated with thick cobbled edges and on the starboard side was an allegorical figure, who appeared in the half-light to be a child, huddled up; a poor, freezing, English child. I almost plunged into the pond head first, fixated as I was on the light that was shining out of the window, coupled with the fact that my last few metres (no, sorry, yards, of course) leading up to the pond itself were heavily obscured by further mounds of used car parts. They appeared to be a little smaller than the cars I had previously thought to be hollow-windowed hearses.

I found my way to the entrance and knocked, loudly and forcefully, expecting a "come in, please" or for a person to appear straight away, be it welcoming or unwelcoming, surprised or terrified, warm or wary, male or female …

Instead I heard a faint voice, barely audible, only understandable because I had my ear pressed against the crack of the door. I placed my camera bag on the ground and listened to the message I received as I slowly attempted to turn the door handle.

"For heaven's sake step away from the door! You're risking your life! Rodney was supposed to repair the cornice over a year ago, every day a few more stones fall down … go around to the entrance at the gable on the left, past the peacock enclosure and into the kitchen … you'll find it …"

Negotiating the cage with the peacocks, which was barely visible, would be my last exam then if I was to successfully gain entry to Rock Cottage. As my coat became caught on the mesh wire, I could clearly hear how a three-corner tear manifests in material. Doesn't matter now, I thought to myself. I couldn't see the peacocks. I'd heard tell that they can be particularly aggressive to strangers.

The door to the kitchen was unlocked, as was the room which lay just beyond it. It was the room whose light had shone down upon me from the window. The second part of my adventure was set to begin. I was about to meet David Scott-Moncrieff.

Only once in my life have I ever greeted him as such; namely, at that very moment when I stretched out a hand and said "Good evening, Mr Scott-Moncrieff, my name is …," at which point he interrupted me to clarify that he wished to be referred to as Bunty, regardless of the occasion.

All right then, Mister Bunty!

Bunty. Not at all as I had pictured him; indeed none of the ideas I had in mind applied even remotely to the gentleman who was welcoming me to Rock Cottage. He was warm and friendly, as if we were old acquaintances. He had received my letter and had been fully expecting my arrival. He told me that the Germans are reliable people, and that when they say they will arrive on Wednesday, they will actually arrive on Wednesday, and not on Friday. Oh yes, and he had no negative opinion on the Germans as a people, "except the Nazis, of course, and a few stupid bandits of that kind," and wanted to know if I wouldn't take a seat?

Bunty, "drop the mister, please," hadn't yet got up from his leather wing chair to greet me, as he was presently disabled. His left foot was in a cast, so far as I could tell, and was raised up high, resting on an ottoman. The rest of his body was clad in a chequered suit of a colour that was hard to define, trousers which went almost as high as his armpits, held in position by light red braces. His striped club tie comprised a collection of patches of different sorts, intertwined by blue and green elements. A silver pin with a pearl rested halfway between his belly and his collar. Above the collar, it was easy to spot the most distinguishing feature of the landlord of Rock Cottage: his face, decorated by platinum-coloured tufts of hair, swollen ears, a swollen nose, a swollen chin and blinking eyes, hidden by mountains of wrinkles.

Somehow, he reminded me of the way apples look when it's two months after Christmas and they're still yet to be roasted. Minus the little red cheeks, of course, but his face was shrivelled and littered with grooves and scars, decorated by a few blotches and smooth spots too. By the time you reached Bunty's water blue eyes, however, the comparison had ceased to exist. They sparkled and twinkled with guile and humour in equal measure, and all the excitement of a child on Christmas Eve; they looked upon me both innocently and yet piercingly, as if they belonged to Santa Claus himself!

However, the faint voice, masked by the unkempt moustache, which played out from somewhere between the swollen nose and swollen chin, wasn't Christmassy in the slightest. The articulation and pronunciation could only be from one place on the British Isles: Cambridge. Not Oxford, nor Eton, nor Harrow …

Bunty talked and talked and talked. Admittedly he spoke quietly, but he was clearly audible. He sentences flitted from topic to topic, abound with meandering stories which had neither start nor end point, punctuated by constant interruptions and parentheses; endless interconnecting tales, which were sometimes so intricately woven together that Bunty indeed found himself caught by their ropes. I had to pay very close attention to ensure I could follow his rich monologue, especially since Bunty's dentures were unable or at least rather reluctant to release certain words.

The living room, in which we were sitting, was peppered with stacks of newspapers and books, boxes and miniature antique furnishings. The doors of the glass cupboards on the walls were all left open, revealing yet more books, documents, catalogues, maps and magazines. Every free inch of wall was decorated with pictures, photographs, bookshelves full of trinkets and pewter tankards and ceramic kitsch, as well as large, old hood ornaments. The majority of these ornaments were the iconic Rolls-Royce Spirit of Ecstasy, of course. But underneath the kneeling, squatting and floating angels was a majestic Mercedes star on a black plinth. There was a very specific explanation for both this and the car to which it originally belonged, but I was only to discover this much later.

"I'm beginning to become rather hungry, my young friend, as I am sure you are too. My darling Averil went to London at lunchtime today and won't be back until tomorrow. Oh, by the way, did you hear about the Great Train Robbery? They were able to get away with over two million pounds! My God, what a heist, eh? Averil is such a lovely lady, may the Lord protect her against misfortune! However, whilst she is away, we have to take care of ourselves, if we don't want to die of hunger. Would you be so kind, my young man, to go into the kitchen and see if you can locate anything edible in there? And make us both some tea."

While Bunty continued to speak uninterrupted, quietly yet melodically as if he were almost singing; piping at the beginning of sentences before his voice sank until it was barely a decibel, I got up from my armchair as instructed and went into the kitchen, finding a light switch but practically nothing that could be considered food. Averil, Bunty's wife, had apparently decided that her husband was in need of a diet. The good chap really had nothing to worry about in that regard. Poor old man … and in his current state it seemed he was so immobile that he couldn't have even fried himself an egg. Aside from the fact that it would certainly impair upon his dignity, I was having a great deal of trouble in imagining Bunty ever being stood at the stove, leaning over a frying pan with an egg in his hand.

I continued to search around. "In the pantry next door, you'll find a round tin, could you bring it in here, my dear friend?" chimed Bunty from the living room.

I spotted it but noticed that it was a shoe shine kit. "Ah, there must be another round tin in there somewhere then. It's got biscuits inside, leftover from Christmas." I eventually discovered the biscuit tin which he was after. It was cornered, not round. The cover read 'The Genuine Joseph Lucas Acetylene Gas Motor Car Headlamp Repair Kit No 5.' The biscuits inside looked like they were still edible, or at least weren't showing any signs of mould. I took them into the lounge and we began to nibble. And by that, I mean Bunty had the tin on his lap and I had to get up after each biscuit and nip in to get another.

They still had the scent and slight taste of the acetylene gas headlamp repair kit no 5 which the box had previously contained. It didn't look as though I was going to be going to bed stuffed.

"Now we should have some tea … can you make tea, my good man? Germans can lend their hand to anything, isn't that so? So, make us a tea if you will. But no teabags please my dear! Should you find any, please just leave them where they are, understood? The teabag was the most wicked invention since hydraulic valve lifters; Mabel brought them over. The devil should come and take the dear cleaning lady away. You should be able to find real tea somewhere in there I think."

If I was lucky, I would at least be able to get something hot to drink! I rummaged around in the Scott-Moncrieff's kitchen looking for 'real tea,' whilst boiling water on a gas stove from the twenties. The water kettle was as black as soot and could easily have been over a hundred years old. I managed to pull and wash two cups from amongst the mountains of unwashed dishes – only the best domestic ware, all Royal Spode of course – and then, under a stack of newspapers on the kitchen table, I located some tea and a sugar bowl.

The process could begin.

"When Averil returns from London tomorrow, she will stop off in Leek and go shopping. There's practically nothing in the house. I forgot to ask Hazel if she could run a few errands for me. Ahh, you absolutely must meet Hazel! We'll have to have our tea black for now, there's no milk in the house since yesterday, sorry, my dear, Mabel is so unreliable! One time in Portugal, aah, mmh, so that must have been in 1954, there was this black tea there, wait a sec, ahh, what was it called, they'd imported it from Mexico, no, Guatemala of course, it was considered an intoxicant there, simply wonderful ..." and so it continued, just as breathlessly as before. I could barely get my words out and thus couldn't interject with any questions, leaving me with no choice but to politely follow the old gentleman's requests.

"Bring the electric fire a little closer to my injured foot please, yes that's it, lovely. Turn the light back off, yes, yes, that's the one! We have to save all we can in these dark times, the government is full of scoundrels and electricity prices are bordering on astronomical! Oh, if only we had your chancellor Adenauer, although he is to resign soon, so I've been told ... and now have a look and see if you can find the bottle of port wine behind it, no, not there, a little more to the left, Averil must have hidden it ever so well, okay well back to the right again and you'll hopefully find some glasses there too, she'll surely not have hidden those as well. That's the sorta thing that Mabel would do, the stupid cleaner girl. Or did you purchase a cheap bottle of something on the flight over in the Duty-Free? Every one of my friends from abroad always brings a bottle from the Duty-Free when they come to visit me!"

I hadn't thought of that at all. My gift for Bunty letting me stay was a book about churches in Munich, written in English. Fortunately, it seemed to interest him greatly as he flicked through it.

"I love Munich. Even on that occasion in 1933 when somebody mistook me for a personal friend of Hitler. Terribly unpleasant I can assure you, but you see I didn't get the chance to correct the mistake. And oh, architectural history is such a passion of mine! On my man travels across this world, I've seen the Notre Dame in Paris and the cathedral in Reims, St. Stephen's Cathedral in Vienna and then, aah, I mean, must have been the Cathedral in Strasbourg ..." and so it continued ...

After we had finished the last of the biscuits and all of my over-brewed tea, we began to drink a 'Tawny Rich' port. Finally, I had the opportunity to ask my first question. "Bunty, is it true that you are the owner of the largest collection of Rolls-Royces in the world?

"Where exactly are all these cars? Could I see them tomorrow and photograph a few of them?"

Bunty failed to answer any of my questions. "Oh, my boy, first of all I simply must tell you the story of the strange Argentinian who was here last week to purchase a Silver Dawn. But before that, another small glass of port, if you please. I take it that you don't really want any more yourself? But if you do, please by all means help yourself … so anyway, this chap came from Buenos Aires, or Bahia Blanca, as far as I'm aware. He was an emigrant in any case, Romanian from birth – I recognised that straight away. I know Romania very well, I travelled along the section of the Danube which flows through there by speedboat in 1941/42. And in a Lincoln, of course. Oh, what a wonderful time it was, my dear, we drank ever so much vodka, as much as we pleased. We only once had to hide from the Germans."

The story was full of punchlines, but I can't follow it for any longer because I need to turn the attention back to the one I set out to write. That aside, Bunty's story about the Romanian Argentinian stopped abruptly and seemingly right before an important part, because his narrative voice and thread were suddenly lost and his head very gently sank onto his chest.

His story had become entangled somewhere, and Bunty had fallen asleep, empty glass of port in his hand. Finally, I had the opportunity to get myself a second glass … but just as I thought this, the moustache twitched, Bunty lifted his head up and yawned, set his glass down, adjusted his scarlet red braces underneath his jacket, rubbed his swollen nose and looked at me. What now?!

"Let's call it a day, my friend!" he whispered as he rubbed his eyes. I helped him to his feet, since the man certainly needed putting to bed. The reason for one of his feet being in a cast was yet to be revealed to me. It was 11pm. The antique electric fire had to be switched off, as per Bunty's instructions, but that didn't seem much of an issue since the temperature it was giving off was just as low as the living room temperature anyway. After doing this, I was confronted with quite simply the most gigantic bed I had ever seen. A monstrosity, reminiscent of persiflage in a Richard Wagner opera, admittedly very short, but with an enormous headboard, covered with ornaments and figures and allegorical decor of the kitschiest variety. Hinges could be seen, indicating that this monstrous two-sleeper was even collapsible. A true wonder of furniture design from the late 19th century.

"Oh, thank you, you are ever so kind …" Bunty had informed me that he could undress himself, which only served to make me believe that he intended to go to bed fully dressed. And, since I myself must be rather exhausted too, I was to head up to the first floor and into the room with the yellow door, supposedly belonging to his son Ambrose.

Ambrose had been residing in France for half a year now, studying the art of viticulture, "Chardonnay and things like that, oh how wonderful!" The bathroom could also be found upstairs. "But you're welcome to stay down here a little longer and read, it's just that the electricity is so expensive here, you know, well, goodnight, my dear chap, see you tomorrow morning!"

Ambrose had left his boyhood room in such a way that it gave the impression he had taken a spontaneous flight without time to even pack a suitcase. The bed laid on for me was visible through the shine of a fifteen-watt lightbulb hidden behind mountains of clothes which had been emptied from the cupboard and strewn out all over the floor. Perhaps this wasn't the work of Ambrose, but rather of his brother Humphrey? Between the piles of clothes lay other curious objects; stuffed bird skins, part of a camping set, mountain boots, books, fresh ginger, and an experiment kit for 'budding chemists from 10 to 14 years,' which was just as pungent as the unmade bed, which looked as though it had been left in such a state for several weeks at least.

Before I lay down, I decided to try and brush my teeth, as I had noticed there was a sink in my guest room. As a matter of fact, the little pipe above the sink jutting out of the brocade wallpaper trickled water constantly, even when you tried to turn it off with the spanner sat rusting in the basin. Whether the spanner was part of a Rolls-Royce toolbox or not would have to wait until the morning sun. I doubted it somehow due to the rust.

While I was dozing in bed, I couldn't help but impose on my current situation with Bunty that question so often used by psychologists: would you buy a second-hand car from this man?

To me, this question was neither here nor there. Given that, as I was soon to discover, the Scott-Moncrieffs sold on average two cars a week, be it handled by Bunty, Hazel, Bernard or Eddie, this psychologists' tool was evidently being routinely answered with a simple signature at the bottom of a contract – a 'yes' in anyone's book.

Great Britain is full of peculiarities. Bunty was one of them.

Although I was a guest of the Scott-Moncrieffs on several occasions, I never had the opportunity to meet Ambrose, who was so often talked about. It was 2012 when I first met him face-to-face, and that was over the internet. He gave an interview about his professional career, and what it means to be an art conservator. He looked incredibly similar to his father and spoke (almost) like Bunty. The pair of us were in stitches about the fact that I had once slept in his unmade bed and attempted to brush my teeth in his wash basin.

A Rolls-Royce ...
what a temptation!

ABOUT HALF A YEAR later, I was toying with the idea of purchasing a Rolls from Bunty, which I could have had for just £250. A mate's rate! A steal in anyone's book! What could possibly have deterred me from acquiring this 1929 model? Now, the pound was worth 11 DM and 20 pf at the time, so investing 2800 DM plus customs and flyover in another classic car was something that I quite simply couldn't allow myself to do. I already owned three vintage cars, and maintenance for all the regular repairs was costing me a stupid amount of money, sometimes as much as half of a typical monthly salary.

As a subscriber to the London-based magazine *Motor Sport*, I was able to keep a close eye on Bunty's public advertisements and ensure that his price wasn't unreasonably high and fell in line with his competitors. I'd found my way into the circulation of Bunty's monthly 'stock list,' meaning I was receiving piles upon piles of Polaroid photos upon request of Hazel or Humphrey or even Bunty himself. In all seriousness, I wasn't actually interested in a Rolls-Royce for myself, but the fascination that surrounded them was very alluring.

To be a Rolls-Royce owner at just one point in my lifetime ... this lifelong ambition of so many, and remarkably this was absolutely affordable for someone on an average salary! (It's still possible to do this today in actual fact, if you do it right).

Bunty knew exactly how to do it right, above all because he typically dealt with American clients. From five cars, Bunty would sell four to customers from overseas. Customers would be very well-advised to come over to England themselves and pick out the Rolls of their dreams to take away that very same day from either one of the sheds at Rock Cottage, or later in the show rooms on Macclesfield Road. If a customer didn't have the time or desire for a trip to England and so simply placed an order for a shipment of one via container after reading the description and seeing a few pictures from an instant camera, there was the risk of bitter disappointment.

Since it was possible to pay via documentary credit in advance, Bunty could have the money at his disposal the second that the shipping company in Liverpool had successfully transported the cargo, allowing him to minimise his risk as salesman.

Just as with any other automobile, even the 'best car in the world' has its foibles and pitfalls when it gets long in the tooth and hasn't been maintained diligently enough throughout its life. Geoffrey and Eddie had done their best to keep the cars which they were entrusted in spick and span condition. It was only the seriously dilapidated specimens that were left to sit and rust. In defence of the Scott-Moncrieff firm, I must add that they always had excellent, first-hand cars, kept as immaculately as chauffeur cars, in pristine condition and fit for the next Concours d'Elegance.

"The first thing I do is look in between the gaps in the upholstery," Bunty said, explaining one of his top tips for affordable car purchases. Searching for coins which may have slipped down there, most likely. "No, in search of confetti, actually … for you see I could then make a reasonable assessment that the car in question had most likely been rented out for weddings, and thus had been used by people who hadn't given it a thorough clean. That is a clear indication of neglect in my eyes."

The majority of people who wanted to procure a car from Bunty were hoping to do so by means of vehicle exchange. Bunty only let himself get caught up in such deals in very special circumstances, however; perhaps if he and Averil actually wanted to keep the traded car for themselves, or if he had an aficionado up his sleeve who would pay over the odds for it. When this happened, Rock Cottage was transformed, like a museum with a rapid succession of changing exhibitions. I went there perhaps seven times, and every single visit brought with it some sort of surprise.

Brave, and quite the swimmer!

BUNTY'S LIFE STORY BEGINS, of course, before he himself had ever existed: a beautiful, warm spring afternoon in 1906.

A shapely, mature lady from Richmond was strolling down Cholmont Walk along the Thames; first name Grace, surname Eustace. She walked this way every afternoon, weather permitting, of course. She wasn't alone, however; her accompaniment was male in sex and considerably smaller than Grace herself. It was a brown-spotted terrier.

It must have been quite a dopey dog at that, for dogs don't typically fall into water on their own accord. And had Grace somehow knocked him into the water with the toe cap of her shoe, he would still have to be considered pretty dim-witted indeed not to have skilfully parried this inadvertent attack. Why would she have done such a mean thing, however?

Let's not attribute this unfortunate event to Grace, for wickedness was certainly not a quality of hers. But it would have undoubtedly helped the flow of the story, had this attractive lady of marriageable age just given the tiny fella a little nudge in the wrong direction, perhaps as part of a study into canine swimming behaviour. That would thus make the terrier just a variable in a scientific experiment, and if this was indeed plausible enough to make a case for, then it could be argued that her actions would be the same, whether the motive was scientific or devious: Miss Eustace had nothing else in mind than to determine the spontaneity, responsiveness and perhaps also the swimming skills of a passer-by, who rushed to her aid immediately, as if he had been waiting for it to happen, discarded his jacket and dived straight into the turbid waters of the River Thames in order to safely bring the thoroughly soaked terrier back onto the land.

Equally, if the dog did decide to take his bath voluntarily or indeed entirely unintentionally, then the young, trim, Egyptologist Phillip Scott-Moncrieff was all too ready to jump in, as this finally gave him the chance to do Grace a favour – a moment that he had waited a long time for. He had passed her here on a number of occasions already, his gaze had met with her beautiful eyes, but he was yet to find the courage to open up a dialogue …

He was not going to stand idly by and let this golden opportunity to spark things off, in the role of the hero to boot, slip through his grasp.

From then on, the pair had good reason to pass time here and there by the Thames together. They walked together, either side of the terrier, just to ensure that he didn't accidentally fall into water once more. That would've been pointless now.

Soon after, Phillip asked for Grace's hand in marriage (which apparently took her very much by surprise), but this was met with a fair amount of reservation from the families of both parties. Grace's parents had long since given up attempting to find a suitor for their daughter, whilst Phillip's parents had been hoping for a slightly younger model for their son to be betrothed to. For you see, Grace was indeed close to twenty years older than her husband-to-be.

Nevertheless, Miss Eustace wanted time to seriously consider the young, dynamic lifeguard and dog lover's proposal, and so, as was possible back then in the classiest circles in England, she booked a voyage to India for this purpose. When she returned to Richmond three months later, she gave the impatient young suitor the yes word, albeit after a further six weeks of consideration. That she was also pregnant at this point remained a secret. It appeared it would have been too late for her to reconsider anyway. The happy couple were betrothed in the London suburb of Egham, where the Scott-Moncrieffs lived, and then, on the 1st July 1907, Grace Scott-Moncrieff brought a healthy, firstborn son into the world: David William Hardy.

That these three, beautiful names were soon to be reduced to nothing more than 'Bunty' can be attributed to Phillip's brother Bill. Apparently, he was the one to start it off from the very beginning and after a while everyone was in on the act. Bunty couldn't ever remember being called anything else by any member of the family. He was to keep this name his entire life, as he found it suited him so well.

Bunty, not Bounty. Even though there'd been a famous ship of this name which had experiences a wild mutiny on board in the South Pacific (which was later turned into a rather grandiose film with Charles Laughton. The association remained close, because Bunty had seaman's blood running through his veins. His grandfather was none other than the master shipwright Scott from Glasgow, who, as a partner of Hercules Linton, had laid the keel for the Shanghai tea clipper known as the 'Cutty Sark' in Dumbarton (which sadly suffered severe damage as a museum in 2007 but has since reopened). That ship would later lend its name to a well-known whisky brand could never have been predicted by anyone in the 19th century, except Bunty of course, who was dead on with his guess. Although he wasn't the greatest whisky drinker; brandy, a good port and French red wine were always his tipples of choice.

A passion for cars attributed to his mother

BUNTY HAD ALWAYS TALKED in awe when discussing his father. But it was his mother for whom he had a special fondness, which she reciprocated with the same intimacy. Bunty was her firstborn, the child she had so longingly desired, and ended up being her only offspring. The pair were so close that he would often cry into his pillow with longing when he was separated from her at Wellington College in Copthorne. It was with complete and utter impatience that he waited desperately for those weekends when she would come and visit him before the holidays arrived and mother and son could go to the seaside together.

Mrs Scott-Moncrieff would collect her boy from college in an old, chain driven, 4-cylinder Mors – a French bolide, which she had purchased from the Mors representative in London; the founder of which was a certain Charles Stewart Rolls, subsequent partner of Mr Henry Royce. Bunty became the envy of every one of his classmates when his mother would roll up in such dashing fashion behind the wheel of this big car, and the fact that she had the courage to steer such a monster as a woman in those days proved to be the decisive factor in sparking Bunty's automotive passion. This 1908 Mors cropped up time and again in Bunty's stories.

At the time, the Mors brand was just as well known in England as it was in France. Their new 4-cylinder, imported in 1907, which featured a drive shaft operation instead of the previous chain drive, was incidentally the idea of a then rather unknown engineer amongst car designers, who had just been appointed as CEO of the Parisian firm. His name was André Citroën.

Bunty was without a doubt the first and only student to own a car at Wellington, even though no-one was allowed to know, especially the teachers. Amazingly, even Bunty's dear mother wasn't privy to this information. She was confused as to the constant financial troubles of her son, especially given that she was convinced he didn't play games, wager or drink. She never landed on the fact that he was using the money to finance a motor without her knowing. It was always the expensive tennis lessons, the excessive amounts of food he gobbled down; in reality, every penny of Bunty's spare change was going on incredibly pricey petrol for his car. The first of many he would go on to own, and he'd built it himself.

In later life, Bunty was often asked why he never considered a career in theatre. His terrific acting talent, his way of arousing attention and drawing in all of his peers to make them wait upon his every word, his aptitude for the theatrical; all of these would have been well appreciated in the art of live performance. His father's sister, on the contrary, claimed to have discovered a future literary talent in Bunty. Auntie May was a writer herself. Yet Bunty had far greater fondness for the spoken word than the written one, even in later life, when he drafted several books and numerous magazine articles.

Inkwells were flying occasionally ...

BUNTY HAD CERTAIN ROLE models whom he tried to emulate from a young age. One example was his Uncle Horace, whose sick humour was loathed by the whole family. Above all, however, Bunty had a serious interest in all things technical. This is why he built his first car all by himself, following a few blueprints, which he would drive around Wellington without the knowledge of his parents or teachers. It operated on three wheels and required a push-start.

Bunty did everything in his power to keep the construction and ownership of his three-wheeler a secret, and as a precautionary measure he kept his little hobby garage at the other end of the city. Bunty would have most certainly been expelled had the tools been discovered. Bunty was also not allowed to drive, of course; it was unlikely that even one of his teachers would have a driving license for that matter. Unlike Mrs Scott-Moncrieff, of course.

Just a handful of students knew about the self-designed three-wheeler, and all were sworn to secrecy. Yet this project was not Bunty's first – it followed another, equally small and primitive automotive. This one was no homemade budget kit car, however, but rather more of a voiturette: a cyclecar. Unfortunately, it was only a single-seater, which was the motive for Bunty trading it in soon after, in exchange for another little speedster known as a Sizaire-Naudin, which he owned for three whole years. He finally revealed this two-seater to his mother one day, albeit still keeping it away from the staff at Wellington College, for that would have certainly led to a somewhat premature and permanent exit from the establishment, something his mother was also aware of and wanted to avoid. She kept her silence, too ...

"Bunty was quite a maverick," remembers Toby Howard, one of his fellow students. "We were slightly in awe of him, because everything he did seemed so risky and dangerous. I was one whom he occasionally took in his Sizaire. He was quite a reckless driver; he always drove far too fast. And when he lost his temper, everyone had to watch out, even the teachers. That was when inkwells began to fly about the classroom ..."

1924, almost 17 years old, Bunty left Wellington along with his custom Sizaire-Naudin. Many of his fellow pupils became lifelong friends with whom he kept in contact: selling them cars and writing them postcards from the most remote corners of the globe. He even had to scrounge money from one or two of them every now and then.

Like many other young men of his class, Bunty set out to shape his fate in his twenties, but he had to do so on very little cash. Sure, there were friendships and contacts in all directions, but Bunty had no desire to use this time to start a working career. His family was well off enough, and when you have enough means to get by, you can always manage. Indeed, even Bunty's father, although a fully qualified scientist, had little interest in pursuing breadwinning in the traditional sense.

Just as his father had an academic degree at his disposal, even though it was only a baccalaureate, Bunty already seemed to have more purpose for society than simply abandoning himself to idleness in his twenties, and so he enrolled at Trinity College, part of the wider establishment of Cambridge University. Quite how he managed this was a mystery to everybody familiar with the stringent selection process which Cambridge operates.

"I was able to convince the chair of the committee that the exploration of mechanical phenomena was my one true passion," read an early passage from Bunty's personal diaries. "It was entirely conservative, scientific phrasing. But they were also rather approving of the car and were impressed by the fact that I was actually able to operate it. I was deemed suitable and worthy of a place on any of the available courses which fall under the general remit of 'Engineering.' I am absolutely delighted about this."

Escape from a police raid in a dinner jacket

BUNTY'S SUBJECT OF STUDY comprised an, at last legitimate, opportunity for tinkering and playing with cars, debates about compression values and oil temperatures, and experiments with different materials, mysterious substances and mechanical equipment.

Cambridge presented him with new adventures – and new opportunities to offload heaps of money. His parents were no longer able to raise enough to cover what the sophisticated student and prospective engineer needed. Besides the pursuit of an advantageous job, Cambridge, like all other elite institutes for higher education, taught Bunty an important lesson: that it is neither customary nor possible to simply spend other people's money, money that was slipped to him by those who loved and revered him. Bunty's well-developed business acumen, coupled with some of his other traits, enabled him to live a pretty comfortable lifestyle. Those who didn't know his true circumstances might have had the impression that Bunty moved only in the very best circles and was well covered by his family thanks to some sort of noble heritage. Indeed, the very fact that the young man owned at least one, if not several cars, among which were often expensive exotic models, would surely lead most to this conclusion.

Using interesting cars as a means to impress, whether bought, borrowed or mischievously ill-gotten, summed up Bunty's eccentric lifestyle entirely. He was a show off, plain and simple. However, his bravado wasn't nauseating, as arrogance often can be. He didn't come across as proud, snobby, or ostentatious, for everybody valued Bunty's warmth, his helpfulness, his good grace and above all his rich and diverse sense of humour.

During his time at Cambridge, Bunty, using whoever's money it was at the time, had managed to procure an American Mercer Raceabout after the sale of his Sizaire-Naudin. Excerpt from his diary:

"What a lovely piece of technology I have managed to get my hands on here. The girls will all be mad after me now! This has to be the only Mercer in England. It makes an infernal racket on the university campus, which is what led to me being issued with a general driving ban yesterday. Mother would certainly be thrilled if she was to see the car …"

In Trinity College, it was very risky to attract unwanted attention. One or two semesters required perseverance, but life at Cambridge was otherwise very entertaining. Particularly the evenings and the nights. The students were strictly forbidden from trying to find jazz club cellars such as the one on Gerard Street, and to enforce such measures, in some cases there would even be police control outside such venues on order of the dean. Another diary excerpt reads:

"We escaped yesterday's raid with little distress. Peter, Thomas and I were able to save ourselves by jumping up onto the musician's podium. We seized some instruments and acted as if we were part of the orchestra. The police obviously believed it because we were the only people in the audience wearing dinner jackets, like the musicians."

Had the names of the three additional saxophonists appeared in the police report the next day, it could've had disastrous consequences for them. By Peter and Thomas, Bunty meant his two classmates Cochran-Carr and Stuart-Fotherington.

Alongside Thomas Stuart-Fotherington, several young men such as Archie Birkin, David Murray, 'Mavro' Mavrodorgato, Bill Dobson, Dick Chapman and Archie Frazer-Nash belonged to an academics' motorcycle club at the university. Almost all of them made a name for themselves in motorsport later on in life.

Bunty was also a part of this club but found motorbiking far too dangerous – as if he had intended to take part in runs or even races! He considered cars to be much safer. He also didn't own a motorbike.

"Yesterday I had to give the Mercer back, I was short of the last instalment," he entrusted to his diary. "A laughable £75 was all I was missing. Completely blank again, I can't borrow money from Mavro anymore. Archie B has already been panhandled by Archie F. It's a curse, being born so destitute …"

Three days later: "The money that I got back by returning the Mercer has been invested in an old Mercedes Tourer. Brakes slightly broken unfortunately, gearshift terribly notchy. Doesn't start well either. How were the Germans able to win the 1914 Grand Prix? They shouldn't have allowed the Kaiser to elope into exile."

A week later: "Accident! Not much happened to Dick or David, but George, Tom and Hugh came out of it with a few small bumps and bruises. Flipped the Mercedes on a hairpin bend by Haverhill, couldn't brake beforehand, no pressure on the pedal. Hugh paid for the tow truck. We'll join forces to repair the Mercedes again. The beer in the pub was lousy, as were the two girls there. Not a very successful day, all in all."

It wasn't just exotic luxury cars which Bunty used to make the counties of Cambridge and Suffolk unsafe. A bourgeois DFP followed the Mercedes, then an Alvis 12/14 hp and a Ford Model A (in which he endured a 'very funny' accident, as Bunty wrote in his diary), and he was even the temporary owner of a Grade cycle car from Germany. He had acquired this very cheaply, because nobody else could cope with its friction gears. A perfect fit, then, for a prospective engineer to whom nothing abnormal could be considered too abnormal.

Despite this, one can make a better impression behind the wheel of a large, chic Austro-Daimler. Not only that: "It finally worked with Margaret, she was captivated. That was her first time in a car. A vehicle of the dimensions of my Austro-Daimler 10/40 horsepower is simply indispensable for certain actions. Popped open some champagne afterwards, unfortunately it was far too warm. I was burping terribly."

Uncle Horace's corrupting influence

IF A MEMBER OF the motorcycle club had won a race, a proper victory party naturally followed. Most of these ended with some sort of tomfoolery, either improvised or premeditated, and Bunty is supposed to have been responsible for the 'assassination attempt' idea.

It was planned in such a way that one of the guests present at peak time at the party secretly set light to a squib whilst another simultaneously burst in through the door to the banquet hall with a dress shirt smeared with tomato paste. Bunty would have loved to play this role himself, but he was aware that the unsuspecting onlookers would have seen right through him. In the end, it was him who bellowed 'Help! An attack!,' at which point someone sprinted to the nearest telephone and alerted the police and ambulance services. As several brave members of the society took on the roles of the tomato puree-covered victim, the press, who had been tipped off already, were straight to the scene, flashed on the spotlight and laughter echoed around the hall. Bunty and his friends had once again achieved what they were after: macabre publicity.

Bunty had most likely developed his taste for such arts from his Uncle Horace. Horace made it his business to take every opportunity to put a bee in the young man's bonnet, and in turn to make him his accomplice. "Horace was the sort of person who would get dressed up as a Sultan by a make-up artist from the theatre, and then proceed to be Emir from Morocco at the Lords Commissioners of Admiralty," Bunty explained to me. "In honour of his birthday, he begged for just one small favour, to honour the Royal Fleet currently staying at the Port of London. He wanted to join in the naval morning colours on Tower Bridge, from the backseat of a Lanchester. And he did it! As true as I'm standing here. I was there as his bellboy, with a bathrobe, golden belt, turban and a parasol! Of course, bets were all completed beforehand, that's what it was all about really. Uncle Horace collected several hundred pounds. I believe that he subsequently donated it all to the Royal Navy Benevolent Trust ..."

Bunty: "Another time, Uncle Horace passed himself off as an electrician, apparently representing a firm for modern security, in order to investigate the alarm in the London Tower. He was allowed to be so close to the crown jewels that he could have stolen them. I know that for a fact, because I was there as his 'assistant.' Of course, we wouldn't have been allowed in the vault alone. My role was planned to involve me having an epileptic fit, in order to distract the guard once Uncle Horace was close enough to the jewels. But I became too scared right before we had achieved our goal, really, we were finally about to commit treason against the Royal Family ... I simply made a run for it, and Uncle Horace followed ... luckily, they didn't catch us ..."

I'd like to query whether Bunty really believed that the audiences to whom he told such hair-raising stories took them at face value. Maybe Uncle Horace had indeed simply told his nephew of this nonsensical plan ... it was certainly the case, that upon arrival at the base of the Tower, the 'electrician' would have been asked for his proof of identity and the company, for which they both 'worked,' would have been immediately contacted. The problem was, Bunty's Uncle Horace stories were simply too nice. It was impossible for you to nit-pick details or demand explanations. Particularly once you had experienced Bunty answer such queries to his stories: "Ah, thanks for bringing that up ... I realised I had missed a couple of important details. Well, this reminds me of a different story ..."

In one fell swoop, he would manoeuvre himself out of the stickiest situation and delve into another, equally baffling little tale.

Just one more about Uncle Horace then: "He had invited me to dinner in Bertorelli's most famous restaurant on Charlotte Street. I was eighteen at the time. After dessert, Uncle Horace wanted to show me the Café Royal, a then rather notorious trendy bar in Soho. It was chucking it down, and we had no luck in flagging down a taxi. Without further ado, Horace yanked open the back door of a car which just happened to be waiting in front of the restaurant, shoved me in and followed suit. Behind the wheel sat a man of small stature with a bowler hat on his head. Back then, the London newspapers were filled with scare stories about American gangsters who carried out all sorts of misdemeanours in the city, so my uncle decided to play a little game, pressing a fountain pen into the back of the poor guy at the wheel and, in a Texan accent, demanded that the man drive us straight to Piccadilly Hotel, without looking round. The threat was that one of our fellow gangsters would pick him off point-blank from one of the hotel rooms if he so much as turned around to look at his passengers. We darted into the hotel under cover of darkness, nipped through the side entrance and carried on behind into the Café Royal. Despite the pouring rain, we managed it incognito and with dry feet – and free!"

The story had a clear hitch. I didn't want to spoil it for Bunty, or else I'd have promptly demurred that interior rear-view mirrors existed in 1925.

Since Bunty loved to romanticise and embellish even the simplest occurrences until they took on an adventure format, the story of the gangster hold-up probably did have elements of truth to it and could most likely be reduced to something akin to a hitchhiking escapade. It would have then been circulated in Café Royal, leading to the tale which Bunty would later share with me.

Purveyor to the nobility and gentry

OVER THE DURATION OF his studies, Bunty didn't waste much space in his diary, in fact he didn't spare any. However, one very important entry had been noted: "Last night I have decided to establish a business of my own."

The entry was dated from 12th April 1927. A year which was later to be found on the letterhead of Bunty's personal writing paper. "Purveyor of Horseless Carriages to the Nobility and Gentry since 1927" was how it would read.

This self-styled title was designed to make light of the famous 'By Appointment to His Majesty the King.' Being considered a purveyor to the Royal Household and thus being able to include the national coat of arms as evidential, privileged branding was the pride and honour of carriage suppliers like Hooper's and car manufacturers like Daimler of Coventry; producers of orange marmalade, soaps, or lemonade such as Schweppes were also part of this elite group. Bunty's understanding was to manipulate this in order to establish exclusivity in his own, typically unique way, based on nothing more than a slogan. It was designed to entice those who weren't familiar with it and, during the course of the next decade, become as popular and well-known as the slogans 'Ask the man who owns one' (Packard), 'Standard of the World' (Cadillac) or 'Motoring for the million' (Austin).

You could say that the nineteen-year-old had decided to become a used car salesman. Bunty, however, had to describe it in a more eloquent and upmarket way – it was simply in his nature.

Bunty's automotive business began with the coaxing of fellow students who were in similarly pecuniary difficulties to him. Most of these already ageing cars didn't actually belong to the students, but rather to their respective parents, who had motorised their sons as a means of enabling them to belong to the popular, to the 'elite.' Better a small second-hand car than a wretched motorbike. Bunty decided to offer a modest twenty or thirty pounds for these boxes, many of which indeed pre-dated the war period, and then to advertise them to circles of younger students in their first semester, who did not belong to the privileged elite, as a means of transport to and from home. The newcomers almost always had enough cash, and when Bunty offered them a Morris, Singer or Whitlock for (from their naïve perspective) a small amount of money, they practically fainted. By taking a short stroll with them, Bunty could succeed in convincing his victims of the importance of being seen as a car owner at Cambridge. And it just so happened that he could source just the thing via a very good connection of his for just £50 …

And so, Bunty's car dealership operation continued from day to day, which took up so much of his time that his studies began to suffer. He wasn't just active in academic circles, either. Bunty would roam through the pubs in the city, trying to discover which groups of people needed cars urgently. One evening, he came across a group of Romanian businessmen, who admittedly hadn't expressed much interest in purchasing second-hand cars but had been so continuously harassed and abused by Bunty, to the point where there was categorically no way that they were purchasing any old car from him the next day. Well, not any old car, but an old Lincoln on the other hand ...

It had to have been a Lincoln, because Bunty had assured them that no other brand could compare. It could only be the American prestige car! Bunty had just acquired the Lincoln extremely cheaply, an eight-cylinder, because there was almost no demand for such cars at the time in England. "They took the car for £500 and besieged me, demanding that I obtain four more, as each of them wanted a Lincoln for themselves ... it was my best business deal yet ..."

Bunty refused to let the enthusiasm of his new clients cool at all, and, since they were only in England on a shopping holiday for gun apparatuses, he promised them he would locate four more of such cars and deliver them to Romania within six weeks for the same price, excluding the travel expenses, of course. And so, Bunty set off with several fellow students to find some more second-hand Lincolns in London. They were fortunate enough to indeed get hold of four – apparently, the entire inventory of vehicles of this rare brand in Great Britain were together. The marque had been in existence since autumn 1920. The purchase had used up all of Bunty's disposable income; the deal simply couldn't fall through. He'd never be able to find anyone else to buy them for a reasonable price. Full of confidence in Bunty's salesmanship, three young Englishmen accompanied to follow his lead in driving the four, eight-cylinder giants diagonally across the European continent; not only did they have the experience of a lifetime, but they came away from it very well off.

"Bunty insisted that our customers pay in British currency," remembered one of the members of the expedition decades later. "Of course, officially, you couldn't get pounds in Budapest. So, the arms dealers overpaid us in Romanian leu and left it to us to exchange the money on the black market. The exchange rate was bad at the time, too. The figures we were offered were gruesome. I would have bet my life that we would be given fake tender. Bunty assured us that he possessed a good knowledge of people and that these gangsters were the honest sorts ... We didn't have anything urgent to do, so we decided to take these supposed pounds to a different pub on the same day and exchange them back into Romanian leu ... to our amazement, we received twenty percent more leu than we had made in the first place! We took this home and exchanged it back into sterling officially in a London bank, because the Romanian currency wasn't actually so poor.

"The biggest worry was getting the bundles of banknotes back to England safely, our biggest slice of luck was that none of us were searched on the train journey home, for we would have certainly had to declare such a large sum of money. We had stowed the bundles in between incredibly pungent garlic sausage packets, which contaminated our entire compartment but fortunately didn't interest anyone else ..."

Bunty and his companions had secured a very good deal and also made the Romanian purchasers very happy – so what?

Bunty had now developed a particular weakness for the Lincoln brand of cars and the distant Romanians. "A Lincoln was always an extraordinarily well-built car," he wrote in his book *The Thoroughbred Motor Car*, "and this, coupled with the attention given to the detail and finish, makes them one of the finest cars ever built in America ... Lincolns are the best evidence that no corners were cut anywhere in achieving this aim ..."

Bunty had to drop out of his degree at Trinity College for two reasons. For one, he was no longer meeting his obligatory attendance targets; he was regularly missing from his seminars. Secondly, his parents were no longer in a position to send their son money. The Scott-Moncrieff fortune had melted away, and Bunty, despite his own profitable car dealership, had an ever-increasing requirement for his family allowance. The money that his avocation brought in would be spent immediately, often reinvested in cars, the sale of which could not always be pushed through overnight. And so, Bunty left his beloved Cambridge, sadly without an academic title to his name.

No knothole for the backside of a carousel horse

IN JULY OF 1927, the former student of mechanical engineering sciences went to London to work at the firm Westinghouse, Saxby & Farmer Ltd. This didn't prevent him from remaining active as a car dealer once he had clocked off, however. The company at which he had found the position produced car components and certified the young Bunty as one of the best, when he eventually left the role:

"I have the pleasure to confirm that Mr David Scott-Moncrieff was trained in the Clappenham works of our company from 15th July 1927 until 15th December 1930, and during this time gained proficiency in mould construction, foundry, engineering, assembly and testing. Over the last two months, he worked in our London design bureau and was tasked with the development of automotive brakes. I must praise his diligence and ability, and I am certain that he has gained in-depth expertise which will prove useful for his future endeavours. sgd. D H Parker, Manager"

The kind words of Mr Parker don't correspond entirely with those of certain colleagues who worked with Bunty. According to an earlier colleague, Bunty did nothing but nonsense and rarely understood any of the tasks which he was given. Additionally, one of his heads of department is alleged to have scolded him: "Scott-Moncrieff, you're so clumsy, you couldn't even manage to use a knothole in wood to make the backside of a merry-go-round horse ..."

This testimony would certainly fit with the suspicions of every former co-worker who had been convinced that Bunty had swiped a letterhead from his employers and simply typed the review himself. Unfortunately, there is no evidence of the true facts in Bunty's diary.

Just as perpetrators are renowned for returning to the scene of their crime, so Bunty returned to Cambridge after his time at Westinghouse's. Picking up where he left off, Bunty attempted to turn the students at Trinity College onto cars. This time around, Bunty cleverly used the service of several informants who knew the financial circumstances of his prospective customers.

Ron Kaulbeck was one such informant, and it was his brother Bill who Bunty had thought to sell a large saloon, an eight-cylinder Delage, in the spring of 1930. The Kaulbecks were well able to afford the acquisition of such a car. The Delage in question also had a famous previous owner: the racing driver Earl Howe.

"A really fine car, I'd have liked to have kept it for myself," wrote Bunty in his diary. "Perhaps a little sluggish ... Howe said that it would do 100mph but it doesn't. But if you drive at 75mph, it is charming and cultured. The suspension is very pleasant, the vacuum brakes excellent. The elasticity of the engine is similar to a Rolls-Royce. The seat upholstery is a little disappointing, though. Why do the French expect their customers to put up with such inferior rubbish?"

The business deal must have ensured the full satisfaction of all parties involved, or at least, nothing can be found in Bunty's diaries to suggest the contrary. But there's also nothing regarding the events which followed, events which were eventually told to me by Geoff Douty – more than thirty-five years later.

I first met Geoff at a convention for more or less established motorists, whose affection above all else was for the Rolls-Royce brand (and to which I had turned up at the behest of Bunty – in a hired Ford). "That was the story with Gilbert Phillips," Geoff explained. "Bunty and the Kaulbeck brothers had driven to Gilbert in the Delage after the deal, he was a mutual friend, who always had a supply of good brandies. They wanted to mark the deal with a good slug at Gil's expense. Gil was American and drove an American car, and anyone with an American number plate in Cambridge was sure to cause a furore. I was also invited, for Gil and I were neighbours. But unfortunately, spirits were far from high that night. Gil was terribly angry, because his name had been mentioned in a newspaper article, and not in a flattering way. I can't remember what that was anymore, but in any case, he wanted to teach the writer, a fellow student of ours, Winyard Brown, a lesson.

"We advised Gil to give the boy a talking to and demand satisfaction by challenging him to a duel. Bunty and I offered ourselves as his seconds. We went to Winyard's the same day with the proposal, which he accepted immediately, although he did profess to finding the whole thing a little strange. As his seconds, he chose John Davenport and another lad, whom I can't remember. As the hurt party, Gil was to choose the location, the time and the weapon of choice; he decided on the following morning, in Madingley Woods Park, with swords.

"Bunty instructed Gil on the finer points of student duels, as Gil hadn't the faintest idea. Above all, we needed to locate a sword from somewhere – Gil had never so much as held such an object. So, whilst we were discussing all of this, there was a knock at the door and John Davenport entered. Winyard Brown, he explained to us, has had a change of heart.

"He'd at last managed to enrol as a student and couldn't put his position in jeopardy by partaking in a duel as it's clearly banned at university. Davenport had another surprise up his sleeve: he wanted to duel in Brown's place! Bunty, Gil and I accepted. Davenport disappeared again, to share this information with Brown.

"The three of us headed to Madingley Woods at seven the following morning.

"Bunty had somehow managed to acquire two antique swords overnight which came in a pretty basketwork box and so we waited, excited just to see if the other party would even show up. It had been over fifty years since there had last been a duel in Cambridge, and never before with swords; such academic practices had supposedly died out in England long ago.

"We had hardly stepped out of the car when the bushes before us separated and through them came a police inspector. With politeness, he asked us what business we had being in the forest at such an early hour. Before any of us could muster an answer, John Davenport and his comrades showed up on the scene. Naturally, Bunty was the first to react, saying: Mr Inspector, we simply want to have a joint picnic here. The cyclist in uniform quite clearly didn't believe us, as a matter of steps later he was at our car, opening the 'picnic hamper,' which of course contained two swords and no breakfast groceries whatsoever. There wasn't so much as a teasmade, which was particularly suspicious.

"The policeman knew instantly what was going on. Why else would he be on patrol at this hour in the forest! He confiscated Bunty's antique swords and box, clarified the consequences of our reprehensible plan, and disappeared on his bicycle with a politely-put piece of advice that it's best to reconcile rather than attempt to murder each other.

"Before we knew it, he was gone and we were standing there, baffled. Bunty, Gil and I wanted to put this whole thing to bed, especially since this act of shameful betrayal, whoever had committed it, had given us an exciting adventure. So, Gil and John agreed that Winyard Brown was to write a second article, apologising for any spiteful remarks; and at the end of it all, I think everyone was pretty relieved that no blood was spilled. We didn't even have any bandages with us! John made the suggestion that we have a nice champagne breakfast, since we'd probably earned it, and it turned out to be a fabulous day ..."

When I asked Bunty about this story later, he added: "It seems Geoff forgot to tell you how I got the swords back! We were on the way back into town, to Winyard's first, to invite him for breakfast, given that the kerfuffle had been solved, when I insisted we stop at the police station to invite the inspector to breakfast too; I wanted him to hand over the swords as I had only borrowed them. The inspector declined our offer, as he was in service and wasn't permitted to afford himself such extravagance. I pleaded with him to drink just one cup of tea with us, and of course every police station had a tea kitchen. He gave us six chaps tea indeed, but as he was alone in the office at this time, he couldn't have eyes everywhere – on us, the tea kettle, the milk, the sugar, the teacups he was filling up – and then the phone rang in the other room, meaning he nipped out in a hurry.

"By this point, I had long since worked out which desk my box of swords was under. Whilst the officer was dealing with his phone call, we dashed out of the building, grabbing the swords on our way but leaving the freshly brewed tea behind and just in the nick of time as well, for there were two more of his vigilant colleagues on their way in to start their 9 o'clock service. We greeted them politely, without letting them get into a game of Q&A, hopped into our car and sped away."

Back then, Bunty must have looked much older – and thus reputable – than he was. The "Purveyor of Horseless Carriages to the Nobility and Gentry since 1927" was adorned by a well-groomed moustache and he loved to wear a monocle, despite his perfect vision. His suits were immaculate; his appearance that of a man of the world, when it needed to be. When such things weren't required, he was as nutty as a fruitcake; a clown, a parodist, a buffoon.

The maharaja's improper wish

BUNTY HADN'T THE SLIGHTEST inhibitions about approaching the Nobility and Gentry as if he were one of their own. He even sold cars to King Peter II of Yugoslavia and the future King Faisal of Iraq. If he didn't come into contact with the monarchs directly, he would certainly be in contact with their closest confidants, and whenever there was a ball or a reception in one of London's many embassies, Bunty would attempt to mix with the illustrious through some cunning scheme. He almost always struck gold when on the hunt for a victim.

This was achieved not least by his good-humoured yet persuasive audacity, and Bunty really knew how to have fun with this. He would recount his adventurous stories, finding plenty of attentive listeners, amongst whom there was guaranteed to be a prospective customer, even though that person would never know it at first. Bunty soon owned London's most valuable collection of business cards belonging to high-ranking personalities. "The best thing you can do, my boy," he revealed to me once, "is to ensure the permanent maintenance of good addresses, for they can be your capital. If you do it right, each address can be worth several thousands of pounds. And more than once, too!"

However, there was one particular man who looked after certain affairs on behalf of an Indian maharaja in London, whose address Bunty did not want to use a second time for business interests. "The man's name was Sikkim Fahanal, and I was introduced to him during a reception at the Dorchester on the occasion of a charity bazaar. Fahanal was interested in purchasing a Rolls-Royce for his employer: a brand new one, of course.

"I volunteered my services to supply him this car, since I had the best relationship to the most important coachbuilders in London, like Park Ward, Mulliners … however, the man didn't just want the usual highly valuable limousine with lots of precious wood and leather in the interior, but rather one featuring a back compartment studded with precious stones and seat covers made of tiger skin. I agreed all of this with him, then calculated a ginormous commission for myself, should I be able to pull off this assignment!"

This wasn't any old assignment; this was about a Rolls-Royce, after all. The first brand new car of this make which Bunty would have the honour and pleasure of selling. Isotta-Fraschini, Delage, Delahaye, Lincoln, Bugatti – Bunty had already orchestrated dealings with cars of this calibre, not to mention the countless manufacturers and models of less illustrious pedigree. He had also been able to sell one second-hand Rolls-Royce by this point in his fledgling career.

However, a newly registered Rolls-Royce was new territory. "Fahanal and I discussed every detail, I must have visited him at least three times at his office in Mayfair. He trusted that I would get everything done as per his requests at Park Ward. He didn't want to make an appearance or be revealed as the buyer for privacy reasons, so he said. This should all be me.

"The two cheques I received from him were covered, I forwarded the payments onto Park Ward. One afternoon in September, the completed Rolls, a Phantom II model, was driven into the garden of his villa. I was one of four people present for the handover, excluding Fahanal and one of his servants. He seemed to be happy. The bright green finished landaulet featured plenty of shiny things, precious veneer panelling and tiger skin upholstery – all befitting his imagination – and which, we were all hoping, would the vision of his master in the Middle East.

"I allowed myself to direct a suggestion regarding this to Mr Fahanal. Your Excellence, I said, now would be a great moment to capture an image of the car to send to His Highness the Maharaja. Our planes can transport a postal shipment to Karachi and Bombay, and His Highness the Maharaja can have the photograph in his possession in three or four days at the latest, giving him a measure of anticipation of the beautiful car which is en route to him overseas in India.

"Mr Fahanal, now wearing a floral white tropical suit, had heard me but was keeping a straight face. Instead, he presented me with a small, pretty box, no larger than a cigar tin, from his servant and said: Good friend, you have proven most accommodating to His Highness and therefore to me, and His Highness would like to show his gratitude. This casket contains the appropriate renumeration for your work. However, it also contains something else. Please open it.

"I was unbelievably taut as I unclipped the cover of the little box. The three men from the Park Ward company were peering over my shoulder, they were certainly jealous by this point. But what did we see? A white envelope, presumably containing a cheque for me, or possibly cash, and a stunning dark red dagger laid on a velvet bed, unbelievably beautiful, like something from a theatre collection.

"What an original and valuable gift, I thought to myself, and I wanted to hold the trinket in my hand. Fahanal asked that I please follow him, as he took me to one side so that the Park Ward people couldn't hear what he was saying to me. "You will be allowed to keep this dagger, which is worth several thousand pounds, my dear Scott-Moncrieff, if you can do His Highness and me one more favour as part of our business. In our country, it is customary that the most beautiful things which are customised exclusively for our Lord may never be replicated. In your case, this means that this car may never be designed and built again. This comes down to the chief engineer ...

"I wanted to swear that it wouldn't come to that, but he wouldn't let me speak and simply said: it's your job, Scott-Moncrieff, in accordance with the tradition of our country and the request of my Lord, to remove the man's eyesight, once and for all. I'm relying on you and wish to ensure this task is carried out. If my instruction is not complete in five days, the fate will befall you instead.

"Charles P, who had carried out such a wonderful job, and I am supposed to blind him? Single-handedly? And this is why I will ultimately be able to keep the dagger? I could hardly comprehend what Fahanal was asking of me.

"Without another word, Fahanal left us and his servant accompanied us to the property entrance. The Park Ward men were sour because they hadn't been allowed to listen to what Fahanal had told me and because they hadn't had the opportunity to explain all of the details of their marvellous build to him, as had been planned. Normally, the client would have a chauffeur present, whom a representative of Rolls-Royce would brief about the car's specifics or even invite for an instruction course. Nothing of the sort.

"I decided against celebrating the sale of my first, brand new Rolls-Royce at the bar in the Savoy, opting instead to speed hastily across the land to seek refuge with friends. For four full weeks, I didn't show my face in London, living in continuous fear that I could be ambushed and murdered at any moment because I had better things to do than poke Charlie's eyes out ..."

I've heard two versions of this story from Bunty. How closely it corresponds to the truth is difficult to judge but is also something I would rather not know (for this reason, I have never contacted Park Ward – now owned by Bentley Motors – to find out if a green Phantom II landaulet was delivered to India in 1931. Since records of all purchases and deliveries are still kept from that time, I'll leave that to you ...) The second version of the story ends in a funnier way than the first, bringing about suspicion that neither the first nor second run-through of events can be considered truth.

Bunty's second variant of the end of the story goes roughly as follows: "The whole business with the eye gauging reminds me of my time at Cambridge, for we were incessantly doing such things there. I mean, we played pranks similar to this, which were always hysterical. Naturally, I hunted down the chief designer at Park Ward the next day and said to him, my dear Charles, please listen carefully to me now, the second part of our business deal is about to begin and you'd better play along, else we'll all be stabbed to death rather nastily from behind. I told him the story down to the very last detail, and then we had to laugh, before thinking up a fine plan and instructing his boss on the matter as well.

"During the lunch break, I picked up a little red dye from the paint shop and, using a few shreds of tissue, I managed to blot his head with the red dye. About half an hour before, I had rung up my good friend Timothy Hornsutter, he had agreed to order an ambulance to the house for 12:30, where he would be waiting with his camera to explain that there had been an accident which he had to document ...

"To the horror of some people, above all the gatekeeper who began to scream as he saw me and my blood-soaked victim stumble into the ambulance, we turned away from the show and Tony frantically snapped flash photographs. He's been injured! He has to go to hospital immediately! I shouted to the porter, who knew me well, since I had been coming and going to-and-fro for a month now, and before he could sound the full alarm, we were out and away. The 'blinded' man took a few days off, and as payment for his grandiose theatre, I shared my commission with him that I had received from the Indian gentleman, a very reasonable sum. I asked Timothy to send the photos Mr Fahanal's address without comment. I never saw them, unfortunate too, as they must have been very strange-looking.

"Ah, the dagger? I gifted it to Charles …"

Never again would Bunty have the opportunity to sell a brand new bespoke Rolls-Royce. The pre-owned Rolls', be they second, third, fourth or fifth hand, however, continued to change owners throughout his activity. Bunty's first ever Rolls-Royce customer had been a lord, whose name I later ascertained from one of his sons after hours of begging, as the name was sworn to secrecy for several reasons. Among these was perhaps the fact that every gentleman who bought a second-hand Rolls-Royce from Bunty was likely to also feel slightly ashamed that he couldn't afford to purchase a brand new one, or perhaps this lord was simply embarrassed to have ever had anything to do with Bunty. Both are valid reasons to remain anonymous. I discovered that this gentleman was Bunty's first client from Bunty himself, who would have had no objections against the mention of the name, given that he loved to boast about the high-profile personalities that he encountered over the course of his life. Selling a second-hand car to the lord in question wasn't the slightest bother to Bunty, firstly because the car was still quite young ("not even 5000 miles") and secondly because it's previous owner had belonged to the Royal Family, as Bunty explained: "The lord was very happy and satisfied. During the handover at his manor in Berkshire, I received a bottle of sherry and my cheque, and after a polite goodbye I headed home on the train."

There is evidence to suggest that His Lordship remembers the encounter with Bunty a little differently, although I didn't get his side of the story first-hand, but rather from one of his sons. "It turned out that the claim that the car had only done 5000 miles didn't exactly correspond to the truth; it was more like 15,000 miles. This was discovered after a query with the Service Department of the factory in Derby. And exactly which relation the previous owner shared with the Royal Family, only Mr Scott-Moncrieff knows. Father was uneasy above all with the insolence with which the young man carried out the whole affair. He was invited for a drink, yet hastily disappeared back to London after delivering the vehicle. He was supposed to be a trustworthy person and not the sort who completed a deal quickly and then would disappear the next day, never to return, said my father. Oh no, he wasn't the sort at all, Mr Scott-Moncrieff had supposedly assured him, smiling, he wouldn't be gone the next day, he'd be gone as soon as possible …"

The fact that Bunty gave such cheeky answers came as no surprise to me, but he would have never intended to hurt anyone. Understanding his sense of humour was certainly not for everybody. Indeed, some struggled to even figure out the point at which the banality of the everyday world prompt him to new levels of clownery, whether his life was in itself theatrical or whether theatre had inspired him to behave in the way he did.

Did he even know himself?

A talented stuntman

BUNTY'S APTITUDE FOR ACTING in combination with his mastery of even the quirkiest automobiles came in handy; above all when it was used to unsettle a car seller. For example, there was an instance when he was able to use his trickery to lower the price of a 5-litre Sunbeam, which, as an Indianapolis race car, certainly had collector's value to such a level that it represented a fraction of the written price. Bunty had noticed well before the test drive that the left front tyre had too little air in it but kept this discovery to himself. The trial run took place on the then still intact Brooklands track. Through artificial cheats such as provoked snake-like movements through to extreme steering locks, ensuring the rest of the air in the tyre escaped, Bunty was able to convince the Sunbeam owner that the car was "very dangerous and as good as unmarketable." The body needed removing to ensure that the car would go straight; the track rod ends of the steering were completely worn out; the wheel bearing was almost knackered, and the brakes were as good as inept.

"I succeeded with some effort to avoid a catastrophe; one of the most dangerous kind, I pretended. Even I, an experienced driver, could have suffered a deadly nose-over ...! The clueless young man was ashen-faced, as he saw me trembling whilst I got out of the car, weak-kneed, a look of pure horror on my face ... He was supposed to be selling the Sunbeam for the renowned firm Thomson & Taylor, and he made the mistake of accepting my measly offer of £150 instead of the £450 he was hoping for, without even ringing his boss. I had made clear to him that I was the only person capable of doing anything at all with this suicide machine ... The Sunbeam was absolutely fine, of course; in fact he would have certainly found a buyer for as much as £600."

Bunty wasn't telling this story for nothing: "Great purchasing proves real mercantile talent, don't you know!"

Fun on the backseat with Loreley

BUNTY WAS ON THE search for a business partner, whose help would 'broaden the foundations' of his business, which was code for being on the lookout for someone with a significantly more sturdy bank account than he himself held; a search which ended with the discovery of a kindred spirit by the name of Bobby Arbuthnot. Unfortunately, Bunty was soon to discover that Tony had even less financial muscle than he did. However, they remained together and came to an understanding that they would concentrate their prospective business policy on a principle that Bunty had used several times before with success. This was to initially find buyers who had already decided what they wanted and were prepared to pay, before then searching for the car which the client had practically already paid for.

Their first customer to be involved in such a trade 'bought' a little red MG sports car, yet unfortunately it was a little over a week until Bunty and Tony were able to locate such a vehicle and persuade the owner to let go of the car cheaply! The deal was close to being completed, when the buyer suddenly drew the curtain over it after the week's wait had given him time to think; just at the moment when Bunty was finally able to bring the dream car to his door. After Bunty had gifted him some immaculate wine – such retrospective practices of candour supposedly helped Bunty recoup lost bonuses through sympathy very often – they even became friends; and it was Dick Chapman who would tell me this story in later life.

"It was my first car, and Bunty had described the MG to me in such a convincing manner that I must have had the impression he knew the car inside and out. And then I didn't hear from him for eight days, I thought my £50 deposit had simply gone to waste … but he didn't disappoint, the car was flawless and brought me a lot of joy. After that, Bunty visited me regularly in Warminster, where I was working in a solicitor's office, and he always came in interesting company and always in a different car.

"There were three categories of companion that he would bring: wealthy or at least well-known personalities, who he knew would be impressed if he introduced them to 'his lawyer,' previous students from Cambridge who were for whatever reason 'in a jam' and whom I was supposed to offer juristic advice, or attractive young women. The latter would accompany Bunty most often to my office. He was well aware that there was a guest bedroom in my flat which he laid claim to numerous times. Bed and Breakfast for two, free of charge, self-explanatory."

One of his guests was introduced to Dick as Loreley Leichner, daughter of a German businessman in London. Bunty appeared with her at his friend's house one Sunday for tea. However, this would be no sleepover, for the flaxen-haired Loreley was under strict parental constraint to be home before midnight.

"We ate in the evening and shared a bottle of wine. Bunty and Loreley drank it almost entirely to themselves, although it was actually I who had wanted to indulge in the bottle of red, since Bunty had to drive the car back to London that night! As a result, he was so spent after the dinner that there was nothing left to do but for me to take up the reins and chauffeur the rather tipsy pair to London in the dead of night. The two of them amused themselves on the backseat, giggling constantly, whilst I felt annoyed at myself for being far too good-natured.

"To top it all, I realised once we'd arrived that I didn't have any money with me and had no idea how I was supposed to get back to Warminster from Paddington on the early train at 5am ... and Bunty was as good as bankrupt. As he thrust the last of his cash into my hand for the train ticket, he said: 'There's no hurry to pay me back. It's enough if you just give me the money back the next time I come to see you.' How I was going to get to Paddington Station remained a mystery ..."

A valuable car for a one-night stand

JACK BARCLAY – TODAY probably England's most prominent Rolls-Royce dealer – once told a story of how Bunty managed to borrow a car on a beautiful day "just for a little spin with my girlfriend … only for an hour or maybe two, I want to show her Lulworth Cove!" Barclay was already a Rolls-Royce and Bentley representative at that time, a very famous one in fact, enjoying a high reputation. Bunty had passed on clients to him now and again for trade-in cars, meaning he would of course lend Bunty a car for "an hour or maybe two," without question. By 'a car,' Bunty had something quite particular in mind: a valuable, impeccable 4.5-litre Bentley Tourer.

Of course, Bunty never intended to borrow this car, rather he had orchestrated to sell it, with the prospective buyer having already paid half of the full price in advance as a deposit.

"It must have all happened at lightning speed, I couldn't have left the man waiting for half a day," Bunty explained. "We're talking about serious money too. The sort of price which I knew Jack Barclay would have gladly let the car go, I was sure of that. I increased the price by a modest £150 and closed the deal. Jack was rather sour after and said he'd have done the deal just as well without me, but once I laid the large sums of cash out on the table in front of him, he came out with the log book, which I still needed to give to the buyer.

"And since Jack had no way of knowing that I had agreed a price £150 higher than the cash I'd laid before him, he begrudgingly pushed a further ten £5 notes under my nose as commission."

Dick Chapman, famed for his eighty-two years in possession of a documentary-like memory, also told me a story, featuring Libby Saintsbury as the prominent figure in a car deal.

This very pretty girl – Bunty only spent his time with girls who looked exceptionally good – was the sister of a young aristocrat, who had inherited a vineyard in South Africa and absolved to undertake a European trip with her.

"Bunty had formed a wager with me and a few of our friends: he would succeed in spending not only an evening, but indeed a whole night together with the goldilocks Libby … We were all in agreement: Bunty admittedly had experience as Don Juan but getting Libby into bed?! He was never going to manage that. We had met Sir Lionel Saintsbury and his sister the day before at a party and despite all her beauty, she appeared to be a prudish, frigid and above all a rather stupid person, who could never be seduced. We wagered £100 with

Bunty that he would never achieve his target. To cut a long story short, Bunty won the wager."

In order to gain permission from Sir Lionel to take his sister for a candlelit dinner, Bunty declared his willingness to source even the most unusual car for him. It transpired that Bunty had actually made this offer to Sir Lionel before making the bet. It's worth noting the conditions of the agreement:

"Sir Lionel offered his younger sister to Bunty on the condition that he procured him a Leyland Eight," told Dick Chapman. "And it should be fast." Bunty had given his word that he could source one of these eight-cylinder 1922 Leyland, but unfortunately, he had absolutely no idea as to the whereabouts of one of the just 18 ever built, nor who their current owners were. He had somewhat overestimated his detective skills and those of his partner Arbuthnot. He can't have garnered much pleasure from his evening and night with copious Champagne and a plenty tipsy Libby, because 5am came around and he still had no idea how he was going to deliver on his promise. Admittedly he had won the wager with us, but he would soon have to face Sir Lionel.

Bunty left his blue-blooded lover in the early hours and set about solving the problem in a way that was particularly painful for him: he could see no other option. He went to the reception of the hotel in which he had shared with Libby one of the two rooms reserved for Sir Lionel and asked to be connected with Tony Arbuthnot. Tony was still sleeping, of course, so it felt like an eternity before the lady at his office woke him and put him on with Bunty.

The instructions were clear: Tony was to drive to the hotel immediately in 'Chitty' and park the car in front of the house – everything else would be explained to him later.

This was no Leyland Eight, of course, but rather the famous Chitty Chitty Bang Bang II, this automotive wonder which Sir Lionel cast his eyes upon as he looked out of the window shortly after early morning tea. Back then, Chitty was comfortably double the worth of a Leyland Eight; the car was legendary and Bunty had acquired it from the heirs of the racing driver Louis Vorov Zborowski, fatally injured in 1927 — and unusually, he hadn't bought this to sell on. With its 18.8-litre aircraft Benz engine Chitty (the second model of its kind, hence the suffix II) emerged in 1921 as the record breaker at Brooklands, with the name derived simply from the sound of the engine valves and exhaust in neutral at low revs.

Now Bunty was a man of his word, trading Chitty II for a night of presumably scarcely enjoyable passion and, despite winning the wager, making a considerable loss in the end.

When I asked Bunty about the story with Sir Lionel and his sister Libby, recounting to him the tale that Dick Chapman had told me, he was not exactly happy. "He should have kept that to himself. The whole thing was a complete catastrophe for me in several aspects.

"For one, the most interesting car I had ever possessed was gone. But I had to keep my word, for it was important to me that Sir Lionel was not lost as a potential customer for future business, as he was clearly willing to part with anything for cars. Furthermore, I actually lost money from a deal for the first time in my existence as a businessman. And quite a lot at that! For you see, the sum arranged for the Leyland was considerably lower than the price I paid for Chitty. Thirdly, the night with the young tart, whose name I have long since forgotten, Linda or something similar, was anything but enjoyable. I'd have had ten times more fun with any parlour maid employed by the hotel. Sir Lionel was the only one who had completely covered all his expenses. It's a shame that he didn't hold onto Chitty for long; he simply couldn't get about in such a car. A rather sad story all round, indeed, a sad story beyond belief. Chapman should never have told you it."

Chitty Chitty Bang Bang II ended up in the hands of a collector in the USA, giving Bunty the opportunity to see the monumental car with chain drive once more.

Meanwhile, Tony and Bunty ceased to sell any cars which they did not already possess or could get hold of easily. If they came across an interesting and at the same time particularly good value specimen, which displayed a 'corporative' concern, as Bunty put it, they would purchase it, with borrowed money if necessary, sheltering such cars in a former carriage shed in Bruton Mews until an aficionado could be found. This garage had space for six cars and was situated in the noble London Borough of Mayfair, between Berkeley Square and Grosvenor Street. An excellent address indeed, since this was just a stone's throw away from Park Lane, with its fine, expensive hotels, in which Bunty and Tony were often found loitering, on the lookout for their newest victims.

www.veloce.co.uk / www.velocebooks.com
All current books • New book news • Special offers • Gift vouchers

A gentleman has come to warn Stalin

BUNTY WAS LIVING IN a tiny apartment in Lambeth at the time, which was not a particularly fine borough by comparison. He had ceased to keep up a diary, for a little while at least, but still received regular post from his mother in Egham. He used to rave about her to his friends over and over, telling them stories of the four-cylinder Mors which she had driven with such style, however he rarely found the time to care for the old lady, who had been widowed for a few years.

In the late summer of 1933, the other cars in the Bruton Mews garage were treated to a new arrival; a 1929 supercharged Mercedes Benz Kompressorwagen model SSK – a large, impressive two-seater. Everyone that Bunty knew had heard that he was planning a trip to Moscow in this luxury car in order to pay his respects to the Kremlin. Legend has it that he wanted to warn Stalin about Hitler. Everybody thought it was simply another of Bunty's jokes, and only Tony Arbuthnot (who unfortunately belongs to the group of people who I am no longer able to meet) knew exactly how serious Bunty was about this, as he was the only one who accompanied him to the office for visas at the Soviet embassy in London.

Since it wasn't the late Tony Arbuthnot who told me this tale, and I also never had the pleasure of hearing it from Bunty, I have to resort to a dialogue I had with Bill Tayleur. This gentleman had residence on the Channel Island of Alderney; he belonged to Bunty's early customers from his Cambridge years, but had frequently sojourned in London, where his father was active in the banking industry. "Bunty was supposed to fill out an application form in the embassy, but he had decided to leave such a menial task to his accompanying secretary – played by Tony. The residence was listed as a castle in Scotland, in order to lend weight to the Scott-Moncrieff name, whilst Bunty's occupation title was dictated as 'gentleman.' Of course, the fellow on the other side of the desk could never accept that and simply said: No visa! At which point Bunty, as cool as anything but secretly laughing, turned to his 'secretary': My dear, please remind me to bring this up at dinner with Maisky this evening.

"Maisky was none other than His Excellence The Ambassador of the USSR in Great Britain. Bunty had never met him in his life. Of course, the official at the desk had heard the quietly, but not too quietly uttered sentence and was obviously impressed. Within a few days, 'gentleman' Bunty had his entry clearance for the USSR. However, the journey unfortunately never took place. Bunty would never have been able to raise the money for it, since everything that he and Tony had at the time had been invested in the Mercedes SSK.

"I can still remember the time that he invited us on a trip in a Vauxhall 30/98. By we, I mean four of his friends, all of whom had to bring two canisters of petrol as a sort of quid pro quo. Bunty was able to scrounge several others from elsewhere. Five people, more than a dozen petrol canisters! We sat on them, held them between our knees, others we even fastened to the running boards using the belts from our trousers. We sped around in the Vauxhall like a bomb on wheels, not allowing ourselves to light cigarettes, stopping every thirty miles to top up the fuel tank. The Vauxhall required enormous amounts of spirit, and Bunty repeatedly demonstrated to us just how easily the 'mobile bomb' could reach 100mph."

There were, of course, periods of relative prosperity, which Bunty knew how to use to his advantage. He would keep hold of a particularly beautiful car for several weeks or even months for himself before selling on, such as in the case of that big Chenard-Walcker of 1924, a French eight-cylinder cabriolet of real prestige value. Bunty would have loved to hire a chauffeur for such a car, for the brand was widely known even across England in the 1920s.

Between seventy and eighty of these cars were being produced by the day in Gennevilliers, making Chenard-Walcker one of the most successful manufacturers in France. In his book *Veteran and Edwardian Motor Cars*, Bunty certifies the model which he had as being one of "extremely high quality."

In the early summer of 1933, Bunty was able to allow himself a prolonged trip through continental Europe for the first time since his Lincoln tour to Romania, without being dependent on external financial aid. The journey took him to Vienna, Venice, Budapest and then to Bucharest once more. In Budapest he made the acquaintance of the stateless night club pianist Ronnie Visky; they remained in contact, and when the war broke out, Bunty's good connection with Ronnie allowed him to obtain a visa for the USA. Helping Barbu Neamtu, a bank manager whom Bunty had gotten to know in Bucharest, proved much less fruitful. Neamtu belonged to an organisation which was not approved by the state, leading to his arrest in 1939. It wasn't until several years later that Bunty discovered where Neamtu had been deported. Freeing him proved to be impossible.

Kiss your hand, Herr Hitler!

BUNTY TRANSACTED CAR BUSINESS on every trip; at the end of the day that was the point of every excursion. He travelled alone and made the journey to Venice in an RL type Alfa Romeo from the mid-twenties, which he'd bought in London and for which he'd been offered a better price in Italy than he could get in the current English market. The prospective for this particular Alfa Romeo was indeed ready to invest so much in it that Bunty found himself in a position to purchase another extremely valuable lump there and then: the very Mercedes-Benz SSK in which he had intended to drive to see Stalin in Moscow.

"I could have bought the big, gorgeous Kompressorwagen from an arms dealer who had worked for Mussolini previously before secretly changing sides. They had sussed him out as a double-crosser, the fascists had threatened him with liquidation. He wanted to disappear to Trieste overnight, and from there travel to Russia. For that, he required money – and admittedly a lot more than he had. I met him the evening before his flight as he was attempting to sell jewellery in a bar, and as soon as he noticed that I was English, he trusted me and asked me for advice on how to sell the Mercedes, which was far too flashy for his planned escape, for cash – and fast! I offered him £400 cash without hesitation, which he duly accepted. But there was still the danger that I could end up in a precarious position for using his Italian registration plates. The fascists were known to be after all six-legged cats, and preferred to shoot the cats first before counting their legs, if you catch my drift. Fortunately, I still had to hand the English plates from my so reasonably sold Alfa Romeo, so I screwed these onto the Mercedes, which now appeared to be registered as a tourist car from England under GN 66.

"Difficulties would certainly manifest later when I attempted to cross the border into Austria, as my carnet was prescribed for an Alfa Romeo. So I decided that, in order to cope with this problem, which had already brought hours of deliberation and would continue to surface several times on the journey back to England, I would simply lose the carnet and request a new one at the office of the Austrian Touring Club in Vienna, which was subsequently carried out with so much charm and politeness that I ended up asking out the lady who had done me this favour for an evening drive in my car, a gesture which she returned by inviting me to a sweet little wine restaurant afterwards. And so on, and so on; I could bore you for hours with the particulars that took place in that week, which I had the pleasure of spending with Susie in Vienna, during which time I made my best efforts to learn much of the language the Viennese use when they have something good or indeed bad to announce. Believe me, these language skills proved very useful to me later on! In fact, they came in handy as soon as I had left Vienna, namely when I arrived in Munich.

"I had only planned to stop in Munich for the beer, it was supposed to be so famous. However, as I went to navigate my way into town I was stopped by the brownshirts who were distributing red flags with the swastika on them. Swastika flags were flying everywhere, in all shapes and sizes. From every lamppost, from every balcony. The browns planted a dozen pennants on little sticks all over my Mercedes; it looked very funny, like a kid's festival. I didn't really know how to behave, all I knew was that I best stay out of political affairs in Germany.

"But there was no escape, and as I journeyed on into the centre of Munich, I was greeted on both sides by hordes of people, screaming loudly, flying flags, laughing and waving and raising their right arms in salute, which was regulation of course. I shouted back again and again, using what Susie had taught me: kuess die Hand dem Herr Hitler! Kuess die Hand! which those closest to the edge of the road must have understood, for they called back: gruess eahna! Gruess eahna! I had to drive very slowly, for in front of me were a number of open-top cars, in which uniformed people were sitting and saluting both sides of the crowd. I could no longer hear what the crowd were yelling, because there was simply so much noise, brass music as well, because on top of which a marching band began to play! To my horror, I noticed that the radiator of my Mercedes began to blow steam and I realised that I had better get the car off the road. I succeeded in doing this, largely thanks to the help of a friendly Obersturmbannfuehrer, who exclaimed 'make way for a friend of our Leader you idiots!' several times and actually caused me some trouble when I tried to get out of the car, because I was wearing a particularly heavy coat and so many people were trying to help me. I fled the crowds and into a cigar shop, spending the next hour trying out many a good Havana until the nightmare was over and I could drive on without fear of being molested."

Thinking about getting married

KUESS DIE HAND (KISS your hand): using manners and polite phrases to his advantage in the right situation, such as a Nazi parade, was certainly one of Bunty's strengths. Cheekiness, when he could get away with it, was simply for fun, but politeness, where it seemed useful, was one of his most effective ways to open doors. Many of his endless connections to princes, counts and barons, to 'nobility and gentry,' to abdicated or deported monarchs, to prominent high rollers or to influential lobbyists could be attributed to his former Cambridge classmates.

Without exception, everybody knew of this entertaining gentleman, who was never shy, full of well-articulated speeches and exceptionally pleasing with his brilliant manners: sometimes Bunty could hardly stop himself from receiving referrals. Embarrassment only occurred when an invitation to a party on the French Riviera came along, as he couldn't usually afford the travel costs. Otherwise, his only concern was that he had only one dark suit, decorated with a few stains on the lapel, making intercourse considerably more difficult in such a high-class society.

A good memory and the aptitude for foreign languages without the need to swot also paid off. Bunty mastered German, and, above all, Austrian pretty comfortably, and he could even manage French and Italian to a certain degree. Bunty had many friends in Germany, so it affected him greatly when, in September 1939, war was declared on the land he cared for so deeply by Great Britain and a large part of the rest of the world. But we'll get onto this later.

Even after the outbreak of the war, Bunty's Sturm-und-Drang period continued unabated. At the time, nothing had changed when, in 1934, Bunty first met his wife-to-be, Averil. Until then, there had been more important things for Bunty than to find himself a 'good partner.' No-strings-attached flings with cute young ladies, for starters, whom he was capable of impressing to a certain extent, up until the point when they would cotton on to his shrewdness and consequences would follow. It would have been difficult to tie Bunty down in the role of a married man, particularly since all of his companions were single and making thorough use of their bachelorhood. But then there were a few – if nothing else rational – considerations, which made the thought of marriage worth deliberating. However, cars remained Bunty's priority as far as his passions were concerned …

Cars continued to come and go at an ever-increasing rate at Bruton Mews, even the magnificent SSK – which, to Bunty's regret, could only manage 100mph due to a little defect – was gone within a couple of weeks. With increasing business, Bunty's takings were multiplying, leading to at least periods where he didn't need to scrounge. However, he had learnt how useful it could be to give the semblance of a man who was 'completely broke once more.'

Everyone accepted him in this role, particularly when Bunty 'outed' himself in the right way, for he was surrounded by people to whom money was absolutely no object. Free lifts to Cannes if a particular party was taking place again on board a yacht, summer night balls in one or other of the castle grounds, Bunty knew how to seize any opportunity – even if he hadn't been invited, he somehow always found access. On some of his trips, his luggage would consist simply of a wash bag with a good aftershave and a dinner jacket. Yet, more often than not, he would leave such events of the High Society having made a sale.

An everlasting love for Mercedes

SINCE HIS ADVENTURE WITH the Mercedes SSK he purchased in Venice, Bunty enthused over the advantages of this brand of car for the rest of his life. Whenever a second-hand Mercedes was on offer in London, he would attempt to get hold of it; and he would sell it on with the same positivity and enthusiasm. Cars bearing the Mercedes name were rare at that time in England. When Bunty resettled in the Lancaster Mews – without Tony, who became self-employed – as many as eight of the ten cars in storage would be Mercedes-Benz. These cars had such an effect on Bunty that he would later go on to devote an entire book to them, which was published under the title *The Three-Pointed Star: The Story of Mercedes Benz*.

The first time Bunty saw a Mercedes in a race was at the Shelsley Walsh Hillclimb, a white, two-litre Targa Florio model. Later he bought several Mercedes for personal use, which he kept for a while. His favourite was his 38/250 model purchased in 1951, which figured as type SS in Germany. He valued this car more than the SSK from Venice, even more than his second SSK, which had belonged to Dorothy Paget, a British racehorse owner and motor racing sponsor, member of the nobility, and which he held onto for a very long time (Mrs Paget wasn't only renowned for her corpulence and her racehorses, but also as sponsor of Tim Birkin, because she had supported him in his efforts to fit four dozen 4.5-litre Bentleys with superchargers. The famous Blower Bentley would never have existed without the financial backing of the wealthy Dorothy). Bunty also became friends with the Mercedes-Benz competition manager Alfred Neubauer, who introduced him to Grand Prix aces Manfred von Brauchitsch and Rudolf Caracciola.

However, not every Mercedes brought Bunty good fortune. It was at the wheel of a Mercedes sports car that Bunty, still a student at Cambridge at the time, had his first severe accident. This wouldn't be his last crash in the driver's seat of a car bearing the iconic silver star. In April of 1936, Bunty spun off the road between Preston Hall and London in what he described once more as "a very bad accident," in an attempt to avoid a motorcyclist who was overtaking a lorry in the opposite lane. Bunty lost control, causing the car to skid into a tailspin and overturn. Bunty was taken to hospital with severe injuries; it was there that he began to keep a diary again. "Once I get out, I'm going to write a book on sorcery," he declared. "Because the fact that I am still alive can only be attributed to magic or miracles."

After six weeks, Bunty was released. He claimed to have actually written the book on the miracle of life and survival, but I believe it only comprised of a few manuscript pages. Bunty spoke often about this book, but I have never seen it.

Do girls' shirts burn brighter?

IN 1938, ANOTHER SHOCKING crash took place in a Mercedes on a mountain pass in Switzerland. The cause? A British tourist by the name of Scott-Moncrieff, seemingly out of practice in the art of driving over Alpine passes, as the cantonal police ascertained. It is worth noting that this was in no way enough to waiver Bunty's love of Stuttgart cars.

Bunty had acquired an old Mercedes touring car in Lausanne, in which he spent a few days meandering through the idyllic Swiss countryside with three friends on board. It is unknown as to where the guys were coming from on that fateful day and where their end destination was. In any case, the car came off the road on a narrow serpentine lane. As there was not quite enough space to steer; the driver would have to stop and reverse a little to make more room. However, Bunty decided instead to try a quick manoeuvre over the embankment, leading the vehicle into a full somersault. By some miracle, nobody in the car was killed or even seriously injured; the boys posed for photographs with the wreckage, laughing about the assurance that comes with travelling under a 'good star.' Bunty: "Perhaps others would have fallen into a crevasse when driving around in Switzerland or would have been shot down by a crossbowman. I was lucky and simply plunged down an embankment … we were trying to get from the Bernese Oberland to Valais. I can't remember what the pass was called anymore. Grimmels or something …?"

It was the Grimsel Pass.

But it wasn't just on the roads that Bunty and his companions survived dangerous situations. Bill Tayleur had the good sense to report a boating accident which could have had a catastrophic ending – caused by pure levity, of course.

"None of us had a clue where Bunty had rented this big power boat from when he invited us out on it. There were five guests: Phil Gillespie and I, along with three girls. Bunty played the role of commodore; turning the rudder with casual elegance, without much regard for where we were actually going – promptly steering the boat into a cliff. We were at Walton-on-the-Naze and the tide had turned, it was going out. The water under our keel was decreasing rapidly, offshore winds were setting in. We were stuck between the reef and a sandbank, and since the boat was listing, water began seeping over the tailboard – not loads, but enough to unsettle us. We used every utensil we had on board to try and ship water back out of the hull. But someone still had to get us out of there, no matter what ... so we lit torches to attract attention. These torches were made from bits of clothing, which we doused with petrol, set alight and fastened to the top of the boathooks, which Bunty then swivelled to and fro. Bunty made the executive decision that the torches be made from the girls' outfits first, because he assured us the texture of female clothing gave off a much brighter light! For you see, the sun was still shining and we weren't certain whether our emergency signal would be spotted at all. Phil and I decided to trust Bunty's scientific judgement, which not only protected our own clothing but also gave us the added benefit of enjoying three beautiful ladies becoming gradually more and more – well, naked, leading to us almost forgetting about the water damage. We watched as the gallant girls, these true heroines, slowly undressed; secretly hoping that any potential rescuers would take their time, only so that we would have the chance to escape by reaching solid ground over the mudflats, of course ...

"It was looking as though nobody was coming to our rescue, and since no more water was flowing into the boat, we abandoned ship and crawled over the little cliffs on the mudflats. First the sweet girls on all fours, then us. Bunty made lewd comments and jokes throughout – he found the whole situation simply wonderful. Unfortunately, this meant that not only did we have a rather unpleasant long walk ahead of us, but the girls, down to their bare essentials on the beach front, blamed us entirely for the whole shipwreck and all the trouble that followed."

London's traffic was brought to a standstill

ANOTHER STORY WHICH BILL Tayleur remembers well is the visit Bunty paid him at his London abode, which Bill shared with his father, on one fine summer's day. "Bunty announced his arrival through a terrifying noise which sounded as if heavy artillery was being fired or a house had been blown up, perhaps as a result of faulty gas heating … I ran to the window, the panes of which were by some miracle still intact, looked down onto the street and saw my friend Bunty getting out of an absolutely monstrous vehicle. Once he noticed that I was looking down, he shouted up to me that I'd better get a move on, because he was intending to take it for a spin into the city and I was invited for a beer!

"Bunty's blunderbuss was in fact the Chitty Chitty Bang Bang II, which he could still call his own at this point in time. He didn't bother turning the engine off whilst he was waiting for me, so the giant six-cylinder roared on before us like a marine vessel, before Bunty gave it full throttle and unleashed the artillery fire on the rest of the world. "ZBOROWSKI MADE IT ALL THE WAY TO AFRICA IN THIS THING," Bunty shouted at me. "SO WE'LL CERTAINLY MANAGE IT TO PICCADILLY CIRCUS!" Parking this vehicle, which was well over eighteen feet long, would be impossible; the City of London was no less busy in the early thirties than it is today. Bunty turned left onto Regent Street, taking the corner far too fast of course, causing the tyres to squeal and the left drive chain to spring free of its sprocket. There was a loud, metallic clang as the loose chain whipped against the bodywork, whilst at the same time the giant car spun a harsh quarter-turn. Bunty stalled the engine. We sat, motionless.

"Surprisingly, everything around us appeared to be magically calm. Traffic continued to flow, albeit in a thin trickle, because the roadblock that was our diagonally slanted Chitty on Regent Street proved rather fascinating to the many other curious drivers nearby. Cyclists dismounted, passers-by rushed over.

"Replacing the chain was impossible without specialist tools. Dusk would shortly be upon us and the Chitty unfortunately had neither head nor taillights, it didn't even have number plates – back then such normally respected regulations weren't highly tolerated by us.

"We had left our seats; I found a few pennies in my pocket, headed over to a phone box and called up our friend Timothy Hornsutter, who I knew had a camera and good connections to the Daily Telegraph. Tony, get over here right away, I said to him, you've gotta see this, it's front page news! But if you leave it an hour, we might be in the slammer by then!

"Within just a few minutes, the traffic blockage was complete. I'm pretty sure that half of London was stationary, for when the Piccadilly corner of Regent Street is congested, traffic cannot move from Shaftesbury Avenue, leading to a queue that stretches as far as Pall Mall.

"The chauffeur of a Daimler limousine offered to tow Chitty, and whilst we were discussing how he was going to get the car out of this chaos, our friend Timothy Hornsutter appeared on his bicycle. He busied himself capturing images of the procedure we undertook to haul Chitty, with its grinding chain, to the nearest possible garage. A large convoy of curious bystanders followed us, it was like a fête! Nobody grumbled, and when somebody impatient sounded their horn, it came from somewhere out of sight, somewhere you couldn't view the magnificent beauty on show. The garage we were searching for was on Brewer Street, which fortunately wasn't far away. Afterwards, we headed for the nearest pub with the friendly Daimler chauffeur, Timothy bought a round of beers and Bunty boasted about his experience with chain driven race cars. Complete strangers to us handed out rounds upon rounds, which Bunty fuelled by constantly telling great stories to the best of his ability. The police showed up of course, but the bobbies had their work cut out, unravelling this traffic pile up and searching in vain for the perpetrator ... Yes, did anybody get the number of that stationary car?

"Which number would that be then, sir?

"Oh, what a joy it had been to be invited along for a spin with Bunty! Unfortunately, we didn't make it into the papers. Timothy told us later on that the pictures had 'come to nothing' – perhaps there was good reason for that. One things for sure, there would be no hiding who the car belonged to had the photos been published ..."

A young lady from a decent family

IT'S HIGH TIME TO talk about Bunty's second great love, after that of Mercedes-Benz supercharged cars or chain-driven monsters with aeroplane engines: his wife.

The thing that fascinated him most of all about this cute (she had to be especially cute of course) young lady by the name of Averil was her passion for fast cars. None of her predecessors were interested in Bunty's biggest passion, but he could share it with Averil. Such large common ground proved the catalyst for a long-term connection. They decided to get engaged.

Averil came from a decent family who would be considered well-off, meaning that future housekeeping money and such needn't be discussed. The 'such' included other pleasures such as the financing of an engagement party.

Bunty's debauched bachelorhood was coming to an end. Less than a year prior to his engagement, he had taken over a lease on a ground floor apartment in Shepherd's Market, which consisted of three rooms and cost £55 a month. Bunty even had a butler at his service at this time. This title was given to an Irishman stranded in London by the name of Byrne, who lived with Bunty and received a weekly salary of three pounds, with free board. Byrne was knowledgeable about cars, and, since he had good manners, could be sent to the leisure classes to collect a cheque or similar.

Byrne was considerably older than his employer, and he was a good cook and housekeeper. Viewed in this light, the last year of Bunty's single life wasn't bad at all. Byrne, of course, could have commanded three times the salary he earned, but he seemed to be satisfied, especially on the day that Bunty treated him to a chauffeur's uniform with a velvet cap. This had been found by chance in the boot of a part-exchange vehicle (Bunty would never have bought such an expensive outfit for Byrne). The jacket and trousers happened to fit the unassuming Irishman perfectly, it was only the cap which was a little too large.

On the subject of jackets and trousers: one morning, so the story goes, Byrne found an unknown sleeper on the sofa in the living room, whose swanky suit lay on the floor. The man looked as though he had been rather severely inebriated and was currently in the process of sleeping it off. Bunty explained the situation: the stranger was a Russian prince, whom Bunty had discovered paralytic on a park bench and subsequently taken in out of sympathy, whilst on his way home from a party at around 2am. Whilst Byrne was ironing out the suit of this supposed prince, he discovered several £5 notes in the back pocket of the trousers and showed Bunty what he'd found. Bunty: "How peculiar. The man told me that he didn't have a penny to his name, said he'd drunk all of his money away and could no longer afford his open-ended hotel bill ... that's the only reason I took the poor beggar with me."

The pair attempted to wake the 'prince' and confront him. "He was in complete shock when we waved the bank notes under his nose: "Oh no," said he, "that couldn't possibly be his money."

"He knew for certain that he had spent the lot. But it then transpired that these trousers, which Byrne had so lovingly ironed, were apparently not his at all. Neither was the jacket ... however, he could give us no explanation as to with whom he had swapped outfits and in which pub this had taken place; he was still utterly dazed and was speaking rather incoherently. It wasn't until after a proper breakfast, praise be to Byrne, that his memory finally returned. After visiting a pub, he had followed the invitation of an attractive lady to head next door for a nightcap of brandy, which she served in her bedroom, strangely enough, where two other ladies and many guys were already present – which, over the course of what turned out to be a rather late evening, must have finally led to the inadvertent clothes swap ..."

Needless to say, such occurrences ceased to happen after Bunty's marriage.

Stranger still was the story involving the horse. Byrne was confronted with one at the front door on an early Autumn morning; tethered to the railing of the steps outside. He gave the animal some flower petals to chomp on, scooped up the legacies it had left all over the place, and then went to wake Bunty. "Sir, I have fed your horse. Where can I find the saddle, in case you wish to ride out?"

"What do you mean 'horse,' Byrne? I don't own a horse!"

Yet there it was, standing there, waiting patiently for instruction.

This time, it was Bunty who slowly but surely remembered the events of the night before as they began to unfold in his mind ... his explanation of the night was as follows: "We were partying wildly into the night, the exact reason for this has escaped me now. On our journey home, we spotted a carriage, standing in front of a house, awaiting command; the carter had fallen asleep. Back then, horse-drawn carriages were already a rare sight in the City of London. Bill and George suggested that we play a prank on the driver, so they began to unyoke the horse. Then we brought it back to mine. But where to keep the nag? We fastened him by my front door and moved to postpone all further decisions until next morning.

"Unfortunately, it was I who was left to handle the details, since Bill and George were long gone. How could I successfully return the horse to his rightful owner and remain anonymous at the same time? It was for problems such as these that Byrne proved to be exceptionally useful ..."

Back in those days, Bunty's telephone number differed by one digit from that of a fishmonger's in the vicinity. Time and again, customers would find their way to Bunty when wishing to place an order, which he would duly note down and then pass on to the fishmonger's at the next opportunity. This kindness was occasionally honoured with a portion of smoked salmon or two. However, on one particular day, Bunty was not in a good mood, leading to infuriation as this mishap occurred for the third time in just a few hours.

The lamentable lady, who just so happened to be the third person attempting to reserve various portions and hoping to collect them the same day, received the following answer from an enraged Bunty: "Certainly madam, so long as you don't mind that the plaice is splattered with the blood of our colleague Hawkinson. A baby shark, on its last legs, has just sliced through his throat with a bite in the cold-storage room about half an hour ago, and unfortunately we don't have enough time at present to clean Hawkinson's blood off of all of our goods, you see ..."

In Averil's presence, such macabre telephone jokes would never have crossed Bunty's lips. After he got to know her, he gradually began to change. Averil Marion Anne Sneyd, born on April 7, 1915, belonging to the family of the Duke of Grafton, had heard of Bunty through mutual acquaintances and wished to meet the young man of the hour at all costs.

Their first meeting occurred at a yacht club, on the occasion of a regatta on the Thames. Bunty was very bashful when he was introduced to Averil. This lad is supposed to be a notorious heartbreaker? Hardly!

A second meet followed soon after. This time, Bunty had brought with him a bouquet of violets for the nineteen-year-old debutante. It was during this date that Averil realised her love of fast cars. And Bunty realised his love for Averil.

And so, it transpired that the connection between Averil and the adventurous spirit Bunty became so strong that it curtailed his escapades to a strict business minimum. The pair undertook certain trips together, partly because Averil was also interested in striking up an acquaintance with the rich and the famous of her lover's numerous connections, and partly since Bunty was indeed extraordinarily proud to be able to introduce this young, red-haired grandniece to the Duke of Grafton as his wife-to-be.

Their first continental excursion together took place in 1936, and it led them to the region of Austria known as Styria, where they were esteemed guests of a hunting party. They came together not only with huntsmen from the region, but additionally had the chance to meet several directors from Daimler-Benz during this light-hearted enterprise. This resulted in an invitation to a facility visit in Stuttgart-Untertuerkheim, which Bunty and Averil accepted with great pleasure. Important business contacts aside, Bunty took back another piece of memorabilia from this trip: original Styrian 'Lederhose', ie knee length goat skin leather pants, complete with all the rich, folkloric ornamentation. Henceforth, Bunty was sure to pack these for every future trip to Alpine destinations, parading them before the indigenous crowds and revelling in the rapture. He continued to wear them for decades. Meanwhile, Averil's wish for a souvenir was confined to a cuckoo clock from the Black Forest.

The spy with the diamond in the soap

IN SEPTEMBER OF 1938, Bunty journeyed abroad once more, this time on a solo mission. This excursion was planned to cover Germany, Austria, Hungary, and his beloved Romania. Sadly, Bunty had to cancel the remainder of the trip prematurely, but fortunately he still had the opportunity to experience Oktoberfest in Munich.

It wasn't until years later that most of Bunty's friends (including Averil) discovered what had caused the cancellation of this trip. Dick Chapman was one of the exclusive group, aware that for once it wasn't business which had given rise to the trip, one year before the outbreak of World War II. "He was travelling in a relatively nondescript car, I believe a Humber or a Wolseley or something similar. Apparently, Bunty had a customer interested in Bucharest. We believed that wholeheartedly, he had a lot of good contacts in Romania," explained Dick. "Many years after the war – and after a bottle of wine – Bunty revealed the true reason for the trip, or at least a story he had the pleasure of entertaining us with. It's always difficult to tell with Bunty where the truth ends and the fabrication begins." (Dick spoke of Bunty in the present here, because he entrusted this story to me at a time when everyone was still in good health.) "Perhaps you also know another version. But the version which send chills down our spines goes as follows."

Everyone who read *The Times* or the *Manchester Guardian* in England could figure out what Hitler was plotting following the annexing of Austria in March 1938. Franco had come to power in Spain, Hitler's friend Mussolini had visited Berlin, the German invasion of Czechoslovakia was imminent. England and Germany had publicly intensified their diplomatic contact regarding this matter. At this precise moment, Bunty decided he would travel to Germany with the help of some friends, and attempt to find out if Hitler was planning to do anything about his sham allies Great Britain. Bunty was convinced that Hitler had plans for an invasion and wanted to occupy England, so he set out to discover when this occupation would take place and where the Germans planned to land their boats.

He thought infiltrating the Nazi party's inner circles would be a cakewalk. He would head to Munich, where more foreign policy is carried out than Berlin, and locate the SA-man who'd been so friendly to find a parking spot for his Mercedes with the steaming radiator so long ago; everything else would fall into place.

I cannot say with clarity whether Bunty was truly so naïve as to think that this mission would prove successful, or whether he was just demonstrating his taste for the theatrical, no doubt acquired from Uncle Horace. Either way, he managed by some miracle to escape from it scot-free once more.

So, he'd arrived in Munich, as a harmless tourist so to speak, which was still perfectly normal at the time. However, every foreigner found hanging around in the centre of brown politics was observed with mistrust; every overnight stay in a hotel meant handing in your passport for the duration, and every evening the immigration authorities would show up and go through the register of guests. Bunty had no chance of moving around incognito.

It shouldn't go unmentioned that Bunty had arranged to meet a man in a little town to the west of Munich, a jeweller who was of half-Jewish heritage and had emigration plans. He needed money for this, and Bunty intended to help by buying an expensive stone from him to take home as a present for Averil. The shop was located inside an inn, which had put Bunty up for the night. No sooner was the jeweller on his way, than two men in police uniform appeared in Bunty's room. As it transpired, however, they weren't there regarding his hitherto unrecorded spy activity, nor were they present to discuss the visitor whom Bunty had received just a few minutes before. Bunty was not to know this when they entered the door, causing his heart to sink. Would he now have to hand over this incredibly expensive stone, were they about to arrest the salesman ...? Just seconds before, Bunty had pressed the diamond into his shaving soap for security.

The police officers asked him to follow them abruptly, without an explanation; he was to drive them in his own car to the police station. Bunty had no choice but to follow this order. Someone at the station would speak passable English; Bunty's German was rather inadequate back then. Apparently, this English tourist had parked his car in a forbidden zone the day before; this was to be met with a fine of two marks (four shillings). In the meantime, Bunty was questioned as to what he was doing in Germany. This questioning slowly transcended into a complete interrogation; and, as Bunty soon discovered, his repartee, humour and art of storytelling didn't work particularly well when put to interrogative Nazi officers who spoke broken English at best. The situation ended with an urgent recommendation that he leave Germany via the quickest method possible, especially Bavaria, because he'd now enjoyed Oktoberfest and there could be no other reason for remaining in this region.

Just a week earlier, Neville Chamberlain, the British prime minister back then, had paid Munich a visit. They reached the so-called Munich Treaty, an agreement for the future destiny of Czechoslovakia. Bunty was aware of the conference in Munich – just as all newspaper readers in Europe were – and he'd intended to begin his spying by claiming that he knew Mr Chamberlain very well and belonged more or less to his confidants; however, luckily, he thought better than to spout this codswallop – it wouldn't have taken them long to find him out!

The police let Bunty go and he returned hastily to his hotel room, to find his bag untouched and this valuable stone – which later decorated a ring on Averil's finger – exactly where he had hidden it. The espionage mission had been a failure; the British nation was no more informed than before and would have to settle for the information Chamberlain had given them.

Into exile with a 12-cylinder motor car

BARELY A YEAR AFTER the prematurely aborted espionage mission, Bunty made plans for another journey to the continent. This time, rather than being cut short, the trip turned out to last a lot longer than planned. Bunty's car was his favourite American: a Lincoln; a noble 12-cylinder model on this occasion, which he had coaxed someone into selling him for just £40. Bunty being Bunty, he ensured he kept regular contact with those business connections to whom he had sold several Lincolns a few years ago for such a profit. His intention was to offer this Lincoln to the same group once more, and for at least the five-figure sum that he had paid for it ...

The timing of the excursion was admittedly not ideal – it was the end of August, 1939, and the invasion of Poland by German troops was imminent. The newspapers in England were postulating calamity. On August 25th, Hitler had received the British ambassador, Nevile Meyrick Henderson, as well as his French colleague, Coulondre, as guests, whilst simultaneously giving orders for the Wehrmacht to invade Poland on the 26th of August (which was then postponed until a few days later).

Bunty refused to let these events stop him from completing his trip: "We were all of the same opinion: that, if it were to come to military action, it would all be settled in eight days. Poland would be annexed by the German Reich, just as Austria was, and that would be the end of it. There would be no chance of a chain reaction as in 1914, for all of the heads of state would have too much common sense for that; especially Herr Hitler ..."

Despite this confidence, Bunty was sensible enough to avoid the risk of stumbling into a conflict zone, opting to change his route through Europe: he decided to head to Romania the long way, through France, Switzerland, Austria and Hungary. This journey lasted until Vienna, and ended on Tuesday 29th August 1939, once again in front of the entrance to a police station.

Thanks to his adventure the previous September, Bunty had learnt how to behave before a German-speaking man in uniform: keep a deadpan face, display no bashfulness, give no jocular answers and, above all else, have a plausible reason for privately cruising around Europe with a British passport. Bunty's transit visa identified him as a tourist.

Since March 1938, Austria had been annexed by the German Reich, meaning that, despite his valid transit visa, Bunty was lacking a stamp in his passport. He reacted with grievous indignation, demanding immediate contact with the

British embassy, or at the very least the highest-ranking officer at the police station. Low and behold, this officer turned out to be a good friend – it was Schorsch, a participant in the hunting trip in Styria, which Bunty and Averil had joined all that time ago. Naturally, he recognised Bunty immediately and promptly ensured that his old friend received the required passport stamp – and several more to boot! An audience with the ambassador had become superfluous.

The uniformed Schorsch was able to help Bunty further still: he arranged him a police escort as far as Budapest and organised a "private" and consequently very cheap exchange of foreign currency. Arrival in Budapest brought Bunty's long journey to its conclusion.

Saturday 2nd September 1939. As feared, the Germans had invaded Poland; just a few hours later, Great Britain declared war on Germany. Hungary was allied with Germany, meaning that Bunty now faced internment, despite his good relations to Vienna.

"A motor race was due to take place on Sunday in Belgrade. I would have liked to have been there, particularly in order to see King Peter of Yugoslavia again; I had sold him an Alfa Romeo once. A continuation of the journey in the Lincoln, which had a British numberplate of course, would be forbidden, and I had no chance of acquiring a Hungarian registration with all the corresponding papers by the weekend. My friends in Bucharest could not be reached and, since they had been counting on my arrival, they had presumably now been arrested ... I left the car with a trustworthy man, whose address I had obtained from Schorsch, and narrowly caught the last train which could take me from Budapest, already largely under National Socialist control, to Belgrade."

The race in Belgrade was set to be the last for many years across Europe, and Bunty arrived in the nick of time to see it.

Averil had to be patient for a long time before she heard a peep from her fiancé. She had already been fearing the worst, when she finally received a letter from Athens, posted on the 8th September 1939 and written on the paper of the famous King George V hotel. He had been gone a good five weeks. The letter contained a short description of the journey up to the time of writing, along with instructions for how Averil could reach him in Athens. "Was in Belgrade at the race, VIP box. King Peter was as amiable as ever ... the young man now owns a Skoda sports car, but still has that Alfa Romeo which I sorted for him a few years back ... also had the chance to meet Nuvolari, that chap's driving is simply magnificent, Von Brauchitsch just couldn't keep up. Of course, we spoke of the war, they were all in agreement that it would be over in two weeks at the latest, provided the Germans succeeded in keeping England out of it.

"Too late now, as you know, my dear! Indeed, it was on that very evening that we discovered that our country is now very much involved, along with the French, which means, my love, plainly and simply, that the Germans will now wreak havoc upon England. They have a hundred times more aircraft and a more modern navy than us, and Hitler appears resolute. His military will attack England, occupy it and plunder. This was what I wanted to warn Stalin of in 1933. I'm begging you, my darling, leave this endangered England and come to me immediately, the very day you receive this letter, or else it could already be too late! Make your way to the American Express Company and buy yourself a sleeping cabin ticket for the Simplon-Orient Express to Athens. You'll have to get to Paris first, but from there you can reach Zurich. The Germans aren't in France yet, so at present you have a chance of getting through unharmed. Purchase all your meals at American Express in advance, you will receive the corresponding vouchers. Hand over your passport to the people there; they'll take care of all your transport visas. Get yourself some change as well, because you'll need about ten shillings for every French franc, Swiss franc, Yugoslavian dinar and Greek drachma. Take as many clothes with you as you can wear, soon it won't be possible to buy any. Should the express be sold out already, purchase a ticket for the Imperial Airways; however, that will cost you £45, about double the price of a train ticket. If you fly, please only do so with Captain Cotheram or Captain Lynch-Blosse, I know both very well and can be sure they will take good care of you. But don't wait for even a day, for the connection between London and Athens could be cut off at any time. I'll be waiting for you, oh and one more thing before you arrive here: would you like to marry me before the British consul general or in the local English church?

"Bunty."

No wedding took place, either in the consulate, nor in a church in Athens, for Averil disregarded all of the well-meant advice of her fiancé and stayed in England.

Caught behind, in front of, and right between the crossfire

AVERIL DISCOVERED THAT BUNTY had headed back to Budapest from Athens and sold his Lincoln V12 Zephyr there (for far less than he had hoped – the interest level for an American Vee Twelve was as good as non-existent in Autumn of 1939), before eventually landing in Sofia. In his letters, Bunty used little more than code regarding what he was driving in Bulgaria and what was keeping him afloat. He brokered cars and motorboats on behalf of anonymous authorities, all the while continuing to beg Averil to come to him for the remainder of the war. But she stayed in England, as of yet unoccupied by German troops, and worked as a waitress in a restaurant – her family's wealth seemingly exhausted, or perhaps access to the family account had been blocked.

Had Bunty, who indeed predicted the German assault on England a good year before the outbreak of war (albeit 'only' through the air, rather than a full-scale invasion, such as the events that took place vice-versa in Normandy during 1944), merely undertaken his journey in August 1939 in order to take flight at the last minute? If so, why didn't he take Averil with him from the start?

What's stranger still is that Bunty had passed undetected into Sofia, given that the Germans were active all across the Balkans and weren't exactly in the business of permitting every deranged Englishman the freedom of fools. In any case, Bunty managed to walk around a free man until early in 1941, before leaving the Continent became a matter of urgency. Since the Germans were still yet to land on the British Isles, England remarkably appeared to be a safer abode than just about every other corner of Europe. Perhaps Switzerland would have been the exception, but Bunty was unable to acquire a visa for a residence.

Hidden amongst scattered tourists, Bunty made his way back to his native England via treacherous, winding paths. He was stopped, held and sounded out on several occasions by officers of various uniform colours – but, fortunately, he was moved on every time. The Yugoslavian army had capitulated and Greece was firmly in German hands. A secret path via Marseille and Bordeaux took Bunty through Nazi-occupied France to Granville in upper Normandy; from there, he was able to undertake the dangerous venture of a journey across the English Channel to Southampton. "I can scarcely explain quite how scared I was back then. Had I been caught, they'd have made short work of me." A ship travelling from Granville to England had to pass through the waters around the Channel Islands, which were teeming with German patrol boats.

The greatest cause of Bunty's suffering: since the sale of his Lincoln, Bunty was carless, meaning that he had to either take trains (and often freight trains at that) or hope to get transported by a lorry driver. His help came mostly in the form of farmers, who accommodated him and warned him of the military control points, or fishermen, who hid him in their boats.

In May of 1941, just a few days after Rudolf Hess landed in England, Bunty and Averil's marriage was arranged in Oxford. The wedding was modest, in a country governed by the disaster of war. Hess had flown to Scotland on May 10 in a Messerschmitt Bf 1102 fighter plane without Hitler's knowledge, in order to speak to the Duke Douglas-Hamilton in Dungavel Castle, for he was seen as the leader of the British peace movement and opponent of Prime Minister Churchill; Hess had hoped to discuss the possibility of ending the war. However, this didn't work out as planned – with Hess being imprisoned upon arrival in Britain. The war continued.

The newlyweds stayed with the parents of the bride in Oxford for a while, before Bunty was eventually drawn back to the vicinity of London. He no longer owned that apartment in the City, and besides, the couple had little desire to live in the centre for fear of bombings from the German Luftwaffe. They preferred instead to find a suburb just outside of London, the search ending in a manner befitting Bunty's style and taste: he managed to convince a friend to allow him and his wife to reside in a sailing ship situated on the banks of the Thames near Teddington. Bunty didn't get this for nothing; the unrigged yawl set him back £400.

When explaining the decision to purchase a ship for residence, Bunty used an argument which would certainly never be cited by anyone other than him. "It was our Siamese cat Ma-Ni, who had the final say," explained Bunty in his book *Escape from Peace*, of Motor Racing Publications, Abingdon, 1949. "There were scare paragraphs in the press to the effect that only those cats resident in ships, warehouses and government offices were to be permitted food. So my wife, who is very devoted to our Siamese cat Ma-Ni said: 'Go out and get a ship, a warehouse, or a job in a government office.' As I am not sufficiently sadistic to sit down and devise new and fiendishly ingenious ways of pestering people, and as warehouses proved on enquiry to be both scarce and very expensive, a ship seemed indicated."

Yet another lovely Bunty story. Packaged cat food being rationed during the war (like everything else was in England at the time) didn't seem that unlikely, yet why warehouse owners would be chosen to enjoy the exclusive privilege of these tomcat rations is a rather farfetched mystery to me. Earlier on that very same page, Bunty hints at the real reason he decided to acquire such a vessel: he wanted to be sure of making a quick getaway if the war were to turn against England.

The war was by no means nearing its conclusion. "We felt more secure on board than on land when the German bombers flew overhead. Above all, our ship enabled us to enjoy the uninterrupted celebration of parties."

Of course, that time period rarely provided humour. And eventually, Bunty too had to join the service of His Majesty, even though his role in England's struggle didn't require him to wear a uniform, nor authorised the purchase of cat food (for which his ship-owner's status was fortunately sufficient). It was peculiar that Bunty hadn't been requested for military service much sooner. He was commanded to work on a shipyard in Fulham, which was tasked with building barges for the Royal Navy, and Bunty belonged to a select few who had to transfer the ships onto the upper Thames at various berths. A job, for which he later credited himself with the 'qualification of master' – a title that he had no right to self-apply.

I had no idea whether Bunty carried out these transfers alone (A) or whether he was simply an assistant on board (B). He never explained this in detail, which leads me to strongly presume it was option (B). Otherwise, the posterity would have surely heard much more about the monkfish Bunty in his early phase, possibly the story of when he came to within a whisker of colliding with a German submarine somewhere in the region of Tilbury Docks, leading him to vehemently swing the rudder at the last second … "it was one of the most dangerous moments in my life …"

Averil also acquired a job which was vaguely related to naval matters: she worked for an authority which supplied food and coal to the workers on the London Docks, allowing the young lady to pinch a few briquettes to take home in her handbag every now and again. Not a particularly comfortable life for pampered people, who were used to trips through the Alps behind the steering wheel of a supercharged Mercedes and celebrations with the Nobility and Gentry.

Only a two-pronged fork

"THE BUREAUCRACY HAD ASSUMED proportions that made me despair. Anything I was plotting was promptly shut down by some office or other. We were piled up with stacks of pointless paperwork, presented to us as if there was nothing more important in the world … I hated our Fabian socialism with which our Labour Party tormented us. I wanted to escape abroad with my wife, for the long term if possible, escape this dismal existence in England. In order to ensure we didn't have to leave our possessions behind, a ship equipped with all these treasures seemed to represent the best possibility."

Bunty wrote this in 1948. Of course, until July 1945, the Conservatives were in power.

Bunty had first thought of South or East Africa, but came to the realisation that many of his fellow countrymen had moved there already after the war – and had already begun to create the precise living conditions there which he intended to turn his back on. As a result, a second homeland in Europe seemed more reasonable and advantageous.

The next consideration was to purchase a little estate in northern France. Bunty planned to earn a livelihood for him and his wife through writing. However, there were so many journalists and correspondents across continental Europe as a result of the war, leaving Bunty to conclude that it was entirely pointless to travel to France. But how many British publishers already had middlemen in … Sweden? Bunty rather fancied his chances of achieving a permanent visa for a journalistic mission to Sweden to live on board a yacht on the archipelagoes off the coast of Stockholm.

The 1912, 24-ton Yawl which Bunty purchased for this new life, complete with a steel hull and an auxiliary engine, contained little more than an old coal oven, a kerosene stove in the galley, an empty fire extinguisher and a fork which was missing two prongs. "The ship was completely ransacked during its final year, and anything that the thieves didn't take off with was left destroyed. We had to start afresh. Averil developed amazing woodworking skills, equipping the bow with a new galley. The old one measured only four feet squared; my wife had refused to prepare meals in such a close cubbyhole. Unfortunately, the deck leaked. Every downpour brought water flowing into the cabin."

Searching for a romantic and gratuitous mooring spot, Bunty decided to anchor 'White Shadow' in Weiden, situated not far from the little town of Windsor, close to the banks of the river Thames. However, in March 1945, the unexpected onset of a flood occurred whilst Bunty and Averil were stopping over in London. When they returned, they discovered their ship wedged in between the trees on the shore, the bowsprit tangled up in the branches.

"Admittedly, we had a few tools we could use to repair our ship, but no pruning saw capable of bringing down a trunk. Unfortunately, such a tool was entirely necessary to free our poor boat from its predicament. We spent the whole night on the salvage operation ..."

The following summer brought about the exact opposite situation: water levels dropped so low that White Shadow's keel found itself on land, causing the ship to tilt precariously to portside. All the local residents assured Bunty that the Thames had never seen so little water, but this was of little consolation. "We needed to find a place to moor in deeper waters, so we had to head further ashore. But how exactly were we supposed to accomplish this? The engine was broken and wouldn't run. We weren't able to afford the service of a tugboat. So we took our little dinghy out and tied a tight line to the Yawl. We found someone who helped us move the ship into deeper waters, through tedious and laborious rowing work, before we were able to drop the anchor."

Bunty and Averil had to accept that they had taken a hammering in trying to ready the ship for sea on their own. So they decided to take White Shadow to a shipyard in order to finish off the work. "As it transpired, the people working there had absolutely no idea of how to do their job. These kids were deemed unfit for military service and frankly they were unfit for anything else too. They were supposed to change some steel plates on the hull, but ended up doing more harm to the hull than good, with the consequence that our lovely Yawl began to fill with water – it was practically drowning."

With little more than the wet clothes on their body, the newlyweds found shelter with empathetic strangers in Staines, who first provided them with a roof, then helped them find a place to stay and finally even gifted them furniture. Bunty's attempts to make contact with his numerous friends of yore always ended in the same vacuum: the overwhelming majority of them were in military service and couldn't be reached. Bunty and Averil were getting rather desperate. "It would be of little use to try and bring about litigation to seek compensation for damages, because they had probably built up a good reputation over years through appraisals and the like. There was only one thing for us to do: collect the ship, sell it quickly and try and acquire ourselves another one."

With heavy hearts, the couple separated from their beloved White Shadow at the end of June, 1943. Finding a new and better ship proved rather difficult, however. "At long last, I had found one. A really fine one at that, mooring in Blairmore on Loch Long in Scotland. Of course, there were numerous hurdles in our way: namely, there was neither a train station nor a bus stop anywhere near to the destination." Since Bunty didn't have a car at the time, it remained impossible to get to Blairmore in order to see the ship, and thus the search continued. Finally, in Greenock Harbour, 30 miles west of Glasgow, Bunty appeared to have located the perfect vessel: a motor yacht from the Camper & Nicholson shipyard, ninety feet long.

"For yachts over seventy feet long, your maintenance expenses go sky-rocketing. But it was all very tempting and we decided to risk the extra size ... the boat matched every one of our expectations, with a beautiful dining saloon, two guest cabins, a comfortable bathroom with hot and cold water, a perfect investment. And a large refrigerator ...," albeit the refrigerator was missing its compressor and thus utterly useless in its current state.

Whilst not as elegant as the Yawl despite its classic vintage build, the motor yacht embodied the type of vehicle which you would expect to see gracing the inland waterways of Great Britain, at least in peacetime.

Averil continued to carry out all manner of improvements and beautifications, and even the siamese cat appeared at home on board the newly dubbed 'White Shadow II.' She also didn't allow herself to be intimidated by the numeral large rats which populated the ship "and laughed in our faces at the traps and poison baits which we positioned around the ship without success."

Averil noted: "Bunty's Auntie May protested when she discovered the new ship. 'Not again!' she wrote to us, demanding that, at the very least I, with my expectant baby, should move to her to live in the castle, until times were better. We politely declined – Bunty was completely sick of living alone from his bachelorhood, and we could enjoy relative comforts on the yacht, as well as proper heating. Our only real concern was ensuring our child's safety around water once he or she was born."

How fortunate Bunty was that Averil had such a passion for sharing this extravagant form of existence with her husband and had no qualms about handling hammers, saws and paint pots whilst pregnant. It soon became apparent that she was much more of a dab hand at such things than her husband.

Indeed, the whole exercise represented a rather strange way of practicing the art of survival in a country desecrated by German V1 and V2 rockets. When Bunty and Averil celebrated Christmas in December 1945, they were as good as a three. On 28th December, Humphrey came into the world. He was born into a time of hardship.

Bunty was incredibly proud to be a father, just as he was to be a husband. Neither of these circumstances, however, were enough to stop him returning to one of his old living habits once the war was over. This began with an effort to find out the prosperity of various friends from university and former business partners from times gone by. Unfortunately, none of them had money for cars, revelry or other forms of pleasure, meaning that they occasionally ended up going round and hoping on board at the Scott-Moncrieffs', in order to carry out a bit of manual labour.

A motor yacht, or a Bugatti ...?

NEW TRAVEL PLANS WERE forged; in under a year, the Scott-Moncrieffs were expecting to finally carry out their trip to Sweden. Bunty was very clear that they still needed the help of two further – and sea-savvy! – people on board. Yet everybody that heard the plans expressed doubt about the feasibility of the adventure. "They predicted every type of shipwreck and a certain death through drowning. But this remained a much better alternative to living in this depressed, post-war England. We, on the other hand, were rather optimistic" – especially given that numerous offers of help to perfect the yacht came in, free of charge. Several others still found it important to stand in their way, typically dishing out superfluous and redundant advice before disappearing down the pub.

Soon, however, three serious hinderances stood in the way of all plans for the White Shadow II's trip to Sweden. The first was the matter of an official registration for the yacht in the ship registry. It was feared that, despite her size, the ship would only qualify for inland waters and not for the high seas. Every experienced captain they had found thus far had declined the responsibility of a blue water journey aboard White Shadow II, but whether this was due to the vessel's seaworthiness, navigation or safety equipment is not known. And 'sea captain' Bunty admitted at the time that he wouldn't have given himself this responsibility. This turn of events was a bitter disappointment, particularly as Bunty had himself instructed a specialist to recalibrate the compass in preparation for the voyage.

The second circumstance looming largely over the ship's maiden deepwater voyage was the financial situation of the Scott-Moncrieffs. They were almost completely out of pocket, with the last of their pennies going directly into the boat. Admittedly, Bunty was working hard, writing articles for a variety of newspapers, but the income was barely enough even for everyday essentials. Hinderance number three was Humphrey. Going on a journey across the high seas with a baby on board was out of the question.

Alas, the only reasonable option was to sell the White Shadow II as well. Keeping the 90-foot motor yacht would have been far beyond the family means at the time. This pained Bunty even more than the loss of his first ship, but there was no other solution.

"We only got a measly £2000, even though we had invested two thousand four hundred, but at long last we had some money. Our first place to stay was in the castle of my Auntie May, an 1860 build. She letted us two rooms, above and below, in one of the castle towers. We were occasionally pestered by the castle ghost, who was always haunting whichever room it was that we weren't presently in. He would throw our belongings all over the place, leaving a terrible mess on the floor ..."

There were also a number of bats in the castle tower. For a family of three, this was far from the ideal living situation.

During this time, Bunty owned a little car, which, in stark contrast to his bachelorhood lifestyle, was characterised by its exceptional economy – for petrol was strictly rationed at the time. Bunty had apparently acquired a ration card for fuel and oil. It was a cute little 1929 Humber 9 hp in best condition. Unfortunately, this pretty car, which he worked tirelessly to restore, appeared to be something of a gauntlet for hooligans, who were plentiful in Glasgow at the time. "Needless to say, they could not start it, so they deliberately set the poor little thing on fire. They were seen running away but the policeman who appeared insisted on taking some twenty minutes copying the particulars of my driving license and insurance into his notebook, and taking a statement from me before he made any pretence of going after them. Finally, presumably to gain further time, the fellow had the impertinence to try and draw me into an argument by suggesting that I had set fire to the car myself!"

Bunty considered getting himself another car. Averil suggested that they should get "the sort of vehicle that is hissed and booed by people standing in queues." He ended up purchasing a 1931 Bugatti Type 46 Coupé. As it turned out, he was right: nobody in Glasgow was interested in an incredibly showy, foreign vehicle. He was able to leave the car on the street all through the night, without ever waking up to a horrible surprise. He managed to acquire the roomy two-seater Bugatti in exchange for a set of lorry tyres, which he had initially exchanged for an old Farymann marine engine he had in turn acquired in a swap for several pairs of brand new army underwear: surplus property of the US Navy.

The car then received a fresh lick of paint, in primrose and black (something which the little Humber had never been treated to). However, it still urgently required new tyres, of the dimensions 32in x 6in, which were impossible to track down in England in the spring of 1947. "We found a garage with its own large retreading plant operated by German prisoner labour. The proprietor, perhaps because he had once had a Bugatti himself, took pity on us and said 'Come to lunch with me and then sit in my garden while your tyres are being done.' In considerably less than seven hours from the time we drew up, our re-treaded tyres were back on the wheels as good as new, and the slit one had been vulcanised."

A stroke of good fortune, indeed.

The journey to Scandinavia

AUNTIE MAY HAD FINALLY prevailed: Humphrey was to stay with her in Scotland. Here, his life was substantially better than in the south-east of London, where Bunty and Averil were now living in a small, poorly heated and scarcely furnished apartment, which they had moved into after their Glasgow intermezzo and a brief lodging in Windsor with Bunty's mother. Groceries were still being rationed (and would continue to be for a long while after), as was petrol, and there remained a higher rate of unemployment – particularly amongst returning soldiers – than jobs. It was through cashless, exchange-based transactions, in which natural produce played a particularly important role, that Bunty and Averil, like thousands of other Brits, were able to remain afloat. The same situation was playing out in many other European countries. Anyone who didn't own possessions that could be exchanged on the black market was poorly off.

Bunty still had plans of Sweden in mind, but returned first to his former metier, the car trade. Given that nobody needed them at the time, cars such as the Bugatti Type 46 could be bought for practically nothing. However, since petrol and oil were still being rationed and sparkplugs and tyres were in short supply, Bunty had little opportunity to make ends meet as an ambulant car salesman. He knew no other trade, except for writing feature articles, which was scarcely more prosperous.

It made Bunty incredibly uncomfortable to have to turn to not only his mother, but also Averil's clan, for financial aid. He sat down and decided to work out which countries had it better than Britain. Germany, France, Hungary, Romania and Austria were unfortunately ruled out. But what of his beloved Scandinavia? Getting into business there could certainly provide success.

Bunty had no pre-war business contacts in Sweden. He had concentrated himself on his native Great Britain, with sporadic contact to central and southern Europe. Instead of attempting to be a newspaper correspondent in Stockholm, Bunty found what appeared to provide an interesting new perspective; the prospect of selling unwanted cars from the UK to the Swedish market. This idea gave his travel plans a new purpose.

"Visiting Sweden on holiday was simply not enough for him," remembers Averil. "He said to me: 'My darling, from there, we might as well pop over to Finland and then onto Russia.' He assured me that there would have to be people in Russia who had earned money from the war, and these people would finally have the pleasure of getting their hands on a genuine Rolls-Royce. This, he considered, was reason enough to extend the trip to Leningrad!"

Bunty's secret hidden agenda here would surely also be to finally achieve his audience with Stalin, which he had botched in 1933, but when I asked Averil, she claimed to be unaware of this. Perhaps he no longer desired this anymore – or perhaps he'd simply forgotten it. When Bunty explained the Scandinavia trip to me, he only once mentioned the planned "audience with Stalin" as a footnote. There is also no record of it in his book *Escape From Peace*, either.

Bunty assumed that a lack of clarity would be prevalent across all borders in Europe in the years following the war, with uncertainty over who had the correct papers, documents stamps and seals and who didn't. He had taken care of the proper tourist visas for Sweden and Norway, but began to speculate about his chances of using obscure letters of recommendation, written on unusual paper with unfamiliar letterheads and translated into several languages, to con his uninformed readers. The letters that succeeded en route could then be used at the border of Finland and Russia ...

At the end of August 1946, Averil and Bunty readied their Bugatti, a straight-eight of 5.4-litre capacity and some 150hp for its long journey ahead. "When order prevails again in Europe, we'll be drowning in paperwork," Bunty said to his wife. "But for the time being, we should be able to get through. Let's use this hour of chaos in Europe, coupled with the sympathy which is brought upon eccentric Brits!"

In order to ship the car to Norway as cheaply as possible, the pair decided to buy four single tickets, because a family of four received a car pass free of charge. In actual fact, they managed to convince two friends to travel from Halifax to Bergen with them, but given that the Bugatti had become a tight two-seater through the sheer amount of luggage on board, it hadn't attracted the attention of the ticket controller during boarding. Bunty's friends had taken the train to Halifax, equipped with two very awkward pieces of luggage: brand new tyres, of the dimension 32in x 6in. Bunty was delighted. "The numerous spare tyres on board gave our car the appearance of a competitor in the Peking-Paris race of 1907 ..."

"The route which Bunty had plotted was rather adventurous," remembers Averil. "It took us from Bergen northwards to the polar circle, onto Sweden to the lakes and then to Stockholm, then onto Karelia in Finland, which was still under Russian occupation at the time. It was there that we planned to find a loophole into the Soviet Union."

www.veloce.co.uk / www.velocebooks.com
All current books • New book news • Special offers • Gift vouchers

Bunty's first book

BUNTY'S FIRST BOOK, *ESCAPE From Peace*, describes a rather different route. There is also no mention of his contact to prospective car buyers, nor of the newspaper reports which he sent to editorial offices once he was en route; compositions with which Bunty had originally planned to finance the journey. Instead of this, the author delves into lengthy and detailed descriptions of hotels and museums, romanticises about lavish dinners and interesting window displays, and waxes lyrical about the conditions of universities and private households. He also cites a long list of all the things that foreigners were not allowed to purchase (mostly textiles), and compares the capacity of Swedish intercity omnibuses with the classic British bus: "They even take bicycles on board! Up to five can fit in a specially designed rack in front of the radiator, and they can also be transported on the roof!"

When I asked if Stockholm became their most important travel destination – since Bunty was so keen on making business connections with Swedish car dealers – Averil couldn't help but laugh.

"It wasn't about this anymore for Bunty. His aim was visiting Leningrad and, if possible, Moscow as well. He wanted to get over there before the war but never managed it. Of course, we were calling in at Stockholm too … but we were now on board the ferry; it was pleasant and we were given something to eat, which was long overdue. In fact, we were allowed to dine at the captain's table." Unfortunately, Bunty was suffering from several symptoms of seasickness during the crossing and, to his regret, had to forgo his beautiful breakfast.

Bunty began to keep a diary again on the journey (it's possible that he had also kept one during the war and shortly after, but I'm unsure), and he did indeed mention the cheese on the captain's table of 'Jupiter' on the first page of his entries: "It is truly excellent and of prewar quality. I made note of the supplier: Tasserington of High Hamsgate." It's worth noting that this entry precedes the unfortunate bout of seasickness …

The Norwegian customs officers weren't interested in the slightest by Bunty and Averil's paperwork once they discovered that the pair were simply stopping by on their way to Finland. Only the spare tyres of the Bugatti were met with an official stamp, apparently in a rain and mud resistant colour. In postwar Scandinavia, just as in Britain, car tyres were considered the most valuable commodity for trade on the black market.

Armed with a number of ration cards for petrol and oil – indeed, they were even rationing in Norway at the time! – and an oversized GB-plate on the rear of the Bugatti, the tourists began their journey. "The car is far too highly sprung, it's frankly rather painful," began one of the next entries in Bunty's travel diary. Several entries opened with "Had to sleep in the car again, sitting upright, because we failed to find a hotel once more. This region is endlessly lonely," or "We must admit to not bringing enough warm items on this trip. This is now the fourth cold night spent in the car …"

Then: "Ferry sat waiting for a whole day on the Sognefjord. It gets dark early." "Could only drive in second gear. Steep mountain paths, like Prescott and Shelsley Walsh in one. We're now in Kaupanger, considering whether to travel down to Oslo. It's only a day trip."

"Oslo, September 22. Among people again! We'd prefer to head straight from here over to Sweden, because the roads are much better. Supposedly, they even have hotels."

The two travellers ended up spending a full week in Oslo, visiting museums and churches. There is absolutely no indication of business transactions of any kind during this time period in Bunty's travel diary. There are also relatively few entries containing information about the Bugatti, leading to the presumption that his vehicle handled its task gracefully, the hard suspension aside. Bunty later conceded that one can get used to certain vibrations. The 46 model has a transaxle rear hub, where the gearbox is interlocked with the differential. This causes the shaft to rotate with engine speed, meaning that certain higher revolution speeds cause rather unpleasant vibrations.

October 3. "Karlstad. Everything is ridiculously expensive here in Sweden. We could only afford to stay in third class. At least the Bugatti is going strong, absolutely no problems." Bunty makes no mention of why it proved to be a requirement in Sweden for the Bugatti to be reconditioned, drilled and fitted with new pistons, meaning it remains a mystery, especially given that the 8-cylinder was in supposedly optimum condition at the start of the journey. The propellor shaft vibrations also aren't mentioned in any case.

"In Norway it was just as in England," wrote Bunty, concerning the attention paid to the Bugatti. "The car was able to glide by, completely unnoticed. In Sweden, it was rather different: here, it aroused great interest."

They travelled through Stockholm and Söderhamn to Umeå. "The most affordable is still to stay on board the hotel ship, which is two shillings per person for a night. There isn't any breakfast, however. Garages are notably more expensive: the equivalent of 10 shillings per night."

Averil often replaced Bunty behind the wheel of the Bugatti, and he attested to her magnificent talent for driving in writing. Averil took great pleasure in her prowess. In Sävar, just beyond Umeå, it began to snow. It then became rapidly clear to the pair that they had left far too late in the year to begin a trip through the Nordland. The car wasn't willing to do so much in low temperatures, and Bunty and Averil began to feel uncomfortable.

Wherever they appeared, the black and primrose vehicle attracted considerable attention. Such a sight was so unusual on the streets of Sweden in early winter that the Bugatti's arrival in some cases brought an entire village out of their houses to take a closer look. "First the boys flocked over, but they didn't ask any questions, rather simply just started, open-mouthed. Then the girls dared to pop their heads out, staring silently at the boys. By the end we were surrounded by every adult in the village. It was rather curious …"

In Bunty's book, which contains a description of the journey, there is only one photo of the Bugatti to be found, taken by Averil (just like all the other photos). This photo doesn't reveal the two reserve tyres strapped to the vehicle, which supposedly gave it the appearance of a Peking-Paris participant of 1907. All that is visible is the replacement wheel on the left hand wing. I can very much imagine that Bunty sold the spares for a good price despite the customs seal, presumably in Sweden, in order to significantly top up the holiday fund. On the radiator there is a plaque from the Automobile Association as well as a badge from the Vintage Car Club.

Don't just give up!

IN LULEA, RIGHT AT the top of the Bothnian Bay, the British travellers were honoured by a reception in the town hall, with music and dance. Bunty's entry: "Wonderful people, good spirits. Feels as if it were springtime! We should rethink our travel plans." The northern winter had caught them off guard. And it was only just October!

But they weren't giving up, not at all. Neither snowy streets, nor dropping temperatures could keep them from reaching the Finnish border. They had covered Sweden up and down, and once they reached the Finnish border control at Tornio, they received a huge and hearty welcome – apparently they were the first foreigners to travel through Sweden at this crossing point since the start of the war in 1939. But what of the German occupants? "They didn't count," noted Bunty. Since the border officials didn't plan for a "sudden sharp increase in tourism," as Bunty put it, they were unfortunately unable to stamp Bunty's and Averil's passports – "They didn't have stamps to seal or even an ink pad; all they had to offer was a healthy slurp from a vodka bottle."

When asked about the condition of the roads further inland, the friendly men didn't respond. Averil: "Bunty's assumptions had rung true: on the Finnish side, we had illiterates, who, despite flicking through our passports seriously, proceeded to hold them upside down when they got to the photo page, whilst spending the whole day in their little hut playing cards and drinking vodka. They weren't interested in world politics in the slightest. Why exactly was there a crossing point here? We discovered it was because of the Swedish lorries travelling between Umeå, Kemi and Oulu. It was very dangerous to come across one, for they drove without lights and gave off thick clouds of smoke, which enveloped us completely. They were powered by wood gas."

Bunty's diary: "Kemi, October 20. We were unable to get further than here, it gets dark by 2pm. Searched in vain for a road map. We should have brought one with us from England … we found a petrol station at least, where we were able to buy some petrol. Unfortunately we can't use our rations cards anywhere here.

"The city is completely destroyed in places due to the war. I'm beginning to ask myself why war even found its path all the way up here. The ruins of the bombed houses here look just as formidable as the ones in London. We found a place to stay with a Quaker."

The Germans had destroyed many of the main roads in Finland, as well as most of the bridges. It was over one of the few remaining intact ones which the Scott-Moncrieffs found themselves needing to cross a river, when they spotted a freight train, closing in on the other side. "It didn't look like there would be enough space for this train and our Bugatti on the bridge. However, just as panic set in, we realised that this antiquated locomotive, which looked like it belonged in an old Western, was moving rather slowly towards us and that we might have a shot at nipping over the bridge and onto the other side before it reached us. We went for it. We were lucky ..."

Kemi was known as the capital of Finnish Lapland, after Rovaniemi was left in ruins. Visiting in the winter didn't bring about the sight of further wood gas powered lorries, but rather a sports coupé – which seemed just about the most unlikely thing imaginable.

Bunty and Averil were introduced by their hosts to the governing President, who invited them to visit the ruins of Rovaniemi, in order to give the two English tourists an impression of the barbarity of war. When he heard that a great number of cities in England had been destroyed in the same manner and that numerous quarters had been bombed to debris and ash, he was incredibly surprised. He'd had absolutely no idea.

He urgently advised the travellers not to take the area known as the Karelian marshes in order to cross the border into Russia. Isolated border posts would shoot at every moving thing in sight (mostly because it could be wolves or foxes), and there were practically no signposts on the roads. The only chance to get into the Soviet Union successfully was from Helsinki, assuming that the Russians were letting anyone in at all.

"We're heading down to Helsinki. Miku Käppättuu reckons we'll be there in five days. Pray it's not too cold!" Who was Miku Käppättuu? Presumably none other than his excellency, the President.

There were no road maps in Kemi either. "Everyone clearly knows their own areas so well that they have no need for street maps," remarked Bunty. "But there's barely even any signs. The likelihood of getting lost is very high, so Käppättuu has kindly offered us his boy, who apparently knows the way, to help us up until Lahti." Käppättuu's 'boy' was a lad of around fourteen years of age, who squeezed in between Bunty and Averil and ended up accompanying them for three or four days longer than he was supposed to. His name remains a mystery, he was simply 'Käppättuu's boy.'

The next day came, and they were no further than Oulu. "Fresh snow has fallen. We had to follow a wood gas lorry for miles. On the recommendation of the boy, we took a side road which features dangerous railway junctions without any warning signs. A small incident of note: we had our tailpipe ripped off when crossing one."

One of the many unrestricted railway crossings prompted a pause in the journey, because a freight train was blocking the way. The train wasn't moving, rather simply a stationary vehicle. Half an hour after it had still refused to move, Bunty got out and made his way to the head of the train to speak to the conductor. "He sees no reason whatsoever to do us the favour of moving on: apparently, there is a problem with a frozen switch further ahead. He says that no car has used this crossing for several years, so, as unusual as it is that one happens to be on the road now, it will have to wait a few hours," Käppättuu's boy translated.

"Kuoppio, October 27. Averil has driven pretty much all day, the competent girl! It's cold as ice; only our feet are warm, because the engine gives off a lot of heat. The boy has taken us to a garage to get the exhaust pipe welded back on. All of the canisters were refilled with petrol as well. Midday saw our first encounter with a Finnish police officer. He claimed there was a parking ban in operation in front of the inn where we ate lunch. Rather pedantic, given that our car is the only one on the road within a one hundred mile radius at this time of year."

In Lahti, the trio spent two nights in the Atlas Hotel. The streets were getting brighter, and were clean for the most part, or free of snow at least. Helsinki was getting closer, which was further confirmed by the increasing prices at petrol stations or guest houses. 'The boy' was dropped off at the train station in Lahti and stuck on a train back to Kemi. There were exactly two cars parked here; both taxis: Mercedes Benz 170. The drivers closely examined the Bugatti with its English numberplate, offering Bunty a few cigarettes.

"Helsinki, October 31. What a miserable city. It's freezing here, too. Averil is currently entering hypothermia. There's no street lighting, no pubs: nothing. Nobody is welcoming, hotel prices are astronomical, and nobody speaks English or German, nor wants to."

"Helsinki, November 2. We can't make it into the Soviet Union without a visa. The consulate insists that it can only be issued in one's country of origin. There are no other border crossings, and every single road, even the ones to Raippo, are closed. We wouldn't even be allowed to use our own car; not in winter at any rate."

Nonsensical chaos at every European border? Bamboozling the Soviet Union border officers with a twinkling eye and a magical charm? Thundering along from Leningrad to Moscow in a Bugatti in November? Come on, now, you had to be kidding, Mr Scott-Moncrieff.

Bunty had to recognise here that, one-and-a-half years after the end of the war, there were different, namely incredibly strict, rules in Russia compared to those in the Balkans or even in France, where he had snuck through undetected (with the help of some guardian angel). He found himself, rare as it was, completely out of ideas. Averil had had enough of being frozen solid, and staying at desolate hotels, shrouded by uncertainty, and longed for a bit of comfort, as much as she might have liked Finland. She and Bunty reached the unanimous decision to postpone the trip to Moscow to another date and different time of year, and booked a freight passage for their Bugatti to Stockholm and, from there, Copenhagen.

Comrade Stalin
will have to wait

WHETHER BUNTY ACTUALLY SERIOUSLY believed that he would be able to enter the USSR without the slightest prior knowledge of the contemporary local living conditions there, sounds rather unrealistic. Perhaps he wanted to meet Stalin legitimately, rather than through the typical Bunty charade of cunning fibs.

The significance of almost every border in Europe at that time became apparent from the lengthy and detailed descriptions that Bunty gave them after crossing through. He spoke with particularly high praise for the Danish border patrol, who had treated this 'British journalist' so kindly, even donating him a full tank of untaxed petrol for his Bugatti.

The couple spent a pleasant two weeks in Copenhagen and on the streets of Denmark's countryside, before the Bugatti eventually reached Scottish soil again in Leith. Here, the unloading of the car down from the ship and onto the quay was delayed by eighteen hours because Bunty failed to formally beseech the port authorities. The captain had apologised profusely for taking no responsibility for the unloading of his ship. The harbour master then had to explain to the furious returnees that, prior to unloading, he had to obtain a confirmation from the delegate workmen, who were unfortunately currently discussing a strike ... "We finally got back to Auntie May's just one day before Christmas. We had brought a Christmas tree and tonnes of decorations back, all of which were foreign to us. Our little son was fascinated by it all ..."

They had been on the move for more than two months, deprived of seeing their son, spared the whirlwind of London life. The time had come to think about finding a house. Particularly given that Averil was now six months pregnant and didn't have the slightest desire to travel another mile in the vibrating Bugatti.

The Bugatti was to be sold. It was undoubtedly a rarity and of decent value, yet nobody responded to the newspaper adverts. Surely an engaged Bugatti enthusiast would be informed by now regarding the present whereabouts of the vehicle.

At that time, any number of 4.5-litre Bentleys, venerable Rolls-Royce Silver Ghosts, distinguished Isotta-Fraschinis, rapid Invictas, even wonderful Austro-Daimlers or Hispano-Suiza Boulognes were being offered for laughable amounts, some with very low approval ratings, which represented great value for aficionados (particularly as they were negotiable!). So, for the time being, Bunty decided to keep his Bugatti Type 46 – which only had a few noticeable disadvantages, namely the vibrating propeller shaft.

As you may have already gathered by now, a great deal of entries in Bunty's diary were at odds with the information published in *Escape From Peace*, or indeed with the facts presented by the author in discussion with Hazel and me. Insurmountable suspicion begins to rise as to the degree of poetic license Bunty allowed himself in certain circumstances, but at the end of the day nobody can criticise him for that – though it is worth mentioning that he also avoided mentioning several personal embarrassments along the way, to which Averil was the only witness. His utter failure to gain entry to the USSR is only very briefly noted in his diary.

Bunty and Averil went on to undertake several more journeys in the vibrating Bugatti, including one through Portugal in the summer of 1948. After that they did indeed find a buyer, causing Bunty to purchase another car immediately "for our personal transport."

Once a Bugatti, always a Bugatti

AFTER RETURNING FROM THE Scandinavian trip, the Scott-Moncrieffs had to think seriously about where they wanted to make their livelihoods. The living that Bunty was striving for would command a yearly salary of just £2000, by his own admission. Britain was starving, whilst a tidal wave of inflation was bearing down upon the country.

Bunty remained convinced that life was better abroad and that he could make a good enough living for his family as a journalist or writer overseas. He was entering the fifth decade of his life; it was time to settle down.

On March 7, 1947, Humphrey's brother Ambrose came into the world. At the time, the family were living in a manor house with ten rooms just outside of Glasgow – precisely where is not stated. Apparently, the annual rent for the estate was just £6. Bunty explained that it was no problem to employ staff members for precious little money, and that the local greengrocers would allow him to buy on credit – "credit, until the newspaper had transferred me my latest instalment" (which seemed to get later and later every month …). The grocer apparently once even offered to lend him a considerable sum of money, although we never got to the bottom of whether Bunty accepted the offer or not. I'll keep my suspicions to myself.

The evening before Ambrose's birthday, the casual contributor and author Bunty surprised his wife with the news of his latest acquisition in the field of "personal transport," another Bugatti – this time a 37A type, a purebred racing car of 1.5-litre formula from the mid-twenties.

Averil was not amused. "We have two little children! The next time you go off on a trip, don't bother coming back. Why oh why did you feel the need to buy a racing car? We need an ordinary saloon!"

Bunty claimed to have several reasons for the purchase. Firstly, for once in his life, he wanted the pleasure of knowing how a nippy Bugatti race car felt. Secondly, the price was an absolute steal – this, coming from the man who currently lacked a steady income! Thirdly, there were tonnes of family cars which were always going to be affordable and likely to resist the upcoming inflation. You could get an old saloon for just ten quid …

The Scott-Moncrieffs left Scotland, taking the children with them as they moved to a small town in Surrey, not far from London. The filigree Bugatti 37A was simply sat on the drive, cheerfully waiting to be taken away, until a sudden twist of fate: Bunty ascertained one morning that there was something 'not quite right' regarding the four-cylinder engine of the car, and that it was thus imperative to take it to the factory in Molsheim, down in the Alsace region of France. The Scott-Moncrieffs were now in a better position financially, so what better way to spend than to take a lovely trip away?

The 37A had coined itself a nickname in the meantime, given to it by Averil. She had christened the two-seater 'La Folie': The Folly, The Whim.

As it transpired, there was indeed something 'not quite right' with La Folie: the engine wouldn't start on the button, nor with the crank handle. There must have been a reason that Bunty was able to acquire the car so cheaply. Any good mechanic in the Greater London area would have been able to locate and fix the cause of the problem, but Bunty was insistent – for him, the Bugatti factory was the only worthy source to analyse the defect and repair it accordingly. Averil, begrudgingly or otherwise, allowed herself to be talked into accompanying Bunty, and so the sons were once again sent up to Scotland to stay with Auntie May.

With as little luggage as necessary, Bunty and Averil began their journey to Molsheim. Being a race car, a Bugatti 37A doesn't afford much in the way of luggage room, so the precious little that the couple decided to bring with them needed to be bound tightly by a leather strap and lashed to the exposed pointy tail of the vehicle. Adventurous cargo indeed!

This trip to the Bugatti factory transpired to be one of the more eventful ones in their young lives. The journey began with the car being heaved up a steep hill with all their collective might, turned around at the top and then given a gentle shove back down. At this point, with the car gaining motion fast, Bunty leapt into the cockpit and turned on the ignition, smashed the gearbox into third and, with a thunderous howl, the Bugatti's engine began to whirl.

Things were going smoothly, until shortly after the town of Chertsey, when the engine began a series of alarming misfires. It was directly opposite Bunty's beloved Brooklands race course that the Molsheim four-cylinder took a last breath and came to a halt.

The approach road to the race course was lined with a large number of garages and work stations, in most cases Bunty knew the owners personally. He went on the hunt for Charles Brackenbury, to plead with him to take the Bugatti in. Brackenbury's team only had petrol on hand, but managed to miraculously bring the engine back to life, though it continued to misfire. Just a few miles after leaving Brackenbury's custody, the Bugatti's engine began to overheat. The radiator required a substantial amount of water – a procedure that they would have to repeat over similar distances. Additionally, the petrol pump would have to be positioned on a slope to ensure that the car could restart, unless some strong hands happened to be around to help push.

Bunty hadn't even reached Redhill by the time it was dark. Admittedly, the Bugatti was built purely for the circuit, but it did have a pair of headlights. The only problem was that they didn't work, and neither did the taillights. After a lengthy search, Bunty and Averil came across a garage which was still open and prepared to 'install' two battery lamps for them. The lights were fastened to the fenders using duct tape, the water was topped up and the pair were back on the road to Dover.

It was of utmost importance that Bunty applied the throttle very patiently and sensibly. Driving too slowly would cause the car to misfire, the sparkplugs to become oily and the radiator to overheat. Yet driving too fast brought with it the danger of misjudging an obstacle or seeing a corner too late, because the light given off by the two side lights attached to the fenders was very weak.

Midnight came and Dover was still out of reach, at which point Averil's resilience came to an end. "The engine continued to misfire and quit working, which meant I had to continue to push. I had to toil to convince my husband that we would be better off taking respite. We parked the car on the roadside and both fell straight asleep in our seats out of sheer exhaustion. A police patrol cycling by woke us, but the pair of them simply wanted to check whether we were actually alive or not. We could feel their disappointment as they realised that we were just asleep! However, they offered to help push the car and oddly enough didn't even discipline us for our auxiliary lighting; on the contrary, one of them left us his service light, equipped with a little red disc, which we attached to the rear of the car.

"By the time we reached Folkestone, the batteries of all three lights were empty. It was the dead of night, but we had great fortune once more: an empathetic soul in a large Lanchester limousine pulled over and offered to tow us to the docks of Dover, which were now just a few miles away. It was around 3am by the time we finally got there, two hours to spare until the next ferry to Calais. We allowed ourselves to stretch out a little on the platform, and when we went to board the ship, half a dozen American students helped us to push the car on.

Their mockery was rather sour ... Oh how I cursed La Folie and myself in turn for getting dragged along on this godforsaken journey!"

Peculiarly, the behaviour of the racing car changed the moment it crossed the border into its native France. Not only would the engine start of its own free will, but the radiator didn't overheat once during the first two hours of the journey.

The next leg towards the south-east went as smoothly as any, causing the couple to begin to question why they were on this trip at all. Averil: "The feeling lasted about two hours, then after that fate struck back. Oil began to leak from somewhere and was seeping in around my feet. Within a matter of minutes, my shoes were completely sodden. We had to pull over again. It wasn't even ten in the morning, but luckily, we found a garage which had just opened. The manager said he couldn't help, offering us nothing more than a roll of insulating tape. Bunty wrapped the tape around the presumed leak on the pipe of the oil tank, and this whole charade took place in the market square of this little town, whose entire population seemed to be watching. There were plenty of strong arms to help give us a push-start once we set off again, since the engine starter had given up the ghost once more. We were less than five miles on, when the next mishap occurred: the accelerator had become caught and the engine was revving, causing the oil pipe to burst in a second place. A car stopped, tossed out a towrope, and took us to a garage in the next town. Bunty and the garage mechanic repaired the accelerator linkage, mended the pipe once more, and topped up the petrol, oil and water. After all the drama of the morning, we decided to find a bistro and order ourselves some breakfast.

"My nerves were shot to bits, but Bunty was rather calm, finding everything perfectly normal and making his typical wisecracks with the host. Since Bunty spoke fabulous French back then, he had hardly any problems with conversation. He even managed to blag us breakfast on the house!

"So, we were pushed off once more and continued this wretched journey ... out of this current town, at least. Oil burst into the cockpit once more, this time soaking my entire wardrobe. Bunty was wearing his lederhose (leather pants) from Styria, which had already resisted one spillage on the journey ... we turned around and went back to the garage. Bunty and the mechanic tinkered for five or six hours, at which point I had reached the end of my patience.

"I headed back into the bistro and explained that we would be spending the night there. The host replied that he, unfortunately, had no guest bedrooms available, but that I may, of course, use the bathroom for an hour, which I did. Bunty didn't even notice that I had disappeared, and come back refreshed and clean. He insisted that we head off right away, despite the fact that it was already very late in the afternoon by this point ..."

Eventually, Bunty also reached the point of exhaustion that meant he too wanted to stop at an auberge and rent a room. It was too late for dinner. The hosts at the inn were originally from England, meaning that the evening became a very long one, despite the couple's exhaustion.

With newfound strength and a refreshed spirit, Bunty and Averil continued their journey the following morning. Molsheim was still a long way away ... but there were no further defects, leading to a wonderful day in the French countryside. Only the radiator provided occasional problems, and even the starter was functioning properly again!

Averil: "We reached Bruges in Belgium, where Bunty knew the owner of a little hotel on the outskirts. We wanted to spend the next night here, and especially try to meet two Bugatti experts who lived nearby: a Monsieur Quentin, owner of a Type 49, as well as the abbot of a monastery there who also owned a Type 49. Monsieur Quentin appeared with Bugatti, wife and child the next morning, and invited us to breakfast; after which we travelled together to the monastery and rang for the abbot. The kind man who answered presented us with a lovely offer: he had some free time and wanted to drive us to Brussels, and Monsieur Quentin was to follow us for safety's sake."

The convoy set off on tour, which was a rather rare sight back then, drawing the attention of two policemen on motorbikes. They presumably planned to pull over the Bugatti patrol and caution them for driving too fast, before the abbot leaned out of the driver's side of his vehicle and yelled "Don't stop us, gentlemen! Don't stop us! We are escorting a racing car from England, this is about victory! We've got a ten-minute advantage, watch out for the vehicles behind us!" Averil: "Whatever the police truly made of this utter nonsense, the monastery brother's guardian angel was with us, and we glided madly past everything in our way en route to Brussels."

The journey to Brussels was effortless, with just one short stop to avoid congestion and to top up Bunty's radiator. Once they reached the city, it was a different story.

"Trying to navigate Brussels in a convoy was like hell on Earth. As if there hadn't already been enough hinderances on this trip, we were facing another. We lost sight of each other in the city, as we were unable to catch up with the mad abbot ahead of us and then discovered that our efforts to do so had left Monsieur Quentin missing behind us. Regardless, we decided to carry on until we found the right street towards Luxembourg. Now, we were just a day's driving from Molsheim … We enjoyed the fact that there were lots of American limousines here, some of which even Bunty couldn't identify. We felt really quite small in our little two-seater. The motor cut off randomly again for unknown reasons, I had to get out and ask passers-by to help push it. Some were happy to help, others simply sneered scornfully. Oh, how I hated those moments!"

Molsheim – finally. With a loud, shocked sigh of relief, Averil escaped the oily cockpit. Immediately, workers from all around rushed over to look at the car and ask questions. "Bunty in his lederhose was the centre of attention of course, far more than our car, as he asked for entry at the factory door."

Back then, the Bugatti works were in the position of carrying out private repairs for customers. Ettore Bugatti had sadly passed on in August of 1947, meaning Bunty and Averil had no opportunity to meet the famous man. There were, however, plenty of experts with whom they could talk shop and discuss the numerous breakdowns they'd experienced along the way.

Bunty and Averil left the car at the workstation and decided to use the time they had whilst it was being repaired to make a three-day excursion to Germany … by train.

On the return back to England, the 37A ran with the proverbial durability of a mechanical sewing machine. Averil was left instigating a rethink regarding her attitude towards small, French racing cars – even the lights were working again! Once they were back home, she demanded that her husband not sell La Folie, but allow her to have it for her own personal use. She had been won over by the little, grey-blue streaker and had forgiven it for all the pain it had caused her on the journey to Molsheim. La Folie became Averil's number one mode of transport.

Flirting with Daimler-Benz

THE TOTAL COST OF the ill-fated journey to the Bugatti factory for repairs was so high that the family fund urgently needed some restocking. Car dealing remained as good as dead; Bunty had yet to receive a single offer for adverts he had placed in the American magazine *Motor Trend*. The hopeful business deals in Sweden and the USA were simply not materialising. In the expectant pursuit of payment through writing, he signed a contract with London-based family mag *Everybody's* – good for one article a month. He applied himself to social and philosophical topics, wrote stories from the life of his Uncle Horace de Vere-Cole and summarised his opinions on how successful the development of a tunnel connecting France and England under the Channel could be. He pleaded for the formation of an Anglo-Franco consortium and warned his readership that work on the tunnel would cost in the region of £6 million. That such a consortium was indeed formed 25 years later and held negotiations in 1973, filled the then 66-year-old Bunty with great satisfaction.

Yet not all of Bunty's lengthy and ornate articles found favour with the editor in chief, Greville Poke. In the period between 1949 and 1950, the total that the author earned through his journalistic endeavours amounted to little over £200. Sitting at the typewriter in his English home wasn't quite as fun or exciting as traveling the world, and the used car trade was providing precious little. Exotic cars were ten a penny, and even when you could find a car-loving prospective buyer, they rarely had the income to finance their passion. These petrol heads, such as those with memberships to the Bugatti Owners' Club, were really committed to their automobiles – organising regular meet-ups and races against each other – and were mostly skilful enough with the toolbox too (very few of them could afford the luxury of taking their car to a factory in Molsheim for repairs!).

Averil had made contact with the Bugatti Owners' Club and went on to take La Folie to numerous race events. At the Bo'Ness Hillclimb, she even set a new record for the fastest time. "I envied her a little," Bunty confessed to me later, "because she was a better driver than I, and it was now my job to stay at home and look after the house and kids whilst writing.

"Averil was always off somewhere with the Bugatti, which I encouraged wholeheartedly because ultimately, I was the one who was able to turn her into such an enthusiast ... But then I got such a surprise, that you would hardly believe. I received a letter from Alfred Neubauer, you know, the race director at Daimler-

Benz, the 'big cheese.' I had written to him to express my disappointment at not being able to meet him during my first visit to their factory.

"Neubauer even responded in English, or at least had his words translated, possibly by Rudolf Uhlenhaut. In this, he was complaining that the golden years of racing were over, and that he feared one day racing would be lost to history forever. This sentence was an inspiration to me. You know what I'm on about here, don't you?"

I knew exactly what he was on about. The inspiration of which Bunty spoke was to write the history of motorsports through the Mercedes-Benz racing car. It was to be as extensive a book as possible, which meant that the author would need to carry out ample background research – at the home of the famous Silver Arrows.

Bunty had even more in mind than simply writing the history of Mercedes. He began to court publishers, settling for nothing less than a contract.

The pair began to plan for a journey to Stuttgart. Averil's Bugatti wasn't being considered for such a long drive, and Bunty wasn't prepared to trust another second-hand vehicle. He decided instead to get himself a brand-new, factory standard car, "A really intelligent, reliable and if possible also economical car. Averil and I thought very carefully about which brand to go for. In the end, we opted for an Austin A40."

In order to pay for this, Bunty would have to publish at least a further six to eight articles, even before Averil's family trust contribution came into it. Unfortunately, no matter whom Bunty approached with his articles, nobody was interested in publishing them. The editorial office of the magazine *Motor Sport* wrote to him: "Many thanks for your reader's letter. We have pigeonholed it in our special section for everything that we find amusing or frightening …"

Despite this, Bunty and Averil eventually managed to purchase the Austin, which they ended up collecting from Birmingham. There was quite the reception at the factory for Mr Scott-Moncrieff and his spouse; for three whole days they were hosted, celebrated and shown around. However, this didn't lead to a discount at the end of it all and, once the purchase was made, Bunty and Averil set off directly from Birmingham to Stuttgart.

Averil: "Never before in my life had either of us sat in a brand-new car and been allowed to enjoy its modern comforts. It was so blissful that we were never bothered about spending a night or two sleeping in the car instead of finding a hotel – our travel expenses could scarcely afford nightly hotel visits. Bunty was very hopeful that Herr Neubauer would offer him a sizeable advance for his book project, we were in severe need of that."

Since they didn't need to stop every thirty minutes to top up the radiator, the kilometres glided by. As they went on, Bunty thought about stopping at every little hotel in the suburban Bruges area, but unfortunately neither Monsieur Quentin, nor the Bugatti-abbot were anywhere to be seen this time around.

Averil: "We didn't bother with a room, deciding instead to sleep in our Austin in the car park behind the house, much to the amazement of our hosts. Bunty insisted upon extraordinary frugality; we had already invested a great deal in the necessary petrol ration cards required for France. Bunty also considered it of great importance that we not take simply the shortest route to Stuttgart, but rather zig-zag though the countryside in the Austin, so that we ended up in Paris, where he planned to redeem a golden cigarette box from a pawnbroker whom he had used fifteen years ago in the absence of a currency for foreign exchange. They still had it!

"Bunty wanted to get hold of a couple more petrol ration cards in Paris, because fuel was only available in exchange for coupons at petrol stations. Our journey continued south, through Dijon and Lyon, before we stopped in Grenoble and Annecy: it was wonderful. And not once did we have to deal with a breakdown!

"We travelled across Switzerland to Germany. Bunty had chosen this route to Stuttgart specifically so that we would pass through Munich and another place where he knew a few people. (It was more than a few people.) We had the entry visa: as English nationals we enjoyed extensive travel freedoms. Everywhere we went, people marvelled at our beautiful new Austin, whilst we in turn stared in amazement at cars we had never come across before, such as a Volkswagen cabriolet and a Mercedes-Benz 170 with a diesel engine."

The arrival of the English couple in Stuttgart didn't quite go the way Bunty had imagined. On their approach to the Daimler-Benz district, they were forced to pull over and get out of their car at the Untertuerkheim gate entrance for questioning. When Bunty explained that he wanted to speak with Mr Neubauer or Mr Uhlenhaut, the security officers responded with ridicule. They'd need more convincing than that …

There were two American officials in the gatehouse near the entrance. Stuttgart was situated in the American zone, and the Daimler-Benz factory was under control from allied occupants just as strict as for every other industrial plant in Baden-Wuerttemberg. On the advice of the two Americans, Bunty and Averil sought the US headquarters in Stuttgart to ask for authorisation to enter the factory. With an official permit from the US military, it would be no problem to enter the site, even by car.

Averil: "We weren't allowed access to Alfred Neubauer, but we were given permission to meet with Rudolf Uhlenhaut, Fritz Nallinger, Max Sailer, and the press officer, Prince of Urach. Bunty was in his element: nothing but world-renowned company! He told them endless long stories of his experience with Mercedes vehicles … they took a real shine to us, inviting us in to stay a few days and make ourselves at home …"

Bunty's desire to bring the story of the Mercedes-Benz Silver Arrows to paper was met with great approval. At the same time, it was made clear to him that he could expect no material compensation from the factory, as this was the responsibility of a publisher (whom Bunty remained yet to acquire). However, they offered him free reign with photos, and Alfred Neubauer himself later promised to write a foreword.

Bunty's admittedly insufficiently thought-through suggestion of taking over the Mercedes-Benz brand dealership in Staffordshire was never pushed through. The English visitor decided to adjourn the topic.

Finding a publisher for his book *The Three-Pointed Star* wasn't easy, and it wasn't until 1955 that Bunty's work was finally recognised. An expanded issue was subsequently released by Gentry Books of London in 1979. Bunty had tried to find a German publisher for the original edition, but his extensive list of German contacts proved unusually useless in this regard. "They shied away from the expensive translation costs," the author conjectured during an interview in 1968, "but I have since been able to find someone who has offered to translate my manuscript for free – and a familiar name to boot! I'm sure that you're friends with him!"

Well, I wasn't friends with him; in fact I had never met him, but everyone in the motoring world knew his name: it was race driver and journalist Richard von Frankenberg. He didn't only translate Bunty's book, he even found a publisher who agreed to distribute it. Unbeknown to Bunty at the time, this act of incredible kindness would end in tragedy.

The only existing copy of the typewritten translated manuscript was in the very car that Richard von Frankenberg fatally crashed on the autobahn between Stuttgart and Heilbronn on 13th November, 1973. His Porsche burnt out during the wreckage. The death of the 51-year-old multitalented ambassador shook the world of motorsport, leaving many more friends than just Bunty bereft. *The Three-Pointed Star* has since then never been translated again.

Bunty was distraught to hear of his friend Richard's passing, with the loss of his translated manuscript heaping on even more misery. Yet he refused to give up. In the men's cubicle of a Berlin-Wannsee pleasure cruiser toilet, on which Bunty and I had a chance encounter, he turned to me: "Halwart, you know my book well, would you be interested in turning your hand to translating it once more? And finding a publisher for it in Germany?" The charter cruiser was hosting a general meeting of veteran car lovers on the occasion of the annual German ASC veteran car rally at the end of June, 1979, and Bunty had driven over in a beautiful Bentley to partake in the Berlin festivities.

I had to disappoint Bunty: I had neither the time nor the desire to take on his book. Furthermore, there were already several excellent books published on the topic of Mercedes in Germany, so I didn't give his 436-page oeuvre much chance of success. So, then I ought to focus instead on his limericks collection, Bunty informed me. Many of them were self-written, and they would surely be highly amusing in German.

Bunty's life in the countryside

THE MERCEDES BOOK PROJECT was rather slow to get underway after Bunty and Averil's return from Stuttgart in the Austin, mostly because Bunty, despite being the owner of an (admittedly old) typewriter, didn't actually possess a desk on which to typewrite. The kitchen table had served this purpose until now. Sadly, the Scott-Moncrieffs were set to be evicted from their London apartment for failing to muster the rent and were thus on the hunt for another flat, as they couldn't exactly live in the Austin. In the meantime, Humphrey and Ambrose were staying with their grandparents in Scotland, waiting to finally be integrated into a proper family home.

They found shelter with Averil's relatives in the northern part of Staffordshire county, where they were let a small cottage near to the village of Basford Hall. The cottage was named 'Sooters,' because of its rather heavily contaminated fireplace. It had a mansion porch and three rooms on the ground floor; the first floor had been waiting for development for over sixty years. Enter Auntie May once more, right on cue – she financed the refurbishment of two rooms for the children and paid for all the most necessary fittings for the whole house, whilst simultaneously organising school attendance for both of the little ones. Averil took on a job as a housekeeper in the neighbourhood.

While Averil's most valuable possession was La Folie, Bunty's was his typewriter: and so it was, that he finally sat down one day to begin the manuscript for his Mercedes book. However, the sheer time constraints of a project of this size, coupled with his ongoing search for publishers and the constant fielding of alternative work offers required Bunty to re-evaluate his timings slightly. Alongside this main project, Bunty released another, smaller book on cars for Batsford Publishing, entitled *The Veteran and Edwardian Motor Car*. This was set for original publication in Autumn 1954, but ended up being put back to 1955, meaning its release was almost simultaneous with that of the Mercedes collection. Bunty dedicated this publication to a high-standing personality who had recently passed on: His Majesty King Faisal of Iraq, to whom he had supposedly sold a Napier and a Rolls-Royce. How and when these transactions had taken place isn't recorded, whilst no contemporary witnesses are able to back up Bunty's claim. When I put this to Bunty during an interview in 1978, all I received in return was: "Now, I've sold ever so many cars to a great number of statesmen, that my dear old friend Faisal is just one of many, you know ..."

In order to share Bunty's unique written (and oral) aptitude for storytelling,

I feel it is appropriate to draw from the foreword of the book dedicated to King Faisal; an epitome of Bunty's fabulously idiosyncratic style:

"This has been a difficult book to write; the great problem was not what to put in, but what to leave out. So, if the reader finds that data about his favourite Vilbrequin-Manivelle (23.8hp, 1906) has been omitted, together with an account of the Bedworthy Magna speed trials (August 1907), I trust he will forgive me. There wasn't anything like room for it all. There are other omissions of quite well-known cars, simply because the documentation does not exist in this country, and I thought that the reader would rather have authenticated facts about less important cars than flannel padding on the better-known ones.

I have had great help from two Americans, John ('Demon') Leathers and Arthur Rippey, and also from many friends on the continent of Europe. In fact, without them this book could never have been written. I am deeply indebted to Walter O MacIlvain of Connecticut for permission to raid his vast store of knowledge for much of the 'Winston Story'; also, to the one and only 'Austie' Clark without whom the book would never have gone to press in time. I am also most grateful to my friend Ken Purdy for his help with the proofs.

"At home, among many others, Anthony Heal gave me invaluable data about Sunbeams, as did Raymond Playfoot about Singers. Arthur Jeddere-Fisher more than kindly took time off from packing his batterie de cuisine and cookery books, necessary for his appointment as Chief Justice in the Cannibal Islands, to write down for me little-known facts about Lagonda. The Victoria and Albert Museum spent an astronomical number of man-hours on helping with research for the chapters on motoring clothing. I virtually established squatter's rights in the VCC of GB library and in the files room of *The Autocar*; and that great historian, John Pollitt, was a tremendous help. Thanks are due also to certain manufacturers' Public Relations Officers, who supplied much-needed data.

"It has been very difficult striking a balance between obscure and fascinating details presented for virtually the first time, and better-known facts, without which the story would have had no backbone. Whether I have been successful is for the reader to judge."

He must have been successful in this endeavour, for the book went through three editions! And Ken Purdy offered his services as editor. He was one of the best-known car feature writers of his time, when he wasn't writing articles for *Playboy*. To be able to mention his name, along with the lawyer – soon to be departing for the Cannibal Islands (cooking books!) – and amateur Lagonda historian Arthur Jeddere-Fisher and the famous Henry Austin Clark Jr was very impressive. I too had the pleasure of correspondence with the Sunbeam man himself, Anthony Heal, and one of Raymond Playfoot's sons went on to become the head of media for the UK BMW imports company.

Chicken farming, piglet fattening, Mercedes dreaming

THE SCOTT-MONCRIEFFS' NEWFOUND-LIVING CIRCUMSTANCES required them to resort to homegrown produce from the garden. Payment for the veteran book wasn't high, and the car dealership business was still failing to flourish. Bunty, however, felt little desire to practice the art of vegetable growing; he was now 45 years old and still remained very much on the path to becoming a famous writer. The cottage lands possessed a stable and a large garden, so the decision was made that, given Bunty had no interest in maintaining the land, somebody would have to be found who would – and this someone was Jack.

Jack was a man of countless talents. His father had actually helped to build the cottage six decades ago, and Jack was well-trained in animal husbandry and the ground rules of vegetable growing, as well as being a skilled mason and plumber. Above all, he claimed no reward for his work, content with simply taking home part of his homegrown natural yield.

The harvested fruit and vegetables helped to save housekeeping money and benefited everyone who lived, or – like Jack – worked, at Sooters. In order to turn the prosperous garden into a profitable farm, Bunty had the idea of attempting to raise chickens – with the plan of selling them at the market in Leek. Once the first generation of these purpose-built animals reached their optimal age, Jack and Bunty loaded their living cargo into an old, rental Ford delivery truck to drive the chickens to market.

Like so many other cars which Bunty had steered over the course of his life to date, the Ford came to a stop after about a hundred yards. After several failed start attempts, the engine eventually decided to kick into life once more. In order to negate the risk of repeating this ordeal, Bunty stepped abruptly on the accelerator and let the clutch up suddenly as he jerked the gear shift into second, with the result that the car took a gigantic and unprecedented leap forward. The momentum of this lightning start flung the rear doors of the truck wide open, sending several cages tumbling out. The cage doors swung open upon impact and there was hardly a young chicken on board who didn't instantly recognise this good fortune as a chance for freedom.

"Our chickens!" screamed Jack. Bunty slammed on the brakes just as quickly as he had slammed on the accelerator; both men dashed out of the car. Comfortably half of the chickens were up and away with no hope of capture. Averil regretted this misfortune very much upon being informed of the unexpected event. Jack simply cursed, while Bunty declared with categorical intent that he would have nothing to do with chickens again in future. From now on it would have to be pigs.

The pig farming went rather well for a while. Bunty found feeding the little pink fellas rather enjoyable, albeit cleaning out their enclosure less so. However, soon the pigsty was put to different use. The year was 1956, when Bunty made the acquaintance of a group of political refugees from Hungary who had fled to England. He offered them quarters … in his boar pen! Not quite as selflessly as it first appeared, for providing accommodation to asylum seekers was met with grants from the state. Bunty sold the pigs, instructing Jack to kalsomine the sty walls and install new windows. The structures for a few camp beds were already in place …

When the attorney came to view the 'quarters' which Mr Scott-Moncrieff had to offer, he declared the space to be unfit for purpose. Consequently, no Hungarians moved into Sooters, and the sty remained a sty. As a replacement for the pigs sold, goats were purchased, who were joined in turn by a terrier and finally a pair of peacocks.

Jack was replaced by Knowles; he was rarely seen thereafter but remained occasionally available for craft work. Knowles wasn't as diversely talented as his predecessor, but he was more sensitive; he was able to help with the children's homework, field telephone calls, carry out the grocery shopping, even cook. Bunty spoke happily of Knowles as a "good friend," Knowles, however, never strayed from 'Sir' and 'Madam.'

It was around this time that the car dealership finally restarted. England turned its attention back towards its proud automotive traditions, the economy was booming (in relative terms, less than Germany for example), and there was great interest again in cars, which could now be afforded once more.

Bunty developed a knack for searching out old Rolls-Royce saloons in the classified sections of the daily newspapers; cars which remained extremely affordable to get hold of. Large, uneconomical cars, above all ones that were defect or had the wrong tyres, were being practically given away. Word soon travelled of a peculiar gent in Basford Hall who was buying up all of these models, with rumours that he had as many as twenty parked up on the property lands. Eventually, news broke to the motor press in both Britain and in America, which was exactly the desired effect: interested parties from all around the world were getting in touch about buying a second-hand Rolls-Royce. Since this brand had maintained a consistent reputation for superior engineering quality, leading to its epithet as the "best car in the world," enquiries continued to flow in, with more and more clients buying into the slogan and parting with great sums of cash to get their hands on one. Bunty was more than happy to oblige. Several beautiful models earned him large amounts, very few cost him much at all.

Bunty put great value on ensuring the cars he offered were roadworthy. If he thought that repairing a particular car would prove too expensive, he would prefer to dismantle it to hundreds of individual pieces to keep in stock for other vehicles. Soon, he had collected an entire depot of used Rolls-Royce replacement parts, thus making him almost independent of suppliers. Two mechanics were employed to work for him, Geoffrey and Bernard. Knowles took care of everything else, such as the goats, who liked to sneak into the house and lay waste to the living room.

The family eventually outgrew Sooters, as Humphrey and Ambrose sought larger rooms, the business needed further shelving for cars and spares, and Bunty himself required a working space and an office. The Scott-Moncrieffs considered moving to a new domicile. Had this gone the way Bunty imagined, the family would have found a little castle with a beautiful reception hall. He would have dearly loved such a hall to use as a showroom, but not for Rolls-Royce motor cars. "A Rolls-Royce is admittedly the cream of the crop," Bunty once said to his secretary Hazel (whose role I will come to speak of soon). "But I would have far preferred to work exclusively with Mercedes-Benz vehicles. They are the true keepers of my heart. Representing Mercedes-Benz in a dignified, English castle: that was my dream!"

In 1955, Bunty finally published his Mercedes book with Gentry Publishing in London. His manuscript had cleared the hurdles of proofreading and editing, and the proud author sent one of the first copies with a personal note to Alfred Neubauer. The paper, on which Bunty wrote his accompanying letter, was inscribed with the Mercedes star.

When asked why he didn't simply become a Mercedes dealer instead, Bunty was (unusually for him!) able to answer in a single sentence: "Do you know, there are simply not enough connoisseurs of such cars in England to carry out worthwhile business." My background research with Eric Johnson, head of media for Mercedes-Benz UK, however, painted a rather different picture. Bunty's wish to be the official Mercedes-Benz representative in Staffordshire was not met with any interest in Stuttgart, while he had been negatively summoned by the import company in London for failing to satisfy a great number of requirements. Bunty had no proof of the necessary financial means; he wasn't considered to be an established businessman, according to the provisos of the SMMT Association, and was deemed to command insufficient real estate for such an endeavour. Despite the appeals of significant bodies in Stuttgart, Bunty's application remained unsuccessful. However, Bunty continued to use the Mercedes star as his letterhead up until 1974, when multiple polite requests to refrain from doing so finally led Bunty to have some new paper printed without the iconic trade mark. He was even further from being an official representative of the Rolls-Royce and Bentley brands, but the copyright holders appeared to take no offence to Mr Scott-Moncrieff using their logos on his business documents.

Nevertheless, the registered company 'Scott-Moncrieff Motors' officially came into existence in London in the year 1960, even featuring a temporary address there. They had located a garage with space for a car and an office, to which Bunty or Averil would commute once or twice a week (a trip which Averil would gladly make in her Bugatti). London brought prosperity, with customers attracted to more expensive vehicles that would have otherwise gone unsold in Sooters ...

The company name evolved three years later into 'David Scott-Moncrieff & Son' and established itself in the small town of Leek near Stoke-on-Trent. Averil was responsible for correspondence, Bernard and Geoffrey busied themselves with all things mechanical, Knowles took care of the house and good old Jack pitched in here and there with the construction of a stone wall or a shed. Bunty even referred to him as "our gardener." Two ladies, Hilda and Mabel, also assisted Knowles from time to time with the housekeeping.

Bill Boddy's visit to the squirearchy

AVERIL BECAME THE PROPRIETOR of the cottage in 1960 through inheritance (along with a remarkable sum of money to boot). This was used to extend the house, by installing several garages and an office space, along with a large studio room (even if this was actually just a corrugated iron shed which Bunty had acquired cheaply from military stocks). On an adjacent plot of land, which also came into Averil's ownership, stood an old tower, which Humphrey moved into; there had been a motorised pump in the cellar since 1892, which filled a fountain with drinking water. Nobody was concerned that it might one day break and no such replacement parts would exist anymore – Jack would know how to repair it.

The extended house, with its new attachments on the right and inherited tower on the left, needed a new name. Sooters became 'Rock Cottage.' In plainer English, Bunty liked to refer to it as the 'estate.' Averil bought herself a new (used) car; a Lotus Mk 9 with a 1250cc MG engine. A miniature monoposto, as this more adequately pandered to her passion for racing than the Bugatti.

One of the first to be permitted entry to Rock Cottage in its new format was William Boddy. 'Bill,' who was the operating editor-in-chief of the respected magazine 'Motor Sport', had witnessed several of Averil's successful appearances at various club races and was headed to Basford Hall in order to interview the young lady. In a patriarchal racing scene, a highflying woman was quite the anomaly. He was accompanied by a pretty assistant with pen and pad in hand, as well as a photographer from Australia.

Averil barely spoke; it was Bunty who seized the moment and dictated whatever popped into his head to the polite young lady with the pad. Before this chat, Mr Boddy had invited Averil and Bunty to lunch in a restaurant in Leek, after which he wanted to get down to business. Lunch dragged on rather longer than anticipated of course, because Bunty spoke incessantly. It was critically important that his guest not misinterpret the mess on the 'estate,' he stressed; he was very close to closing a contract deal with Daimler-Benz and thus was in the process of converting the whole property. You see, both sons were currently on a break from attending the best boarding school England has to offer, and his Rolls-Royce collection … and so on, and so on. You get the picture here.

When Mr Boddy was presented with the bill, he glanced over it quickly before handing it to his assistant, who was clearly responsible for managing the day-to-day finances. Bunty, who was sitting next to her, caught wind of this and whispered to her: "Give me it discretely under the table, my love, Daddy's paying!" And so, he did, though he asked the girl to leave a £5 note as a tip. This caused her a lot more grief than it would have done to pay for the whole bill from the editorial fund, because £5 was rather a lot for a tip and she would receive no receipt for reimbursement. To further this embarrassment, Bunty had proudly made sure that the waitress thought that he had left the generous tip personally, in order to curry favour with the staff in the hope of saving himself from leaving one the next time he ate there!

Once the crowd reached Rock Cottage in the afternoon, it was the photographer's turn to get a bit of a fright. Cannibalised Rolls-Royce limousines and hearses everywhere, ankle-deep mud leading up to the sty, several inquisitive goats inspecting their new visitors, and two naked boys, playing in the garden pond, in front of a dilapidated building … "So this how the English squirearchy really live?" Mr Boddy asked the landlord, to which Bunty replied: "When they're involved in the second-hand car trade it is!"

Through a cowpat in a TVR

ACCEPTING THE AMBIENCE OF rural life was a concession that city boy Bunty had to make for an orderly family life. Rock Cottage wasn't actually as isolated as one would be inclined to presume, as the 'estate' could be reached through a driveway leading up from the woods. A different entrance route meant travelling through two farms and their muddy paths, often desecrated by animal excrement.

One of the farms was owned by the builder Thomas Brasserington. A cracking chap, with repartee to rival Bunty's, and the pair were often embroiled in heated verbal exchanges. 'Brasso' gave Bunty plenty of reason for this, as he liked to keep his cows free-range, whereby they naturally revelled in the unmaintained grass of their neighbours. Inevitably, the cattle would deposit their legacies directly in front of the back door. Time and again, Bunty would storm furiously into the farmhouse and demand that Brasso stop his damned animals from roaming freely into their garden, to which Brasso would also respond in anger, tossing his hat to the ground and stomping on it for emphasis whilst the shouting match ensued. The pair could be heard for miles.

However, the shouting was regularly followed by a reconciliation party, typically commencing when Bunty would turn up at his neighbour's doorstep with a bottle of brandy ... The 'reconciliation drink' once ended up appeasing Bunty's troubled feelings twofold (according to a story from Hazel).

Bunty was en route with his bottle, but, rather than carry it on display under his arm, the bottle was in a paper bag for discretion and decency. Suddenly, the peace offering arced out of the bag and flew high up into the air, before colliding with the ground to smash into pieces. Its carrier, already deep into enemy territory, had slipped on a freshly laid cowpat. With pithy curses on his lips and a rather interesting blend of fragrances coming from his robe, Bunty entered Brasso's kitchen. After explaining what happened, it became apparent that it was over to Brasso to open up the secret compartment to his kitchen. Additionally, he offered to cover the costs of the dry-cleaning for Bunty's recently spoiled suit.

Bunty's fondness for the paper bag occasionally led to him being spotted shopping with one, which had the consequence of an overfilled bag ripping on more than one occasion. The contents of old ladies' shopping bags smashed to the floor with alarming regularity too, as Bunty, ever the gent, would hold the door open for them upon leaving the supermarket; the problem being that he carried out this favour with such clumsiness and impetuosity that it often did much more harm than good. Emptying elbow-height shelves stocked full of tin cans was another of his talents. Certain shopkeepers, who knew Bunty well, would take the preventative action of leaping from behind the till the moment he entered the store! As long as he was on the shop floor, the damage could be contained.

Bunty also liked entering shops with a lit cigar, which brought regular complaints. A good cigar, the pricier the better, brought him great happiness. In later life, when he used to frequent the post office to collect his monthly pension, he would say to the lady at the desk: "Oh what a modest penny indeed. That ought to be enough to cover one good cigar this evening." The employee found this to be highly inappropriate and one day asked Averil if she would ensure her husband refrained from this motto in future: "There are several pensioners in the local community who receive far, far less and are expected to make it last an entire month!"

Behaving appropriately where it was expected of him, such as in the grocery store or the post office, didn't come particularly naturally to Bunty, and he considered it to be beneath his dignity to be seen paying for banal items like washing-up liquid or toilet paper. If he was able to palm off Averil's requests onto Hazel or Knowles, then he did so gladly.

There were two cars which Bunty acquired through favourable circumstances and subsequently didn't intend to sell immediately – a Lancia Artena and a TVR. The 1934 Lancia proved itself to be a very reliable and comfortable holiday car; Averil in particular enjoyed it, leading to La Folie being slightly side-lined. The TVR was one of the very earliest editions from 1955. The sports cars, manufactured in Blackpool by a young man named Trevor Wilkinson, were 'kit cars,' meaning vehicles which one purchased as a construction kit (greatly helping save money on the notorious 'purchase tax,' which increased prices for new cars considerably). Bunty and Averil knew Trevor, and even helped him out by taking a small percentage share of the company – even though they themselves were rather strapped for cash. Bunty grossly exaggerated this in later life, declaring that Trevor "would never have afforded to take the plunge into self-employment without my generous support."

One day, a customer rolled along to see a Rolls-Royce that had been listed, but then turned his fancy to the (unlisted) TVR coupé. However, as he peered in for a closer inspection, Averil noticed to her delight that the man began to turn his nose up at the idea.

The car stank horribly, outside and in, of cows. "I'd driven it over with wellies on, which I always wore outside, since I had no intention whatsoever of giving up the car …" Every car at Rock Cottage smelt a bit musty, for a wide range of reasons. But the cars listed for sale were spotlessly clean. Occasionally, the boss himself even picked up the leather cloth.

A soft spot also for Lagonda

ON ONE OF HER frequent club races at the track in Mallory Park, Averil met a man who has been cited several times already in this book: Bernard Worth.

Bernard was a gifted mechanic and offered his services to help the Scott-Moncrieffs at the weekends. He would have gladly taken a full-time job, but he had to work at his uncle's business in Lincolnshire. After about a year, he gave this up and became a fully-fledged member of the team at Rock Cottage.

Averil traded the Lotus for a Cooper Climax, that had previously belonged to Stirling Moss. The 'Manx Tail Monoposto' was a well-known and successful racing car on the scene. Bunty followed suit by getting his hands on a supercharged eight-cylinder Auburn. In doing so, he made sure he received just as much attention in the paddocks as Averil did behind the wheel of her Stirling Moss racer. Bernard owned an HRG with a Lea Francis engine, a car which he never drove on country roads. He would transport it to races in a trailer, using a 1933 Lagonda M45 saloon.

Since Bernard received no wage for his weekend work (eventually he would be put up for free at Rock Cottage), nor viaticum when it came to races, he had learnt to prepare himself for it: he would show up with a fully-stocked provisions basket. Bunty regularly laid siege to this, devouring the lot with enormous appetite, leaving poor Bernard with precious little. Regardless of who had eaten what, however, the last hard-boiled egg or tuna sandwich would always go to Averil.

Bernard's Lagonda was a powerful carthorse, which Bunty tried to mooch for a laughable offer of £30. Bernard stood firm; he was never parting with the car for such a pitiful amount. That Bunty wound up as the car's owner on a beautiful Sunday afternoon, with Bernard's willing consent, can be attributed to a particularly palatable Madeira wine, which Bunty kept stocked for very special purposes. This event brought a second misfortune to poor Bernard, who was found snoring away in the Scott-Moncrieff's guest bed until late in the afternoon. The uncle in Lincolnshire must have been rather sour when discovering his nephew was nowhere to be seen.

"I already had a longstanding place in my heart for Lagondas," wrote Bunty in his third book, published by Basford in 1963 under the title *The Thoroughbred Motor Car 1930-1940*. "I'm very fond of these cars, with the exception, perhaps, of their twelve cylinder. It's a good car, very good even, but not the best car of all time, as many have suggested, and which a constructor by the name of Bentley had expected. The M45, which I rate very highly, wasn't actually a build of the immortal W O Bentley; the 1935 successor, the LG45, was his first version of these cars to be presented to the world. I later purchased a V12 with a coupé body by Mulliner; I would have liked to know just how high the price of one of these cars would have been new. A simple touring car cost £1285 by this point already. The vehicle had all the gimmicks in the world and drove superbly; only the steering was sometimes sluggish. I could easily reach 100 miles per hour, though I tried to avoid this if possible, as such high speeds used up enormous amounts of petrol."

The very same day that Bernard had sold him the M45, Bunty succeeded in acquiring another bargain. He was able to obtain an Alfa Romeo 6C1750 Zagato from 1929 for very little money. The two-seater's six-cylinder OHC engine had a defect, admittedly, but it worked. Bunty placed an advert to try and sell on the Alfa (he kept the Lagonda for himself for the time being), to which a British European Airways pilot responded, who was prepared to part with a great deal of cash, and could hardly wait to come over and speed off with it. It was his first Alfa Romeo.

Just a few days later, he returned to Rock Cottage, full of frustration. "I told him, plainly and simply, that you have to be extremely cautious with such cars, treat them like an Italian princess," explained Bunty in response to the pilot's grievances about the engine having no power. "You weren't willing to listen to what I had to say, Sir! You drove too fast; presumably you didn't centre the camshaft rotation beforehand either, or extrapolate the engine simulation. Now the engine is broken … I will of course take the car back, but I will have to ask you to accept a little deduction from the refund for the repairs …" And he offered the poor man, who was completely unsettled by this gratuitous use of highfalutin old-timer vocabulary, just two-thirds of the money he had originally paid only a few days before. So the Zagato Alfa returned to Rock Cottage for a second stay, practically untouched. In many similar situations, Bunty would succeed in selling a customer like this a second car, but he would only do so if absolutely certain that the second car was perfect. A customer who had two successive reasons to complain was a customer lost forever.

A fascinating, insufferable boss

AT THIS POINT, IT'S time to talk a little more about Hazel – a woman who truly has my utmost admiration. When I first met her, Hazel Robinson was a single mother of a little son named Peter, rather than Bunty's first secretary and assistant.

Hazel applied for the role of all-rounder with Bunty in 1962, having already heard a lot about him. She was an admirer of the gentleman and imagined it would be wonderful to work for him. Over time, Bunty went on to trust Hazel more than every single person in his vicinity, even more than his beloved Averil. Hazel's loyalty wasn't always repaid, however; she was frequently the victim of his inane jokes.

Before the Scott-Moncrieff firm moved into new rooms in the Hope Mill building, Hazel's office was situated in an uncomfortable outhouse at Rock Cottage, built by Jack from hollow concrete directly next door to the garage workshop. There was electricity for a lamp, a kettle and a radiator. Such luxuries weren't always available in Bunty's business premises.

"His charm, his storytelling, his cheerful effrontery – they outright fascinated me," Hazel explained to me, "and I was impressed at how everyone admired him. He possessed a reputation as a worldwide businessman, on first-name terms with oriental monarchs as well as prominent race drivers because he knew them so well and had command of several foreign languages. He could speak French and German very well.

"Still, our first meeting must have served as a warning, for Bunty's behaviour was anything other than nice. It was at a birthday party of a mutual acquaintance, and there were around fifteen of us at a festively decorated table. The dessert was a fruit salad, everyone received a portion, handed out in a glass bowl. In the middle of the table, there was a jug with fresh cream. Bunty took it upon himself to serve first and poured practically the entire lot over his fruit – the rest of us were left with little more than a few paltry drops to share.

"Bunty didn't acknowledge this whatsoever, savouring his dessert with great pleasure as he told Mercedes stories without interruption, unabashedly burping at the end. I really don't know why this man fascinated me so …"

She wasn't just fascinated by him; Hazel also knew exactly how to respond to Bunty's nature. Before long, she was an indispensable asset for his growing business and never looked back. Eventually she took over management of the accounts – with Averil's full permission, handling customers and organising the work in the garage. Hazel's calm, balanced and always friendly temperament, her great respect for her boss and maternal care of him, her good memory, her negotiation skills, coupled with a decisive disposition and diplomatic nature, made her an invaluable member of the team.

Hazel commanded a reasonable salary. But her arrival meant the departure of another member of the business: Knowles. Hazel deeply regretted being responsible for his redundancy but being in business does require maintaining control on staff expenditure – the Scott-Moncrieffs were fortunate to only have to do this once. A butler and a secretary couldn't work in the long run.

"At first, I was only working part-time. On my very first day, I remember Geoff Beardsmore, the head mechanic, revealing to me that my predecessor simply couldn't face working with Bunty anymore. He had just finished his manuscript for his book *The Thoroughbred Motor Car*, which she had been asked to type up, and his constant changes were utterly exasperating – apparently, she had to type some pages as many as seven times …

"But when the book was released by Batsford a year later, everyone found it wonderful. Bunty ordered fifty copies, signed them and gifted them to various people with pride and joy. In a way, the book was part of his life story, as it described almost every important car which he had owned at some point. Only Auntie May didn't share in the admiration of his claque. She discovered the amount that Bunty had received as payment from Batsford and found this laughably low sum to be anything other than fair for the penmanship of her gifted nephew.

"Soon enough, my boss was begging me to work for him on a full-time basis; he offered me £12 a week. I could get by on that. But I hadn't signed up for an office job whatsoever: I was expected to clean engines, visit customers and collect cars, stave off suppliers when we had outstanding payments to make – essentially carry out all the unpleasant duties which Bunty didn't fancy.

"When he received word that there was a particularly interesting old prewar vehicle up for sale somewhere, he would send me off with a few pound notes, whereby I was expected to summon my womanly charm and negotiation skills, in order to bring the car back to Basford Hall as cheaply as possible. For as long as nobody in the field knew me, I could succeed in appearing as a 'private' buyer. Bunty, infamous for his business acumen, had difficulty in persuading the majority of sellers into offering him a rarity for mates' rates …"

Left: Bunty.

Below: A number of luxury car wrecks laid to rest in front of the garden gate, a waterless goldfish pond and a couple of corrugated iron sheds, discreetly grounded in the fog of the English Midlands: an ambience which serves up quite a fiendish fright for a strange guest, attempting to locate the mystical and well-hidden Rock Cottage on a November night.

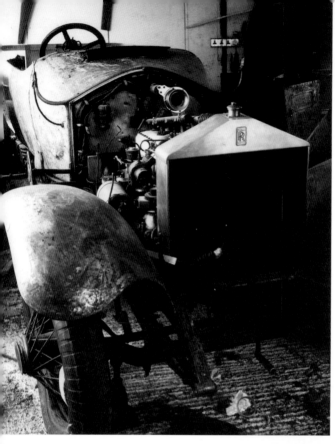

Left: This Rolls-Royce Silver Ghost dares to dream of a second life, after it takes a last breath and claims mandatory retirement from its current role of grand limousine, or rather mortuary vehicle.

Below: This great piece of furniture could be found in the Scott-Moncrieffs' bedroom. Both the head and foot of it could be individually hinged from underneath. It was a so-called 'lit-bateau,' built by the Sawla Frères. The odd furnishings in the house were made up of predominantly English antiques; an alternative setup would have been impossible to imagine.

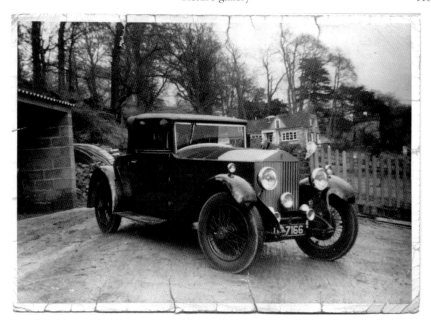

Above: Bunty had entrusted me with this pretty, two-seater Rolls-Royce 20hp from 1929. I could have had it for £250. A bargain, since, by comparison with the many others he had in this price class, this one was very well maintained. I resisted, however, not least to avoid burdening our friendship through the risk of business.

Left: Had one of the objects that Bunty acquired over time spent longer in the scrapyard or in the overgrown shed, he certainly paid less for it. In 1960, England was certainly full of such automotive gems.

Above: Bunty with cleaning equipment? Surely only for the photograph! He would typically, very willingly, leave it to his agents and volunteers to care for the appearance of his cars. And such activities were not to be exaggerated, either: "We are honest people … our cars can't exactly look new, can they, otherwise we'll give the customers the impression that we are blowing smoke!"

Right: The little rascal that was Bunty at 14 years of age. In true English fashion, he's decorated with a tie and pin. A stylish wardrobe (or at least, what he considered that to be) was to later take on great importance in Bunty's life.

Left: Bunty had a very close relationship with his mother, Grace, née Eustace. She was one of very few women who owned a driving license in England at the time, let alone a high calibre car. She financed her son's Cambridge education and various escapades, as far as her funds allowed.

Below: After a self-built three-wheeler, this single-seater was the second 'automobile' that Bunty owned, the acquisition of which he kept secret even from his mother, out of fear that it might get around Trinity College and lead to his expulsion. The monocar had the sad disadvantage of lacking a passenger seat, meaning that guests (particularly female ones) couldn't be taken out for a spin.

Above: A collision, 1927, caused by Bunty with a 2-litre H.E. As with most of the transport accidents that he was responsible for, nobody was injured. Importantly for him, a photograph was taken to capture the situation: less for insurance purposes, more for the album. Bunty kept such images the way that a hunter collects trophies.

Top right: This photo was captured by a certain Mr Stella in the Cambridge landscape in 1928, where Bunty had flipped this Mercedes with Leo Shallit (centre) and Donald Stewart-Fotheringham on board. Presumably, black ice had been determined as the cause. He and another companion survived a similar accident in an even older Mercedes on a Swiss mountain pass road.

Bottom right: In a quite theatrical pose, Bunty presents himself to the photographer here in front of a Ford Model A, whose broken front is playing on his conscience. The disproportionately large headlights exhibited by this car are notable .

Above: Bunty in the backseat of a De Dion-Bouton with Branbury Tighe at the wheel. The young lady with whom the monocle-wearing protagonist is flirting, is Branbury's sister, Sheila; one of Bunty's ever-changing girlfriends.

Left: Of noble French heritage, the Chenard-Walcker with which Bunty (a few years older by this point) posed for a photograph in the style of a successful businessman. This was a car of similar value and prestige to a BMW 5 Series of today. Bunty named the car 'Anna Porka.'

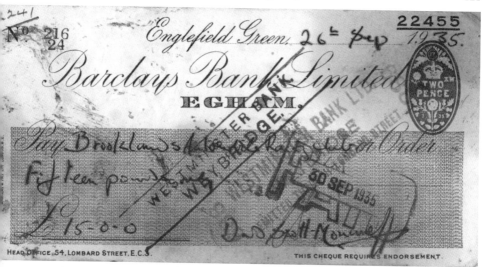

Above: Bunty was a member of Brooklands Racing Drivers' Club, costing him £15 a year, as this cheque proves. He liked to keep meticulous records of all payments. Being part of a prestigious team was important to him.

Right: A little less gentle than most of his scrapes, this newspaper excerpt from September 1933 describes and pictures an accident in which Bunty suffered severe head injuries. He had swerved at high speed to avoid a motorbike.

A CAR OVERTURNED while travelling at high speed on the London Road, at Preston Hall, on Monday. The driver, Mr. David Scott-Moncrieff, of Berkeley Square, London, endeavoured to avoid a collision with a motor cycle. He received serious head injuries.

Above: London-Edinburgh Trial, 1935. Sat at the wheel of an American Stutz Blackhawk, Bunty is seen here taking part in the saloon category of this trial. He enjoyed such events, at which there was ample time to make a good impression on an interested audience, whilst other drivers posted better times. Bunty still took part in contests with antique cars in his seventies.

Above: Bunty loved his high-calibre exotics. The top image is of a customized Mercedes special motorized with an aero engine; the bottom is Chitty Chitty Bang Bang II, captured here in Dover, 1931, with Bunty's friend, Peter Hales.

Left: This image captures Bunty in the supercharged Mercedes-Benz SSK which he bought from an arms dealer in Venice. On the way home, he got himself caught up in a Nazi parade in Munich in this impressive old car, but this photo dates back to just before that, in Vienna, where he managed to acquire travel documents via a sneaky trick in order to pass the car off as UK-registered …

Right: On the reverse side of this photo, Bunty noted: "This Targa-Florio, which would make every vintage enthusiast green with envy, was driven by one of the directors during the war period: he said it was a lot of fun. The car is currently housed in the Stuttgart works museum."

Below: Bunty in the driver's seat of his favourite brand of car at the start of a hillclimb. He took part in events such as this whenever it could be arranged, in expectation that he could find a buyer for the car by the end, or at least make the acquaintance of wealthy individuals whom he could interest in another of his vehicles.

Above: Unusually, Bunty is not in the driver's seat of this breath-taking chain-drive Benz known as the Brooklands Special (1921), featuring a Zeppelin engine under the hood.

Right: Bunty and his wife on holiday in Turkey. They are pictured here standing before the tomb of Kemal Atatürk. They took numerous trips together; only when Averil had important tasks to carry out for her company did Bunty begin to explore the company of rather younger ladies … which his spouse met initially with mixed feelings, but later with serenity.

Right: Bunty didn't have to pay too much for his Bugatti 37A – and for good reason: the engine was suffering from an array of defects. In order to repair the racing car once and for all, Bunty decided that the only option was to take it to the Bugatti factory in Molsheim.

Right: The Scott-Moncrieffs with their problem car in August 1947 en route to Molsheim. Note the scarce amount of luggage on board.

Above: Butler Byrne at the wheel of a 4.5-litre Bentley sports car in front of the house at Shepherd's Market, where Bunty lodged in the early thirties. They didn't need to buy the chauffeur's uniform – they found one, plus an oversized cap, by coincidence in the boot of a vehicle that Bunty had recently purchased.

Right: If you love your car, you'd better be prepared to push it! Bunty is wearing his original Styrian lederhosen here. He and Averil somehow managed to get to Molsheim, where this picture was taken. By looking at the fenders at the front, one can see the makeshift lights, fastened with duct tape. The large electric lights in the centre had given up the ghost before the Bugatti had even left the UK!

Right: This Bugatti Type 46 was the model that Bunty and Averil took to Scandinavia in autumn of 1946. However, it failed to get them into the Soviet Union …

Above: After the Bugatti 37A, nicknamed La Folie, had taken its trip to the factory, it worked like a charm. The sporty two-seater, pictured here in a photo dating from 1950, fast became Averil's favourite car, causing her to forget all about her problems with it before it was repaired. She used CLG 707 at every opportunity; even taking it shopping in the local village.

Life's handicaps
(according to Rudyard Kipling)

THE MOUNTING CONSOLIDATION OF his business with a core team of reliable and loyal workers enabled Bunty and Averil to holiday more often and take part in more races (Bunty was just as content to fill the role of co-driver, supporter or all-purpose, solo entertainer on race day). However, attendance at an Edwardian car rally in 1963 would have severe consequences for Bunty. He had spent the morning participating in a rally on the coastal resort of Brighton with his friend Stanley Brunt; by late Sunday afternoon, the cars were being readied for their commutes home. Stan drove a big Isotta-Fraschini, Bunty was his co-driver.

Bunty got out of the car in order to stop the oncoming traffic while Stan completed a rather awkward reverse manoeuvre out of a confusing exit to the course and onto the main road. All the cars were very courteous in their stopping, except for one, whose driver spotted Bunty too late to realise he was on the road. This led to an accident which was almost fatal for Bunty.

Bunty remained in hospital in Brighton for eight weeks, where he was gradually put right. Averil would come to visit him at the weekend, keeping the business running with Hazel during the week. She would stay overnight with the Lightfoot family. Tom Lightfoot owned a 1903 Mercedes, and saw himself as a sort of artist. Bunty was eternally grateful for Tom's help, and decided to reward him by later commissioning him to paint the walls of his showroom on Macclesfield Road in Leek with chubby little figures of angels.

After his release from hospital, Bunty had to suffer heavy plaster casts to lug around with him. He was only able to work two hours a day, spending the rest of the day in a Victorian bath chair in the lounge of the house, making phone calls and grumbling.

"It wasn't easy to get on with Bunty at that time," confessed Hazel. "He was understandably often very ill-tempered. Since he was out of the loop with the way the business was playing out, but continued to carry out telephone conversations with customers, there was endless confusion. He would make the most impossible promises, which we would then have to revise the next day …"

There was one particular telephone deal which Hazel and Averil were unable to stop: it was made with the owner of an old mill building in Leek. Bunty explained to him over the phone that he wanted to finally purchase this long-fancied property located on Macclesfield Road. The remarkably cheap price for 'Hope Mills' was paid for by damages received from the insurance payment of the driver responsible for Bunty's accident. Having a real showroom in the city to house the best cars they had to offer was a longstanding dream for both Bunty and Averil.

At long last, the doctors finally removed the last steel nail from Bunty's left leg. Bunty kept the plate henceforth as a ruler in his office. He also insisted that his mackintosh never be dry cleaned – not just for reasons of Scottish frugality: the blood and dirt stains in the fabric were to remain in the family!

The renovation of the mill building, the installation of three offices and the decoration of the showroom brought together all available manpower. Old Jack pitched in, as did Geoffrey, who discovered his talent for laying tiles. The grand opening was set for Bunty's 57th birthday on July 1, 1964, but unfortunately work overran considerably and so the building's inauguration had to wait until October.

When the day finally came, Bunty had invited over a hundred people, many of whom had travelled great distances, as it was a rather rare occurrence for Bunty to be throwing a party. Everyone who attended the party wondered whom Bunty had acquired as a sponsor, because there was an abundance of food and drink ... one cast iron bath tub, half-filled with ice cubes, contained two dozen bottles of champagne on demand (his favourite brand was Krug), while feasting took place on several sorts of pastry, salmon and other delicacies. A particularly important guest for Bunty was Hermann Scott, the librarian at the Royal Automobile Club in London. Hermann knew little about cars but had a great knowledge of literature and was able to help advise Bunty on publishing matters. Like all the party guests, he felt great admiration for Bunty, who was able to move again completely now and was thus able to fully entertain his guests.

Humphrey, by this point fully incorporated into the company register as a partner of his father, gave a transient guest performance at Macclesfield Road when his father wasn't present; assuming the role of junior manager, he would help himself to daddy's cigar box and cause quite a stir when he spoke to a customer, smoking and rocking back and forth in his chair. Curly-haired Humphrey already had two years at Wellington College behind him at this point and was very friendly with a young girl by the name of Mareijke. He was supposed to be headed to London, on his father's request, to complete an apprenticeship at a Rolls-Royce dealer. Ambrose, as his parents had long been aware, had entirely different ambitions. Cars didn't interest him in the slightest – he wanted to study History of Art.

The weeping worm and a rather bitty beer!

BACK TO BEING SOMEWHAT mobile, Bunty decided to take part in a vintage car rally in the south of Germany. For this, he selected a 1921 Rolls-Royce Silver Ghost whose point of interest was its enormous height. It was almost possible to stand upright in this giant coupé. Bunty described it as his 'giant chicken coop on wheels' and took Geoffrey with him as a precaution; the car was admittedly an original, but its mechanics were rather unreliable.

"After his return, he was back to his old self," explained Hazel. "He had regained his full mobility and spoke for hours about his experiences in the chicken coop, and the admiration that he and his car received while he was gone. He dictated two dozen letters to me, to be sent to friends to whom he wanted to report every last detail of the rally in Bavaria. Being back in his beloved Munich was a great occasion for Bunty."

The car dealership was running so successfully by this point, that Bunty could allow himself to purchase cars for his own pleasure rather than to promptly sell. These personal purchases included models by the brands Delage, Alvis, Lagonda, Alfa Romeo, Railton and Invicta. A particularly exquisite gem which Bunty kept hold of for two whole years was a 1929 Hispano-Suiza. He only really took this beauty out for short spins, but he did so with childlike joy; and whenever a problem occurred, Geoff was quickly on hand to help.

The half-page adverts which the Scott-Moncrieff Ltd would leave in the British motor press made worthwhile reading even for non-enthusiasts of vintage cars. There was a Bentley saloon, whose engine ran like "Swiss clockwork," or Rolls-Royce tourers which were built "in the style of Vanden Plas." However, if one came across the line "we believe that, with just a little effort, this car could become a priceless, high-quality gem" – then this would be immediately accompanied by a serious warning: the 'little' effort could amount to a huge sum and finally that the advertiser was allowed to estimate whatever price he wanted!

"We believe ..." and other similar expressions, commonly preceded an entirely noncommittal statement regarding the Scott-Moncrieffs' content: we believe that the car only had two previous owners ... It seems as though the car may have completed less than 20,000 miles ... It is our understanding that the car was previously the possession of the Duke of Cardigan ...

Hazel: "If a car was really run-down and couldn't be enhanced through fancy words, then we would be honest and describe it as such. Bunty offered cars like these very cheaply, for £200 or £300. I remember a pitiable man, who bought our worst object for precious little, a 20/25 Mulliner saloon. Of all our cars, these were certainly the worst. Most of these jalopies had been utterly cannibalised, but, on the occasion that they were roadworthy, they always found buyers. The one who bought the 20/25 Mulliner came to us five times, and every time he failed to drive away. Bunty hadn't deceived him – "You're buying a wreck!" he'd said to him. We nicknamed him 'the weeping worm,' because he always came crawling back with watery eyes to collect this car, which stubbornly refused to work for him, then went away weeping, only to try again the following week. One time the starter failed, another time two tyres were flat, on one occasion there was dirt in the carburettor. The weeping worm didn't want help, because he would have had to pay for our mechanics' time. He also clearly didn't have money for a trailer to transport the car anywhere …

"Another poor, unlucky fellow was the buyer of a much more expensive car, a 1956 Bentley Continental which had only just arrived in our showroom. A Chelsea-based practitioner was interested in it. When it came to accounts in the high-end price range, Bunty would invite the client back to Rock Cottage, to close the deal over a slurp of brandy. The buyer of the Bentley didn't want a brandy, however, simply asking for a cold beer. Bunty was more than happy to oblige, collecting a bottle of lager from the fridge and fishing out an antique pewter tankard from the shelf, to fill with the content of the beer bottle. Bunty sipped his brandy and the doctor drank his beer with equal contentment. Out of nowhere, he suddenly grimaced, taking Bunty by surprise: had the beer not been cold enough? Upon closer examination of the glass, the doctor's displeasure became apparent: the cleaning lady Mabel had long since been using the tankard to store paper clips, safety pins, thumbtacks and other lost property, unbeknown to Bunty; who was under the impression that it had just been serving a decorative purpose on the shelf. It hadn't even entered his mind to check inside before serving to guests. The doctor regurgitated everything before the objects made their way to his throat, while Bunty did his best to explain to the client that there was no assassination attempt taking place here … he must have succeeded in any case, as the Bentley sale went ahead as planned."

500 ten-dollar notes down the trousers

"WHICH OF YOUR MANY Rolls-Royce customers most endured in your memory?" I posed this question to Bunty several times throughout the course of our friendship. As expected, his answer was never limited to just one individual.

"There was that married couple with the two large paper bags from the supermarket. I picked the pair up from the train station and wondered to myself why they had decided to lug their weekend purchases around when they were intending to test out a Rolls-Royce. They left the bags in my office, before we went out for a test drive. The car was exactly as they had envisaged; they accepted my listed price of £2800 and we drew up a purchase agreement. I handed over the log book and the car keys, and was now waiting for him or her to pull out the chequebook. Instead, the lady got up, went over to the two paper bags and shook out the contents on my desk: two-thousand-eight-hundred one-pound notes, each bundled into twenties. Nobody had ever unloaded so much cash onto us before ..."

The man who had five-hundred ten-dollar notes also left a lasting impression. He was the second buyer to pay cash for a four-figure purchase. "He was American and asked that we collect him from the Birmingham airport. He looked incredibly portly, but then many Americans are. His head was rather small and didn't really fit his giant body. He wasn't immediately inspired by the car of his choice but came around to it in the end. Well, we soon realised that this good chap wasn't the least bit corpulent, but rather was actually well padded – with dollar notes. He insisted, just as the paper bag couple, on paying the price for the car immediately and fully in cash, so he subsequently undressed in the lounge of Rock Cottage, right down to his underwear. He had doubled up on these, and between the two pairs lay hundreds of flat banknote bundles. The majority were in the region of his undergarments, the outer pair of which we had to ladder with nail scissors. He must have been terribly uncomfortable sitting on the plane. Why he hadn't wanted to declare the money upon arrival and why there were no larger notes – we had no idea. There must have been a reason."

Back then, there were no full body searches on plane journeys, and arrival in Great Britain only prompted questioning when small pets were brought into the country.

"In any case, we were delighted to see that his head matched his body far better, and $5000 cash was a good reason to celebrate. Especially as the American asked to only receive a receipt for half of the cash handed over."

Humphrey and Hazel were present when Bunty delivered this story. Hazel asked Bunty not to tell the other trouser-based story (which she didn't stay to hear the end of, either because she already knew it, or because she found the topic to be rather embarrassing). But this was a signal for Bunty not to hold back. "I once owned a pair of suit trousers, which I really loved, anyway one day my ladies were of the opinion that they belonged in the dustbin. Well I found them there in any case. So, I fished them out again, but I discovered that all of the buttons had split off, so I carried them to the dry cleaners in Leek, whereby I also asked that they sew on new buttons." Hazel had left the office, when Humphrey decided to continue the story: "Daddy wouldn't dare tell Hazel what he said to the lady in the cleaners, as to why there wasn't a single button on the fly of his trousers. He told me though. He's supposed to have said that such an unbelievably good-looking lady, wearing the shortest miniskirt in the world, came into the garage yesterday, giving him such an explosive excitement that all the buttons on his trousers blew off ..."

Bunty just giggled, saying nothing.

Out and about with the dashing Charlotte

SUCH AN UNDERSTANDING, TOLERANT, companionable partner as Averil was more than Bunty could have wished for. Admittedly, she wasn't the definition of a storybook English housewife, but then Bunty wouldn't have married her if she had been. Averil needed above-average empathy and patience for the escapades of her husband, and didn't begrudge him other female travel companions when she had to stay at home: be they Lucie, Else-Marie or Rosemary. However, there was one other great love in Bunty's life: the milk-coffee-brown Charlotte.

Bunty's fascination with Charlotte was first explained to me in a letter I received from him, before a stay in Ireland allowed me the pleasure of meeting her in person. The following is an excerpt:

"We will meet you at the Cork Harbour this evening, Eddie will accompany us, he's already coming with us because of Charlotte. Eddie, the good lad, he has also grown fond of her, at least as much as I … and you will fall in love with her, too! I am so lucky to have met Charlotte a few years back: she's the type that you'd want to grow old with, she's truly a dream. You'll immediately recognise why she is so endearing. Perhaps I'll relinquish her to you for half an hour. She's coffee brown, even in the places that aren't visible upon first glance; Eddie and I will show you everything. She does have a rather remarkable temperament for her age, you'll definitely want to photograph her from all sides, and I'm certain that you'll find her most attractive from behind. All the boys at the company think the same, not just Eddie and I. I solicited the help of Eddie to give her a personal sponge bath every evening and look after her cosmetics a little. What to do about Charlotte has, of course, required thorough consideration from me. I had to decide: Charlotte … or my good old, faithful, dependable Rolls-Royce Silver Ghost. The decision had to fall in favour of Charlotte, for I would never allow this opportunity to escape me, and you will soon acknowledge why."

Four weeks later, we met on the harbour of the Irish city of Cork. Bunty proudly presented his Charlotte to me: she was simply a dream. Amazing proportions, if built a little broadly (it later transpired that, as Eddie had assured me, this was precisely what gave her such an advantage), coffee-brown and, as I had the pleasure of noting during an outing in the countryside, just as lively as Bunty had described her ("Don't be shy, give her a little go …"). Charlotte could have been of noble heritage, and she was incredibly photogenic, not just from behind, but from all angles. Not every 4.25-litre Bentley was as attractively put together as this fine cabriolet, which Bunty had christened Charlotte: his vehicle of choice for trips abroad in later years. In order to raise the funds for Charlotte, he had to part with not only his 'chicken coop on wheels', but also with the Hispano and the Invicta. He didn't have to wait around very long for buyers.

Apparently, the Vanden Plas beauty had belonged to a headmaster, who "commanded such a low salary that it wasn't sufficient to cover the maintenance costs of the car ... it probably only just stretched to the petrol costs. Vanden Plas build truly wonderful cars, but always down to a price, so they often use a rather inferior quality of wood. We had to completely replace Charlotte's body frame, an insanely expensive endeavour ..."

Hearses never bite the dust

I'LL RETURN TO THE beautiful Charlotte later. Now, the focus will be turned to cars whose charm is of a different nature: hearses. Bunty had discovered the latest resource for good business. He bought up numerous obsolete Rolls-Royce hearses, which were plentiful in England at the time. These cars, typically from the 1930s and often born as splendorous state vehicles, could on the whole be acquired relatively cheaply.

Humphrey, who had finished his apprenticeship in London, was made the specialist for tracking down such cars and could be seen driving a hearse into Rock Cottage almost every week where its hearse body would be dismantled. Also, when necessary, these cars would be mechanically overhauled. On one occasion, Humphrey was pulled over by the police while at the wheel of a hearse; excessively high speeding was the complaint. Humphrey admittedly lacked the quick-wittedness of his father, who would have surely given the police officers hair-raising subterfuge as to why he was travelling at race tempo … however, the junior manager succeeded in charming the constables and thus avoiding the fine.

The worn-out mortuary vehicle trade provided plenty of impetus for macabre stories. One of Bunty's very favourites was the tale of the not-quite-laid-to-rest coffin, that he was understood to have found in a hearse that he had spontaneously purchased.

"So here's how that came about," Bunty detailed: "A funeral director in Stockport had a fleet of around five or six vehicles, all Rolls-Royce, and they stood in a row on the company grounds. He wanted to offload the oldest one, a 25/30 from 1933. A wonderful model, if a little way from being the most beautiful. We agreed a fair price, shook hands and were about to go out into the yard, where he intended to close the deal with me, when the telephone rang. As the conversation was clearly nowhere near reaching its conclusion, he decided to wave me on and allow me to drive off without further formalities. At this point, I found myself instinctively climbing into a rather lovelier model, its roof decorated with a lot more silver jewellery, and so I made my getaway, without making sure the rear department was empty … because, well, how was I supposed to guess that precisely this car had been readied for the final voyage of a faded Earthling on that very afternoon? I regretted my momentous mistake rather a lot, and there were a number of telephone calls between Stockport and Leek …"

Bunty had successfully ruined a funeral.

The 'mistaken' car was collected the following morning, contents included, and the correct one was delivered simultaneously. Hazel: "Bunty made sure to get away with a few amusing remarks during this whole ordeal. The bottom line, however, was that we had to pay a lot of money, because Bunty had caused an utter disaster."

Many purchasers of two-seater sports cars or touring cars "with a new, custom-fitted body from a renowned coachbuilder" had no idea that their car had performed as a hearse in its first life. If one came across the word "original," it referred only to the chassis and the engine. Suspicion was typically left unaroused, for the vast majority of restored Rolls-Royce vehicles received an entirely new coachwork … unfortunately the proportions didn't quite match up between a deconstructed hearse and a touring car, even less so for a two-seater.

Then again, most procurers didn't seem particularly bothered by this; the fact that these were Rolls' vehicles at a very affordable price made this a worthwhile endeavour, even if it was a semi-replica.

To mark the occasion of the company becoming 'limited' in July of 1966, Averil, Humphrey, Geoffrey and Hazel were officially made 'directors.' This looked fabulous on newly printed letterheads. Alongside remained that immortal line, printed in italics: "Purveyors of Horseless Carriages to the Nobility and Gentry since 1927."

"You reckon your title is an honour? Your boss will just expect more from you than before," asserted Humphrey, once he discovered the news. The directors now outnumbered the mechanics, a workforce which consisted of just Tony and Eddie alongside Geoff. In Hazel's new office at Macclesfield Road, good old Jack, responsible as ever for the installation of electronics, had made a rather serious error. Whichever device you plugged into one of the sockets resulted in a short circuit. No kettle, no light … Hazel was left to work at her (manual) typewriter using nothing more than a paraffin lamp for lighting from the afternoon onwards.

In the meantime, Bunty's popularity had grown to nationwide proportions. The press came to Leek and Rock Cottage, and Bunty loved to tell the reporters new stories every time – about himself, his cars and his adventures. The Daily Express dedicated a two-page spread to an article about the Scott-Moncrieff firm, which meant a lot of work for the family. All forty available Rolls-Royces had to be lined up together for a photograph in the open field, meaning all vehicles had to be cleaned and all glossy parts had to be polished to a shine. The directors and the workforce sweated and cursed, as it was hot out and not every car was roadworthy … only Bunty managed to enjoy the occasion, putting on his usual show. With water buckets and cleaning apparatus to hand, he posed as per instruction in front of the cars, making it later appear as though he had done all of the work himself. "We were infuriated that he didn't waste a single word on how many diligent hands worked to keep his company going," Hazel later revealed.

There were also negative consequences after the article had been published in one of London's most popular daily newspapers. A number of begging letters arrived, along with anonymous abuse: "You lot are all imposters and good-for-nothing spendthrifts ... we're looking at the arrogant rabble here, who allow themselves to be chauffeured around in Rolls-Royces all day!" Bunty also received an amusing application letter from New York. "You don't know me, sir. But I'm allowing myself to write to you despite this. I am a street sweeper and came across the newspaper featuring the article about you in the gutter, which is a part of my job really (I would consider it a luxury to buy a newspaper, since I can read all the international presses daily and free of charge from Manhattan's waste containers). My greatest wish would be to own a Rolls-Royce. Since my understanding is that you currently command at least forty of these vehicles, I figured it would surely not be too much of an issue for you to gift one to me and send it over to New York. I live near the Eastern Docks and can help with unloading, just let me know the shipping route and estimated arrival time."

No viewing pleasure whatsoever

BUT THINGS GOT EVEN better. A film crew turned up in Leek and asked whether Bunty would be available for a few yards of celluloid – admittedly without payment, but there was simply no better publicity for his business! In those days, cheerful short films like this were common practice in cinemas, the golden years of television and video were yet to begin. Bunty was only too happy to consent. For a day and a half, he was allowed to speed down narrow, winding ravines through the countryside in an open Rolls-Royce: the cameraman filmed from a car in front. An exciting (and above all dusty) endeavour; the many gallons of petrol cost him as much as an expensive dinner in a restaurant and numerous whiskies, but Bunty enjoyed his role as the daredevil behind the wheel of an open Phantom II Continental so much that he didn't regret the expenditure.

Hazel: "When he discovered, three-quarters of a year later, precisely when and where the film would be shown, he invited us all to accompany him to the cinema. A great contingent of us headed up to Manchester, and Bunty didn't just cover the cost of our tickets, but also insisted on the most expensive seats. When the footage of Bunty and his journey rolled – all one and a half minutes of it, sandwiched between two newsreel reports — it was met with great disappointment. Bunty leapt out of his seat, angrily yelling 'If that was it, I want my entrance money back!' and stormed out of the theatre. His convoy followed him, if a little reluctantly, renouncing the feature presentation. However, the box office had already shut, so nobody was able to refund us our ticket money … he also ranted incessantly the whole way home, until someone made the suggestion that we salvage the evening by getting fish and chips. The prospect of a takeaway calmed him. We stopped off at a fast-food restaurant, Averil bought us all something to nibble on, and we agreed to never discuss the ordeal again."

Would you be a sweetie?

BUNTY WAS LEFT WITH a slight handicap from his accident in Brighton: the complex bone formation in his left foot was no longer as it was supposed to be, requiring several follow-up operations. He found it difficult to endure the repeated immobility linked to this. When I first encountered the great man, he was in one of these such states.

He didn't like to speak about his suffering, glossing over it and refusing to acknowledge the pain publicly. And as if to prove that he certainly wasn't disabled, he took long footpaths in his stride and never shied away from steps. When it came to driving, nobody would assume that Bunty's clutch foot was impaired. Those who were aware would likely attribute his driving style to this unfortunate circumstance, which was incorrect: since he was a youngster, Bunty had practiced a driving style modelled on the legendary Tazio Nuvolari.

"Would you be a sweetie?" Hazel asked me once whether I had noticed that Bunty used the term 'sweetie' every time he asked someone for a favour. At first, Hazel assumed that this term was reserved exclusively for her, which soon turned out to be a fallacy. Literally-speaking, this is rather hard to translate into any other language. Bill Tayleur confirmed that Bunty used this set expression as early as in the thirties: "I remember that he begged the owner of a car in the car park of the Racing Drivers Club to leave his car somewhere else, so that Bunty could park in his spot. This was my first encounter with Bunty. When he began the request with 'would you be a sweetie,' instead of the common 'would you be so kind,' my first thought was that Bunty must be gay. My club friends explained to me that indeed the exact opposite was the case, Bunty was a real womaniser, and expressions like 'my sweet' or 'my darling' commonly preceded his wishes or demands."

Let's return to Charlotte: when I first caught sight of her at a rally in Ireland, I could immediately understand Bunty's enthusiasm for this sublimely beautiful car. Averil, Eddie and Hazel were accompanying him, and Geoffrey made up the fifth member of the party in a second car. He was in charge of a 1924 black 3-litre Bentley, and had no passengers on board, just half a tonne of spare parts. These weren't for his car, rather for Charlotte, should anything happen to her.

The brown 4.25-litre Vanden Plas drophead was really a flawless beauty of wonderful proportions. Bunty's fears that his car wouldn't get adequate viewing time amidst the sheer number of rally cars were unfounded. This was because a sailors' strike had led to no more than seven, instead of some fifty, vintage cars being present in Ireland, leading to the event being cancelled at short notice. Instead of using one of the expensive car ferries, Bunty had arranged a transfer aboard a cattle freighter, and the other five cars, my 1931 3-litre Lagonda included, all landed a good five days before, because the crews wanted to allow themselves a few additional days of holiday.

The little group of Ireland explorers consisted of the Schultes' from Elmshorn (near Hamburg) travelling in a tiny Hanomag and an old Fiat, Axel Grüning and his wife from Hamburg in a beautiful 1912 Benz, Bunny Tubbs and Dennis Field (the latter played an important role in the Veteran Car Club: he was responsible for the historical classification of vehicles) as well as Frank Davis, the millionaire, returning from long-term residence in Australia, accompanied by his family. One of his teenage daughters was known as a calculated Snow White, something she wasn't happy about at all. We all headed to hotels, which had been reserved for the good one hundred rally participants, and the pre-prepared buffet in one of them was exclusively reserved for us. The feasting threatened to reach dangerous, and above all tiresome proportions, but fortunately we had Bunty and Frank with us. Bunty, accompanied by Frank's two cute daughters, put on an edifying entertainment program for the troops. The girls through their appearance (the temperatures were at a summer-high, and the teens offered their services to wash the cars every afternoon, which they carried out not only with great fervour, water hoses, sponges and leather, but also dressed in nothing more than tiny bikinis), Bunty through stories from his adventurous life.

Bunty's last evening was our penultimate, because he was flying back from Cork to Manchester with Air Lingus on urgent business with Averil and Eddie: leaving Hazel condemned to spend another day on the green island with Charlotte, until the ferry men had ended their strike. We also had to endure these extra 24 hours.

Introducing Timothy, the glass-eater

ON THAT FINAL EVENING which Bunty spent in Ireland, he absented himself with the company of Averil and his friend, Bunny Tubbs. Bunty wanted to visit relatives on his mother's side, based in Waterford. The following day, after the Scott-Moncrieffs had said their farewells, Bunny detailed to us his account of the reunion party in Waterford to us.

"The meeting, which was just as boozy as it was merry, was attended by a number of nieces and nephews whom Bunty had never met before, and who were relishing the chance to finally meet their famous uncle. But, unusually, it wasn't Bunty who delivered the highpoint of the evening. This was left to his nephew, Timothy, who, in his thoroughly drunken state, informed us that he had the ability to masticate and assimilate shards of glass. Such a thing is occasionally available for viewing at a cabaret, but we were left incredibly surprised to hear that one of Bunty's relatives was capable of such a feat. Naturally, the proof would be in the pudding. In order to enable Timothy to perform a spontaneous demonstration of his art, Bunty – who else! – gathered a crystal glass bowl from the family trinkets on display in the vitrine, dropped it to the floor and challenged the young man to show the room his talent.

"The hostess, dashing in from the kitchen after being disturbed by the sound of what was clearly a fragile object smashing, unleashed a screaming fit once she saw which expensive heirloom lay in pieces on the floor. Her screams, loud though they were, were scarcely discernible against the chants and applause of the guests; she, like the rest of us, was witnessing a quite remarkable operation, the uniqueness of which soon eclipsed the apparent value of the bowl. Timothy bit into one of the broken pieces, which sounded even more horrible than the initial breaking of the glass, before gulping the shards down. 'Now let's make him walk barefoot across hot coal!' shouted Bunty, but, since there was no burning coal readily available (and besides, the house was heated with gas), and above all because Timothy asserted that he had never tried his hand at such a skill, the show stopped there. Had there have been some hot coals available, Bunty would presumably have spread them across the dining room carpet. I also assumed that Timothy had avoided the suggestion because he had holes in his socks, he was that kind of guy, and so it would have been quite embarrassing for him had he been forced to take his shoes off …"

Bunty's plane had scarcely departed when trouble struck Charlotte. Fortunately, Geoff was on hand with the vintage Bentley, tools and the spare parts; Hazel was jolly relieved. The petrol attendants had fallen into line with the sailors' strike. Later, there were further problems with the coffee-brown beauty, whose allure was admittedly downplayed by Bunty, but annoyed Averil so much that she refused to partake in any further rallies in it. She bought herself an OM touring car and ensured that this remained in impeccable nick at all times.

Bunty provided Charlotte with a general reconditioning. However, this displeased the Junior Manager; who considered it a waste to spend all week using all available manpower in the company to work on his dear old father's private vehicle. When it was all completed, Charlotte should hopefully at last be as reliable as she was beautiful! However, before the dream-mobile was roadworthy again, there was another rally, which Bunty would have hated to miss out on – one which was taking part on German soil once more.

Above: Bunty made the decision to buy a brand-new car for the first time in his life, opting for a proven model: the Austin A40. To achieve this, he drove all the way to Birmingham, where he enjoyed fabulous service from the directors. Whilst this did turn into a three-day stopover, he failed to get even a penny's discount.

Right: Bunty, as he lived and breathed – a photograph dated November 1959. He was rarely caught tinkering with camshafts and the like, or with an oily rag or tool to hand, as you may be misled into thinking from this image. The only thing he would allow to spoil his suit and tie would be cigar ash, or the spillage of gravy or vanilla cream.

Above and left: Averil's passion for cars went beyond her convalescent Bugatti 37A to include racing cars of other makes. Bunty was occasionally allowed to drive her 1951 Lotus (pictured above). She was noted for driving incredibly boldly and occasionally rather aggressively, while Bunty sometimes preferred more elegant cars like this 6C1750 Alfa Romeo.

Above: Bunty's secretary, Hazel, also greatly
enjoyed fast cars. Here she is seen in 1971,
posing with her son, Peter, in front of their
Mini Cooper S (complete with a cracking
license plate), along with all the trophies that
she won across a diverse range of events.
Hazel didn't just know her way around cars
from all over the world, she was also able
to expertly handle international clientele,
which proved exceedingly valuable to Bunty.

Right: Hazel Robinson applied to work
for Bunty because she had heard so many
fascinating stories about the man that she
simply had to know him. However, Hazel's
loyalty and sacrifice was not always
appreciated by her boss. I have Hazel to
thank for many of the stories contributing to
this book.

Above: Bunty could only let go of certain Rolls-Royces if he accepted another car as a trade-in, such as this 1935 Citroën, nicknamed 'La Rosalie' (top). The rather dull but impeccable RR Freestone & Webb Wraith saloon (bottom) was one of Bunty's favourites. Sometimes these cars would be stood outside for months awaiting a buyer. Not all received the privilege of a dry home under a roof.

Above: This fine Bugatti, type 50 (5.0 litre straight-eight, 225hp) had belonged to the British world-record setting driver Sir Malcolm Campbell. However, Bunty wasn't the sole proprietor of this noble car, as he shared the prize with his friend, Harry Heathcote. When Bunty encountered financial trouble once more, he sold his share to Heathcote.

Below: Another Bugatti in Bunty's possession at the time was this Type 44 from 1930. Admittedly, the engine had 'only' a three-litre capacity and 80hp, but this drove like a sports car, commanding a fee of £1500 in the 1960s. This can be taken to mean that Bunty made himself a tidy profit indeed when he finally sold this car.

Above: Junior manager Humphrey Scott-Moncrieff, cock-of-the-walk in a 3.5-litre Bentley. The young lady on the right is his girlfriend, Mareijke, whilst the girl in the middle is Mila Schrader. The photo is taken in front of the showroom on Macclesfield Road in Leek, 1973. Humphrey was far from a subservient partner to his dad: he rightly criticised his father's often reckless financial management.

Right: Humphrey in discussion with Geoffrey Beardsmore, the head mechanic. Geoff accompanied Bunty on many trips, and was indispensable when it came to diagnosing and resolving breakdowns. Humphrey avoided partaking in rallies; this was one aspect of his father's passion which he didn't share. If he was caught moving an old Rolls-Royce, it was strictly for business purposes!

DAVID SCOTT-MONCRIEFF & SON LTD.

Showroom & Office :
2 Macclesfield Road,
Leek, Staffs., ST13 8LA
Telephone : 053-82 (Leek) 4300
   or : 053-82 (Leek) 4020
Cables : "Buntycars, Leek"

If closed apply until 9.00 p.m. to :
Rock Cottage, Basford Hall,
Leek, Staffs.
Telephone : 053-831 300 after 6 p.m.
   until 9 p.m.

STOCK LIST   JANUARY, 1973
SELECTION OF ROLLS-ROYCE.

1. 1928 21.6h.p. fixed head two door four seat coupe by Southern Motors.
Most attractively finished in Lonsdale yellow and Navy blue. Grey trim
in real hide. Offered on behalf of a valued client for £3650.

2. 1934 20/25 two door coupe by Barker. This rare and lovely body with
moulded wings and a large projecting rear trunk has recently undergone
considerable restoration. We also have details of a recent engine overhaul. A large amount of history comes with this car which is finished
in Primrose and black with a beige hide interior. A very low mileage car
and real collector's item at only £3950. AYW.25.

3. 1934 20/25 with very interesting two door coupe coachwork. A most unusual small Rolls-Royce which has a very good chassis. The bodywork is
partially restored and we hope to complete more work on this car. A
complete repaint, retrim and other quite extensive work is necessary,
once this is done, it will be a very beautiful and expensive car, but
in the meantime we can offer it as it is to an enthusiast wishing to do
the work for himself at £1038   MS.9000

4. 1935 Phantom II "TA" series limousine by Hooper, the Royal Coachbuilders.
A magnificent formal limousine in very very fine order. Finished in black
over Napier green with the front compartment finished in black leather
and the massive rear compartment in Bedford cord. This is a very rare
car and is priced at £3955. BLU.661.

5. 1937 25/30 with very handsome semi-razor edge sports saloon by Thrupp and
Maberley. One owner for the last sixteen years has kept this rare car
in excellent condition. Finished in cream and light brown with very
good paintwork. The interior is upholstered in brown hide in fine order
with matching carpets and the car has a sunroof. Mechanically far above
average. This very good looking car is only £3535. EXH.132.

6. 1938 (late series) Phantom III twelve cylinder with elegant four door
owner-chauffeur drive four/five passenger semi-sports saloon. Coachwork
by Barker who have been building carriages for top people since the
eighteenth century. Tastefully finished in cream and brown with brown
real hide trim to match. This car has been carefully stored for a long
time and is both mechanically and bodily in above average condition.
Particularly powerful quiet engine. Almost certainly the finest but not
the most expensive Phantom III on the market today. The engine has been
completely dismantled and rebuilt, for which bills are available.
£6,125 EXY.685

7. 1957 Silver Cloud I - HONEYMOON EXPRESS. Possibly the most famous post
war Rolls-Royce ever built. See pages 62 and 63 of the book "The
Elegance Continues". Finished in Dusk over Peruvian Gold. One of only
two two-seater Rolls-Royce built since the last war. This fabulous
collector's piece has power assisted steering, electrically operated
windows, full cocktail cabinets and is in beautiful condition throughout.
VERY expensive. Coachwork by Freestone and Webb. AM.2375.

Left: One of the so-called stock lists, which Bunty regularly sent off to prospective buyers. They're very enjoyable to study. All objects are supposed to have survived in collectors' hands.

Below: a 1949 Bentley Mk VI standard steel saloon, which could be affordably acquired at any time from Bunty and other second-hand car dealers in England.

Left: Mechanic Eddie Berrisford in a 1923 two-seater Rolls-Royce Silver Ghost, which the Scott-Moncrieffs held in the family for a very long time, and was thus never for sale. It was one of only a few cars built in this series to have front wheel brakes. The Ghost was only ever taken out of the garage on the express wishes of a client.

Below: A 1932 Rolls-Royce 20/25hp with a close-coupled saloon body by Carlton. Such a car was difficult to sell in England in 1974, but the Americans invested in these cars with pleasure.

Above: This drophead Rolls-Royce Silver Cloud with oversized tailfins was one of only three specimens built by Freestone & Webb in 1957 (see p151, no 7). Humphrey sold the 'Honeymoon Express' two-plus-two-seater in March 1974 at an auction in Geneva, when the author had the pleasure to meet him.

Below: An elite collection of the finest Rolls-Royce and Bentley cars in the new David Scott-Moncrieff & Son exhibition rooms, 2 Macclesfield Road, Leek, Staffordshire. Around 20 cars situated were here in the former watermill. Many celebrities were present at the grand opening in 1971, and a bathtub was filled with champagne on ice.

Right: This 1932 20/25hp model was specially built as an estate car or station wagon for a customer in Kenya. Bunty paid a lot of money to bring this rarity to England, and he immediately found a very wealthy buyer.

Below: Always elegant; always befitting his social status. Since he stopped wearing his Styrian Lederhosen, Bunty was often – albeit certainly not always – seen in a fine suit. This photo, featuring the Bentley by the name of Charlotte, was taken by the author in Blarney, Ireland, in 1966, on the occasion of the FIVA rally, which is held there but was unfortunately cancelled in May of this particular year due to a sailors' strike.

Left: A 1927 3-litre Bentley Vanden Plas Tourer. One of the best-kept models that David Scott-Moncrieff & Son Ltd ever had on sale.

Right: On the go in the Bentley Vanden Plas drophead named Charlotte, visiting ancient sites in Greece. Here, Bunty is enjoying the Greek rally as co-driver, whilst Averil sits at the wheel. It was rather rare for them to share a car: typically, they would choose to drive their own vehicles.

Above: A contemplative Bunty casts his gaze over a particularly beautiful 1938 Bentley 4.25-litre with Thrupp & Maberly coachwork. It was sometimes hard for the old gentleman to let go of one of his prized cars. Given his aptitude for eloquent description in advertisements, most of Bunty's cars changed hands remarkably quickly.

Below: In the former 'Britannia Works' machine factory, Bunty and his team established their repairs and restorations workplace. The touring car parked in front of the facade is an example of a mutated hearse.

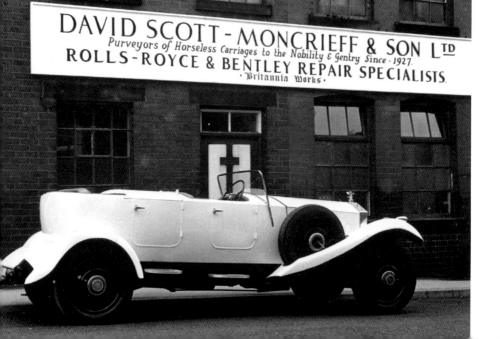

Left: A 1924 Rolls-Royce 20hp, downgraded to nothing more than a pick-up truck. Bunty purchased cars like this without hesitation, turning them into attractive tourers.

Above: Averil and Bunty in South Africa in a 1929 OM T665. They are on their way to Umtata. It wasn't just Averil who found it unsuitable that her husband was sporting a topi, a symbol of earlier colonialism. She was a passionate and savvy driver, without whom Bunty would never have managed many of his journeys in antique automobiles.

Above: A rather inglorious view – the supposed 'best car in the world' on the hook of a tow truck … But no time for false sentiment: if Bunty, Geoffrey, Eddie, Tony or Hazel were unable to bring a cheaply-bought old Royce to 'Britannia Works' on their own, then they would bow to the inevitable.

Below: Perhaps he's just called her 'sweetie'…? Bunty and Averil as guests at a party in Stuttgart, 1964, photographed in a rather unflattering light: Averil is about to use a lipstick from her handbag, whilst Bunty, with a cigar in his left hand, has removed his jacket. Bubbly, sherry and the local Dinkelacker beer are being drunk.

Above: As time wore on, Bunty had to take to the role of passenger at vintage rallies. Here, he is posing for a photo in the dickey seat of his Rolls-Royce Silver Ghost; normally, he would be sat next to Eddie in the front passenger seat. Eddie Berrisford had taken on Geoffrey Beardsmore's role as breakdown mechanic for all the vehicles and was a good soul indeed.

Left: Here, Eddie Berrisford is seen chauffeuring his boss in the OM T665, once belonging to the racing driver Dick Oates. Bunty always had a weakness for cars of the Italian OM make. This very car – which is indeed the one in which he drove to Munich in 1970 – was exhibited and auctioned off in Paris (Rétromobile) in February 2004. The fact that Bunty was a previous owner failed to receive a mention.

Above and right: After successfully crossing the North Sea, the crew on board 'Bunty's Ark' made it to Haarlem thanks to supernatural forces. Averil and Eddie had passed the 26-hour test. Bunty was very proud of them: he spent the majority of the journey in a bunk with seasickness. Next stop was Amsterdam.

The ambassador of British automotive culture

IT WAS THE TRADITIONAL Travemuende Rally of the Allgemeiner Schnauferl Club, ASC for short. From his on-sale collection, Bunty selected a Rolls-Royce Silver Ghost, while Averil came in her OM. Geoffrey, meanwhile, politely turned down the offer of accompanying the pair. This wasn't just so that he could continue work on Charlotte – an excuse which Bunty wholeheartedly accepted – but also because he was rather sick of having to jump to the rescue of other attendants at every event. What, you're having difficulties with your engine? Our good old Geoffrey will be right over to help you! He's the best mechanic in the world ...!

Bunty happily loaned his people out for free, which distinguished him as a benefactor, but meant Geoffrey being kept in suspense all day and night, for there were constantly people refurbishing, altering and checking up on their vehicles. From cleaning the carburettor to changing the rear axle, from fine-tuning the ignition to repairing the radiator, "our good old Geoffrey", was ready for every breakdown emergency that reached Bunty's ears.

So, Eddie was set to take Geoffrey's place, but that also didn't work, as co-partner Humphrey was strictly against the idea, for reasons of business considerations. "Father, participation in a rally abroad costs us a lot of money. We fix up the cars using company money, have to pay for expenses and book ferries. You can't visit such an event every month."

The apprehensive Junior Manager didn't refer to his mother's hobby here. She took care of her OM personally, just as with 'La Folie,' and didn't charge her travel costs to the company account.

Bunty, still the managing director of the David Scott-Moncrieff & Son Ltd by trade, saw it rather differently. "My dear son, each of my foreign excursions is a promotional tour for our company. I always return with contacts for new clients, I am the best representative of our house, an ambassador of British automotive culture. Everyone knows my name; my advice is valued as expert. Isn't that so?"

Humphrey didn't share this opinion. The once so economical Bunty had turned into a wasteful spender. Humphrey was backed by his mother and Hazel; Daddy had to be restrained. The 'best representative of the house' promised everyone everything under the sun, but the days of customers being swindled by Bunty's infamous tricks were over.

Humphrey had succeeded in making amends with many former clients: it was only if they weren't careful that Bunty could still wreak havoc. Such as the time that he was left alone in the office for a few hours and sold a customer a Phantom III for cash – a considerable amount too – which he then didn't hand over. Humphrey didn't explicitly voice that awful word 'embezzlement,' but he legally relieved his father of every authority over the company, reopening a new account to which only he and his mother had access. He couldn't change the shareholder agreement, but he thought up tricks to push his father further aside.

As the date of the Travemuende event approached, a customer for the Silver Ghost appeared, the same car which Bunty intended to drive on tour. He was forced to change his arrangements and select a replacement for the Rolls-Royce veteran. He opted for the old Lancia Artena, a real non-seller which had stood in the Rock Cottage shed for years and appeared unmarketable. Humphrey thought it was a sensible decision, especially as his father promised to find a buyer for the vehicle in Travemuende. Astoundingly, the Lancia's engine sprang into action at the push of a button, performing as admirably as ever on a test run.

Hazel and her little son Peter travelled in Averil's OM, whilst Bunty took the mechanic Tony along for the ride. The two gentlemen started a day earlier, for safety's sake: the Lancia needed driving gingerly, for it had a long history of stationary inactivity behind it …

The Hotel St George in Bruges was the stopping point, as had been agreed. The Lancia had experienced a few pitstops en route; Averil, Hazel and Peter were first to arrive in Bruges. It wasn't before midnight that the men arrived, and the house had long since closed. They succeeded in trespassing their way into the hotel through an unlocked kitchen door, after which they occupied the first, decent-looking empty room that they came across. In order to achieve this, however, they first had to open a dozen other doors, provided they weren't locked, so as to ascertain whether someone was sleeping on the other side. This also meant turning on the lights in every room they entered, which led to several loud screams upon interruption of sleep … or certain activities … "If people were disturbed, they have only themselves to blame, as far as I'm concerned," proclaimed Bunty over the communal breakfast the following morning, audibly enough for all the other guests to hear. "When I was at the age at which one books a hotel room in order to have fun as a couple, I always took the precaution of locking the door …"

In Travemuende, Bunty was received like a state guest – in other words, exactly as he expected to be. Nobody took the slightest notice of the OM crew. Bunty was the centre of attention everywhere, finding patient ears in the veteran car comrades Max Rauck, Werner and Alex Gruening, Paul-Heinz Röhll, Michael Wolff-Metternich, Julius Ammon and Gerhard von Raffay, who attentively listened to the 'Ambassador of British Automotive Culture,' as he reeled off a succession of endlessly long stories.

The sale of the Lancia had seemingly ceased to occur in Bunty's mind, but then it would presumably have been of little interest to this crowd. Only Rauck and Röhll went on to later become customers of the Scott-Moncrieff firm; Rauck was interested in a Silver Ghost rolling chassis, which later found its way to the Deutsche Museum, and Röhll acquired a Bentley sports car.

The day after the event, Bunty felt little desire to return immediately to England. He preferred the idea of taking a detour to Denmark, to see his friend Baron Raben-Levetzau, who presided over an extensive car collection in Nyborg. In order to get to the ferry in Puttgarden across the Baltic, Tony pushed the accelerator a little too far – with the consequence that the Lancia engine's head gasket blew. "We'll just keep going!" ordered Bunty, accepting that the radiator would have to be topped up every mile and a half. Fortunately for them, a moat ran parallel to the country road. The only problem was that there wasn't a decent receptacle on board the Lancia or in the OM which could be used to fill with water and carry over to the car. The only possible suggestion was a bottle of cognac, which was currently still half full. Bunty and Tony had no choice but to empty it – and they had no intentions of gifting its expensive content to the Schleswig-Holstein countryside. Averil and Hazel contributed a couple of substantial slurps and now the bottle could be filled and its contents poured into the radiator. A process which was repeated several times, albeit with gradually deteriorating concentration … They missed the ferry of course, and the next one didn't leave for another twelve hours. Waiting for them on the other side was Johann-Otto von Raben-Levetzau with a tow truck to take the broken Lancia to the museum work space, where it resided for several months. Bunty and Eddie fittingly flew from Copenhagen back home, while Averil, Hazel and Peter plodded back in the OM.

(The valuable Levetzau collection was auctioned off at the stately home in 2012, a sad end for this car collection maintained with such rigorous commitment.)

An opportunity overslept

AT THAT TIME, HUMPHREY'S younger brother Ambrose had passed his A-levels and gone to Montpellier to enrol in an oenology degree programme as per his father's instructions. This in no way corresponded to the ambitions of the young man, who wasn't the slightest bit interested in becoming a winemaker or vintner. Bunty, on the other hand, found the idea of having one of his sons in this business a very pleasing prospect. He pictured discounted bottles of a particularly good Bordeaux, and perhaps even founding a quaint fine wine merchants further down the line. Through Ambrose, he would have an expert in the family.

When Ambrose returned home after a very brief stop in France to announce that he actually wanted to attend an art school, Bunty was left very disappointed. However, he backed down and accepted this. Ambrose would later go on to become a restorer in a large London gallery and finally the conservator of Southampton Art Gallery.

In London, he met Claudia Mary Delphine Petre, a gifted artist, whom Bunty liked so much upon first meeting with her that he retrospectively forgave his son for choosing a different career path to that of the winemaker.

On the 1st July 1967, Bunty celebrated his sixtieth birthday; it was a fabulous party. Only the continued tension between Humphrey and the senior was enough to dampen the mood slightly.

In the meantime, a new and very diligent car mechanic had started working at the firm; a man by the name of Raymond Allen, who was seventeen years young. Averil had taken the bookkeeping tasks off Hazel's hands, as Bunty had taken to dictating myriads of letters. He let all and sundry know when and where he intended to show up. He had become surplus to requirements in Leek, since he was kept well away from all business matters and didn't have much desire to constantly quarrel with Humphrey, particularly as he would never win.

Travelling alone wasn't an attractive proposition for him, so he attempted to integrate his spouse into his travel plans. Averil, on the other hand, had become indispensable as the company's financial director. Bunty had realised this of course, and so one day he entered the office and informed his wife that he had heard from a young lady, who happened to be searching for a new position and had all the necessary qualifications that the job required. She was coming in for an interview on Thursday.

Bunty had spun this very neatly indeed, for he was fully aware that the entire crew would be unusually out of the house on that particular Thursday. "What, none of you are here?" reacted Bunty with apparent ignorance. "Then I'll just have to judge the young lady on my own ..."

After heading home that Thursday evening, Hazel and Averil returned to find a very disappointed Bunty. The young lady had seemingly failed to make an appearance. She popped up the following day and subsequently explained her version of events. She claimed to have indeed arrived at the house at the agreed time, to discover Bunty fast asleep and snoring in an armchair and nobody else around. Not wanting to wake the old gentleman, she decided to turn around and go home. However, since she was so keen on the job, she decided to return the next morning and was delighted to see that there were other 'managers' besides the old snorer in the corner! She got the job.

Oversleeping the interview appointment was entirely Bunty's misfortune. Jean had correctly assumed that this would be carried out by an older male interviewer, and so had opted for a rather racy miniskirt, in the style of Mary Quant.

Averil and Hazel were delighted with Bunty's discovery, for Jean soon proved herself to be an excellent bookkeeper – not just a pair of tremendous legs! The first task for the mechanics was to lay a new electricity cable connecting to the office. Hazel's office, or rather Averil's in more recent times, had remained short of power since Jack's faulty wiring over three years earlier, but expecting the new colleague to settle for working under a kerosene lamp à la Charles Dickens was a presumption that none of the staff wanted to make!

The customs catastrophe

THE APPOINTMENT OF THE new bookkeeper afforded the self-proclaimed Ambassador of British Automotive Culture the chance to partake in rallies with Averil again. However, they continued to travel in separate cars, something which Averil insisted upon. She made sure to take part in her trusted OM and Bunty was so impressed with the reliability of the Italian sports car that he pulled out all the stops to acquire a second OM; something which proved far from easy. Cars of this make were, and still remain today, a rarity. As it happens, he succeeded in finding a second model, a former Tourist Trophy racer even, once driven by Dick Oates.

In these two 1926 OMs, Bunty and Averil (Eddie was alongside as mechanic and chauffeur, Hazel and Peter completed the team) took part in the 1967 Sardinia rally. However, the day of departure arrived and they were still yet to receive any confirmation from the organisers as to whether their entry had been accepted. "It'll be lying in an Italian post office, they're on strike again," claimed Bunty. "We'll set off regardless."

Hazel had booked spaces on the ferry from Genoa to Cagliari. En route, the OM team made frequent pitstops in continental Europe to visit friends and acquaintances; Bunty had notified them all of his party's arrival. It became a lovely and eventful journey.

Then came a little incident on the border of Austria and Italy. Bunty and Eddie had joined the queue at passport control; they were followed by the ladies' car. As an official began to approach the first OM, Bunty noticed that some smoke had started to billow out of the dashboard. "A catastrophe! Our car up in flames! Can you imagine?" As it transpired, the situation wasn't nearly as grave as Bunty had initially pictured it back then. Panicking, he frantically began to rip out any electrical conductor wires in sight; assuming it was an electrical fire. Eddie leapt over the sideboard, presumably also believing that the car would go up in flames at any moment. The border official set about trying to save Bunty's life, desperately dragging the old gentleman out of the cockpit by his trouser suspenders. Unfortunately, this failed, as Bunty still had a firm grasp on several bundles of wiring, which refused to relent despite his yanking and jiggling. Peter sprung up on the back seat of the car following behind, in order to get a better view of the spectacle taking place in front. Averil and Hazel, in their bucket seats, were dying with laughter. From a comic perspective, this situation was hard to beat.

The smoke soon dispersed; no explosion followed. Eddie got back into the vehicle and, despite the jumble of cables on the dashboard, the journey continued – to a very thorough passport control …

In Genoa came the moment of truth. The ferry reserved for the rally participants took the pair of OMs aboard without question, but the team soon discovered that their entry had been declined by the Italian club for whatever reason. Time to make a U-turn? Oh no. Bunty had other plans: he was to ensure that his crew be accepted as guests!

At the meet in Cagliari, Bunty proved that he still had his old tricks. He made himself known to the town mayor and coordinated a private reception to honour a British team who had travelled all the way from the United Kingdom in two rare, Italian OM sports cars in order to pay homage to the beautiful country of Italy. The Dottore had managed to whip up more local VIPs for the reception than the rally organisers had for the official participation at the event that same evening, and there was a lavish dinner followed by a police escort through the city the next morning.

Bunty could get over the fact that neither of the two OM teams, nor any other non-Italian team for that matter, were awarded a trophy. Plus, since they were already in Italy, it seemed rude not to attend another rally the following weekend, also without competing. It was a Fiat rally in the city of Turin.

In order to avoid discovery of another late cancellation, Bunty took the precaution of registering for their next rally – the annual FIVA World Rally – as soon as he returned home. When he discovered that it was to take place in Australia, he promptly withdrew his application. That would indeed have been a little too expensive for a holiday … Humphrey breathed a sigh of relief.

An opportunity for better investment than air transportation of veteran cars presented itself locally. There stood a small, empty factory hall, located in the centre of Leek. The 'Britannia Works' was up for sale, and since the showroom at Macclesfield Road had for a long time been outgrown, while the sheds at Rock Cottage were precious more than primitive, the company grasped this opportunity with both hands. This former factory offered eight to ten work spaces. Unfortunately, Eddie left the firm in order to go into business alone; Humphrey's staff thus consisting of just Hazel, Jean, Tony, Geoffrey, Ray and Derek. Soon, new workers arrived: Brian, Ted and David. Business was going well, the refurbishment and resale of rickety old luxury cars was more fruitful than ever before. With the appanage that was afforded the company founder, Bunty could even partake in a vintage cars rally in South Africa. For the first time, he and Averil travelled together in just one car – because the event organisers would only cover the costs of shipping one car by airfreight. Yet, several of their freshly-made friendships in South Africa threatened to go to pieces just as soon as Averil and Bunty had arrived …

The echoes of Umtata

AVERIL: "IT WAS TERRIBLE … Bunty wore a topi in South Africa, a symbol of the colonialism of old, which is universally frowned upon there. You're just inviting mockery and scorn. But Bunty insisted on wearing it, despite people drawing his attention to its inappropriateness. He further offended our hosts' moral sentiments with a pair of shorts from Humphrey's time in the Scouts: they were far too short and tight for Bunty. I was embarrassed by him, milling around in such an outfit … worse still was when he sat down … During our visit to the caves of Umtata, I would have loved nothing more than to sink into the ground myself when he lost control of his bowels and let out a wholly audible noise, which then proceeded to echo for an entire minute around this famous labyrinth … our guide had to stop his scientific lecture because nobody could hear a word he was saying. The sound of Bunty's flatulence echoed and reverberated from all sides, and the only person who found this remotely funny was Bunty himself."

Three years later, Bunty and Averil made a second journey to Africa. They didn't travel in a vintage car on this occasion, but rather in a contemporary Mini Cooper S. The first leg took them through France, the second through Switzerland. In Liechtenstein, they paused to visit the principality's No 1 car celebrity Max Heidegger, to whom Bunty had sold a Silver Ghost long ago. The route to Africa was anything but rectilinear, as the next stop was a detour to Munich, where I had the pleasure of organising their accommodation at the Hotel Zum Tannenbaum again, before we visited Max Rauck, Hanns-Otto Geigenberger (in whose garage stood a Bugatti type 101 – Bunty was delighted!) and Gottfried von Wedel, owner of a Rolls-Royce 20hp with rare Kellner bodywork.

Bunty abandoned the plan to journey to Africa by land and sea. He dumped the Mini, together with all of the expedition equipment, in my garage and organised plane tickets for himself and Averil – to Tel Aviv. In a succession of diverse hire cars, all of which broke down in their stewardship, the couple visited cities steeped in history, at which point Bunty announced he was particularly eager to visit Sodom, in the hope of inspiring a few limericks that he so loved to write. In Jerusalem, the pair both suffered an unfortunate bout of diarrhoea, which was rather detrimental to Bunty's good mood, and Bethlehem also holds rather bad memories for them too, because the inn that housed them kept smoking oil lamps which induced prolonged dyspnoea …

At long last: Africa. The next set of stops were Addis Ababa, Nairobi and

Johannesburg. All contained fellow students, acquaintances, even former customers. And not only happy ones at that: Bunty had forgotten that he had once delivered a Rolls 20hp without a piston in the engine to one such client; here, the welcome wasn't quite so warm. In Pietermaritzburg, they met a farmer who owner a Packard from the 'twenties which Bunty would have liked to have purchased from him immediately. Incidentally, he wasn't the only one.

As Bunty so often experienced in his life, one of his old friends appeared in the same place at the same time. Often under entirely different circumstances, admittedly, but even so: he seemed to cross paths with acquaintances as if it had been coordinated with exact precision... This time it was the turn of Johann-Otto von Raben-Levetzau, who happened to be sojourning in Pietermaritzburg at the same time as Bunty and Averil. The Baron had been invited to a party down this way, and since he had also heard tell of a man with a Packard, he had similarly decided to take this opportunity to pay him a visit. In doing so, he ran unexpectedly into Averil and Bunty. Johann-Otto also failed to prise the Packard away from the farmer.

Another collector whom they sought was Waldemar Greyvenstein in Bloemfontein. He owned a glorious armada of classic cars of Austro-Daimler and Hispano-Suiza calibre, and Bunty was allowed to test drive each and every one. For this purpose, he bought himself a new tropical suit, because several photographers had been commissioned. Averil still thought Bunty's shorts were too short.

In the towns of Monorgan and Sonnenstrahl, there were more cars to inspect, such as Rodney Wilson's 1908 Napier, which Bunty was sorely tempted to purchase. Rodney offered to dismantle the car and send it over to Leek, but Averil was quick to veto this, and so the Napier stayed put.

Taking the tow truck to church

AVERIL AND BUNTY FIRST resurfaced at mine over three months later to pick up their Mini and drive home to England. As I soon heard tell of this, they promptly headed off for another tour just four weeks later.

Finally, Charlotte came into her own once more. The journey being planned was to Greece and would last a month and a half. Back at home, the suitcases were being repacked with only fresh clothes: a rally in Austria was on the cards. Bunty and Tony took part once more with Charlotte, while Averil chauffeured 'La Folie' – who was still on the scene.

There were three occurrences during this journey which are of note. One: for reasons which can be traced back to a non-completed mounting job, the coffee-brown Bentley's boot lid flew off shortly after passing through Rotterdam, landing on the radiator of Averil's pursuing Bugatti. Averil had difficulty in stopping her car in a controlled way; the whole ordeal could have been a lot worse. Fortunately, there was minimal damage, the boot lid was refitted – and properly this time.

Number two: a chance meeting occurred with a horde of adventure-seeking compatriots. More specifically, a convoy of ten Morgan three-wheeler drivers on their way from the Nürburgring to the Salzburgring race track in Austria. Joining the clamorous three-wheeled fleet afforded the team a great level of attention and the two groups had a tremendous amount of fun together. The Nürburgring management had recently hosted their annual vintage cars race, after which one and a half dozen of the participating teams had followed the invitation to a similar event being held at the Salzburgring the following weekend.

The colourful convoy used our place in Munich as a stopping point. Bunty and Averil in Bentley and Bugatti aside, the group had picked up several followers along the way, including a French couple and a crew from Belgium. Their departure the following morning made just as spectacular viewing as their arrival the evening before; an unforgettable night for us and no doubt for our neighbours as well. There wasn't a window in sight without curious onlookers peeping through the curtains at the array of cars pulling up on their street, nor a balcony in the neighbourhood bereft of owners leaning eagerly over the parapets, shaking their heads with disapproval at the late-night disturbance playing out before them. There were at least ten people staying overnight in our kitchen and lounge, a further ten had pitched little tents on the nearby village green of the Harlaching Menterschwaige, four or five crews, including the Scott-Moncrieffs, were looking for a hotel and even somehow succeeded. After all that, it was long past midnight.

Among the Morgan Three-wheeler entourage was Jacques Potherat in his old MG P-type sports, upon whom we bestowed the honour of parking under our balcony. This French rogue, who – just like Bunty – took every opportunity for outlandish pranks, was a collector of obscure cars from the 1930s, an ambitious motor journalist and author. In Paris, he had founded the 'Syndicat Cyclecariste' and was seen as one of the top experts on French automotive history. In the 1980s, he was a reporter for 'l'Express,' attending the Paris-Dakar rally twice and even hosting his own TV series, before an undiagnosed tropical disease sadly lead to him requiring a permanent wheelchair. He had a 4.5-litre Bentley adapted for hand operation to allow him to continue driving right until the end of his life. Jacques passed away in 2001; he bravely compensated for his illness with trademark buffoonery until disease finally got the better of him.

'But this reminds me of a different story,' to use Bunty's best-known phrase; and I haven't elaborated in this instance.

Occurrence number three: Bunty met Mercedes competition director Alfred Neubauer once more in Salzburg. For Bunty, this represented the high point of the trip, and the chat they shared sparked Bunty's intention to finally bring his Mercedes-Benz SS sports car up to a roadworthy condition, a car which he had kept hidden away like a secret treasure stash for over twenty years, just waiting for the right moment to restore it to running order. The reason for this hesitation was plain and simple: Bunty was terrified of the enormous costs that were connected with such a project.

Before the Mercedes project finally took shape, Bunty wrestled with several other cars, including an impressive 1924 four-door Panhard-Levassor. He had acquired the dilapidated saloon with its low-revving sleeve-valve engine for a knocked-down price. Humphrey didn't stand for this bizarre vehicle being displayed in the showroom, particularly given that Bunty didn't even want to sell it. A few days later, the Junior Manager received a request from a friend, whose daughter was getting married, asking if he could hire a car befitting the occasion ... he had a Rolls-Royce in mind ... "We don't let cars as a matter of principle, my dear," Humphrey answered, "but Father has something suitable for the newlyweds ..." – and so Bunty headed out in his Panhard saloon to act as the wedding chauffeur.

May the marriage of the betrothed take a happier a course as their journey to the church. Bunty had decided to take a shortcut up the motorway en route to Manchester. In doing so, he pushed the poor Panhard to speeds it was completely unable to handle. After two simultaneously blown out tyres and a ruptured exhaust manifold, the Panhard sat on the hard shoulder, patiently awaiting the arrival of the tow truck which would subsequently tow the Panhard, chauffeur Bunty and the engaged couple to the church. After a considerable postponement, the marriage ceremony finally took place. The Panhard eventually made its way back to Leek, where it was dumped in a corner of the garage and never spoken of again.

Bunty rules the waves

IN THOSE DAYS, BUNTY began forging plans which he initially kept a secret. He intended to acquire a boat; a former fishing trawler or something similar. His family knew nothing about this, as Bunty only conducted phone conversations with yacht agencies and boatyards when he was sure that nobody was around. His intentions only began to surface publicly as the postman was delivering more and more letters containing pictures of ships, which Hazel routinely opened.

Bunty's love of being afloat stemmed not just from his grandfather, who was a shipbuilder, or from his father, the heroic protector of little terrier dogs in the Greater London area. Memories of the abode upon the Thames, where Bunty spent the years shortly before and after his wedding, fuelled his desire to devote a second period of his life to maritime living.

The heavy correspondence that Bunty maintained not only with boatyards but also with friends all over the world, and the numerous acquaintances that Bunty and Averil had made on their travels over the years were not without consequences for the commercial future of Rock Cottage. The notion of purchasing a ship wasn't entirely superficial.

More and more estranged visitors would appear, sometimes uninvited and unannounced, and stay as long as they pleased, accepting carte blanche to make themselves at home. Rodney from South Africa stayed a particularly long time. He had discovered a new passion in England: antique doll's houses. He set them up in his hosts' house; playing with them, repairing miniature furniture and painting tiny patterns on thin silk strips. After Rodney had purchased his twentieth Victorian doll's house and still had yet to consider booking a return flight, Bunty and Averil could think of no other solution than to leave the house themselves: they booked a trip to the Caribbean, on a banana steamer which represented particularly good value for money. The cruise took them to Jamaica, Barbados and Haiti. Everywhere they went, they met past clients of Bunty, to whom he had sold cars long ago, or came across vintage cars which Bunty dearly yearned to bring back to the UK with him.

The first Caribbean cruise was swiftly followed by a second, but Bunty undertook this one alone. For a full two months, nobody saw or heard anything from him – apart from a postcard greeting, which he sent from Martinique to all his friends. Everybody received the same postcard – even I got one. Bunty must have bought out the entire stock of this particular motif. This colourful picture displayed a half-naked Creole with a banana in each of her hands.

As his worldwide contemporaries discovered three weeks later – once again via postcard – Bunty had managed to book a cheap flight to Florida to stay with a friend in Miami. It was rather astounding that the US embassy in Port-au-Prince had provided him with a visa for entry to The States at such short notice, especially given that visitors in those days had to provide prior proof of their return journey before entry.

Bunty was in the USA for the first time in his life, and, armed with a Lincoln Continental rental car, he set about making The Southern States unsafe. However, what he was unable to know was that Averil had suffered a severe road accident and was in hospital. Bunty didn't discover this until he finally invested a few dollars in a telephone box in Memphis, Tennessee. He took the next available flight back to England, and when Ambrose collected his father from Heathrow, he had further terrible news to share: Bunty's mother was dying.

The passing of his mother affected Bunty greatly, for he had so much to thank her for. Staying true to his character, however, he did his utmost to turn his grief into joy through the comfort of a beautiful old car. Someone had offered him an affordable Vauxhall 30/98, a fine example of the legendary sports car which was revered at every racetrack across Britain as the pinnacle of automotive engineering at the start of the twenties, before Bentley came to the fore.

The funeral of his mother and the current circumstances of his wife were enough, however, to stop Bunty from testing the Vauxhall out in Silverstone personally. He entrusted Eddie to carry out the test drive and to purchase the car, providing it ticked all the necessary boxes.

Eddie did what was required of him and returned with a new car for his boss. The Vauxhall proved to be a good investment. Bunty had previously owned a 30/98, but only for a very brief time, after which he sold the car for a good profit. The quality of the high-capacity, four-cylinder engine provided fond memories. The new owner took his new acquisition to numerous vintage car rallies, for which he required a license that the RAC issued. Bunty's driving style horrified all the other drivers; he would allow this heavy car to drift around corners, turning leisurely without dropping gear, and then rapidly accelerating upon exiting the corner, thus blocking the faster cars in pursuit from overtaking ...

Shortly after the acquisition of the Vauxhall, Bunty finally purchased the boat that he had dreamed of for so long. His decision fell in favour of an ark from the 'fifties, built in the style of a small fishing trawler according to the design of naval architect Soresby, famous for his whalers. 'Anin' came from a renowned shipyard in Yorkshire, but was found in a very rundown condition. As a result, the trawler was also remarkably cheap: Bunty purchased it from a bankrupt's estate.

After Hazel had seen the ship, she predicted its imminent demise. "I couldn't imagine that such a thing would even be able to float. I was terrified that Bunty would drown on his maiden voyage."

The trawler's new owner christened it 'Bunty's Ark.' The ship was given a thorough overhaul in Yorkshire. "For Bunty, the purchase of the trawler meant the start of a new chapter in his life," explained Hazel. "In the spring, Bunty had been informed that the RAC would not be renewing his racing license; he had refused to provide a doctor's certificate, which was obligatory for applicants over fifty, so he was no longer permitted to take part in vintage car races. Admittedly, he was later granted the license as a show of goodwill, but for the time being, Bunty was offended. He submitted a membership application to join the Royal Thames Yacht Club, which was accepted, and so this passionate motorist became a passionate skipper ..."

He had always been a passionate sailor, claimed Bunty in later life, as he played on his maritime heritage and his 'experience' in that regard. He certainly deserved some credit for his bottle.

The task of making 'Bunty's Ark' seaworthy was taken on very earnestly by the shipyard in Whitby, Yorkshire. Bunty could scarcely wait for the maiden voyage. He didn't have a pleasant, gentle introductory sail planned, however, but rather a tangible sea expedition. End destination: Haarlem, Holland. Distance: 311 nautical miles, 360 English miles or 580 kilometres. A stiff job indeed for starters.

The ark measured 30 feet in length and wasn't built as a sailing boat, but rather as a power boat, with a corresponding hull. The spacious construction offered plenty of room, the stern had two davits for a dinghy (which was preferred to a life raft). Bunty invested a few pounds in a stronger engine; he was recommended to install a 78hp four-cylinder Farymann diesel, an honest, reliable slow runner, good for an average of twelve knots, which could be obtained second-hand for next to nothing.

Bunty's companions for the journey across to Haarlem were Averil and Eddie. The journey was seen as a test run for an extended journey through Europe's inland waterways. The newfound chief Mr Commodore was certain he had the necessary nautical know-how, even if this experience was thirty years out of date and gave him no basis whatsoever to commence a North Sea crossing. For as long as the land remained in view, the three musketeers were able to fumble their way south. However, after passing Lowestoft, the English coastline disappeared over the horizon, at which point the terrestrial navigation came to an end.

None of the three had experience of the high seas. They had of course used compasses and maps before on land, but this was an altogether different challenge. Moreover, Averil and Eddie had left Bunty solely responsible for management of the ship's course. The captain unfortunately surrendered himself to seasickness halfway through the voyage, seeking respite in one of the bunks whilst bravely fighting this sudden bout with a glass of brandy. The weather was beautiful, the sea relatively calm. They weren't forced into any complicated manoeuvres by bigger vessels, and, as it became dark, they turned on the canonical lights and sailed peacefully onwards.

Presumably this was pure fortune, for the North Sea is renowned for being one of the busiest waterways. At approximately seven o'clock in the morning, the Dutch coast came into view. Another coincidence – or was this divine intervention? – ensured that 'Bunty's Ark' reached the yacht harbour in Haarlem at precisely the same time that breakfast was being served in one of the clubhouses. Guests of the Royal Thames Yacht Club were covered of course.

Averil and Eddie had passed the 26-hour test. Bunty couldn't have wished for a better crew; even the mooring at the jetty did not cause any significant difficulties. After a few days, they continued onto Amsterdam. "Eddie will develop into a good navigator, I believe. He spends every spare minute studying maps and handbooks," wrote Bunty in his logbook. But also: "Eddie is a little sloppy … he's lost one of my good pair of loafers …" Eddie interpreted that in an entirely different way, however: "He had thrown it at a rat, who was trying to nip through the fairlead to try and get at the docking line by the bow. He'd missed of course, but the shoe and the rat had disappeared into the water of the Ijsselmeer …"

Onwards to Vienna
– for the red-light district?

BRIMMING WITH CONFIDENCE, BUNTY planned the continuation of the journey forthwith; the crew would be making several stops en route, travelling as far as Istanbul. At least.

I had received word of Bunty's travel plans, and he wanted me to provide him with detailed information about Germany's inland waterways. He told me of his intentions to reach Istanbul, and how he still had fond memories of the red-light district in Vienna, which he had "experienced" on his previous trips to the Balkans. Bunty's letter wasn't censored by Averil before being sent; I've taken the time to do so now.

When Bunty asked me to send him charts of the German waterways, I turned to Heinz Fluecht of the Deutsche Motoryachtverband (German Motor Yachting Association). A handsome package was sent across to aid the journey. I, like my colleague Fluecht, had previously been an editor for a magazine for amateur sailors, and felt competent enough to give Bunty a few useful tips. Bunty confirmed receipt of the maps but insisted that I sent him another which he was missing: that of the Rhine-Main-Danube Canal. I called him up and explained that such a canal didn't exist at present; it was admittedly in the works, as planned by Bavarian President Franz-Josef Strauss, but that it would be another decade easily before this important connection between the rivers Main and Danube would be open.

"My dear friend," Bunty instructed me, "I am extraordinarily sorry to have to correct you here. I know that you live in the very country whose waters I am intending to cross, and you certainly know your way around there. But the canal of which you speak, the one you claim does not exist, has been in existence since the early 19th century! I want to use it to reach Passau from Regensburg. You simply have to find out for me whether it is suitable for ships with a ten-foot beam and a draught of four and a half feet ..."

My question as to where Bunty had learnt of such a canal was met with great satisfaction: "One of my nephews is employed at the Royal Geographic Society. I know from him that this canal exists. The Society is one of the most reliable institutions in Great Britain ..."

I promised to enquire. And I discovered that there had indeed been a fragmentary connection between the upper Main and the Danube two hundred years ago, but that, of the sections which had previously existed, only a few had linked directly and that the majority of these impressive, man-made ditches in the landscape had been recaptured by nature and returned to the local habitat. So, Bunty would indeed have to wait ten years before Mr Strauss would have the opportunity to realise his ambitious plan.

Bunty didn't care to acknowledge my findings. After a break of three weeks, he travelled to Haarlem with Averil and Eddie, paid the accrued mooring taxes with a heavy heart and then continued his journey.

He planned to sail up the Rhine until he reached the mouth of the Main. I was supposed to hear from him in Wuerzburg one day. Thus far, he had bumbled comfortably along the canals of Holland for a week and navigated several stages of the French waterways before heading down river Rhône to Arles. Since they had to pass four to six locks every day, daily stages were kept short for the most part. The regular mooring and unmooring and the subsequent jostling with quay walls, lock gates and passing barges gave Eddie plenty to do; his artisanal abilities were taken advantage of daily. 'Bunty's Ark' bore many wounds from this.

Almost every evening, Bunty would invite guests on board. Sometimes these were acquaintances, whom he had informed of his arrival in advance, other times they were neighbouring yacht captains and their crews. They never stayed for just one drink.

Upon returning from his second stage, Bunty discovered that an American DJ had purchased the 'old chickens house', which needed driving to the London Docklands in order to be shipped to the USA. Bunty insisted on completing this final journey in his beloved Silver Ghost personally. Equipped with a train ticket back to Stoke-on-Trent, he set off on his own.

Nobody had seriously believed that Bunty would make it to Stoke-on-Trent station the following day as agreed. When he didn't show up the day after either, people became slightly uneasy. Late that evening, he finally appeared, behind the wheel of a rickety old Bentley Mk VI. He had bought the wreck from a friend, whom he had met through the yacht club. Humphrey wasn't exactly enthralled by the Bentley but paid his father the expenses and hoped that the old gent would return to his boat trip as soon as possible.

At this precise moment, Bunty no longer wanted to return. Searching for unusual cars now stimulated him more. So, one day, he returned home with a 1957 Reliant Three-wheeler, which finally managed resale two years later (Humphrey would have gladly given it away, simply to have been rid of it), and after that he got his hands on a Citroën DS23 Break. Two Germans had arrived in this car, bought a Bentley and paid for it with the French vehicle. Humphrey was completely against the deal, but his father, who always made a habit of 'coincidentally' being present at such times, gave a decisive thumbs up: "I must have that Citroën!"

Bunty discovers his passion for Citroën

A CAR WITH LEFT-HAND drive, German registration plates, no proper papers for English road law – where on earth to start? Humphrey drove the car to an auction, but didn't sell it, to the delight of his father, who valued the car very much.

At that time, Ambrose married his girlfriend Claudia. The wedding party was joyous and raucous in equal measure, with Bunty chipping in a third of the costs. Bunty got to play the protagonist once again at another event around this time.

This peculiar incident wasn't at Bunty's expense, but rather the expense of around thirty people, who hadn't the faintest idea whom to thank for this presentation on the adventures of an old gentleman on Europe's inland waterways.

Bunty had been given the opportunity to hold a slideshow about the first part of his sailing trip in front of friends and acquaintances in the function room of a hotel that had been rented out for the occasion. As Bunty prepared to show his slides, there were just a few people present, none of whom Bunty recognised. He was disappointed that so many of his guests had not yet arrived, despite having shown such interest in the presentation beforehand, but he didn't want to wait any longer, so the lights were switched off and the slideshow began. At that moment, the doors opened and closed again; hordes of people entered and took their seats – at long last, the room was now full. After a little while, one of the new arrivals turned the lights back on. Bunty paused his humorous presentation and was confronted with thirty or more people, all dressed in traditional Japanese garments. Not a single face was familiar to him.

The explanation? Bunty had set up his projector in the wrong function room. This one had been reserved for a Japanese dance troupe, who were intending to rehearse a piece. However, for the first half an hour they were too polite to interrupt Bunty's speech. Meanwhile, his friends and admirers were patiently waiting in a neighbouring room, believing that the he'd stood them up.

The great Citroën proved itself a worthwhile acquisition. This comfortable and roomy vehicle ensured long journeys could be carried out effortlessly, whilst the left-hand drive proved to be a sizeable advantage on the continent. Both Gerhard and Thomas van Ackeren, the brothers to whom the car previously belonged, joined for the next journey to the ark's mooring spot. Gerhard even accompanied the team on a leg of the subsequent voyage, which led them down the Rhône, while Thomas chauffeured the Citroën to the next stopping point. It was Arles.

In order to handle the rapids at Givors, it was mandatory for the group to take a pilot on board. Upon arrival in Arles, Bunty claimed to feel as comfortable and at home as the great Vincent van Gogh and began behaving rather peculiarly (which can probably be blamed on the numerous apéritifs he enjoyed before every meal), proclaiming that he would have made a superb artist, thanks to his fabulous vision. Luckily, he didn't proceed to slice one of his ears off.

Arles was initially the final destination; Jules and the Citroën were waiting here. Since it was nearly Christmas, a prompt journey home was on the agenda. Bunty begged forgiveness for not being able to offer any Christmas presents this year: he had ordered a bespoke, dark blue suit from the famous London tailors Gieves & Hawkes, in order to make an impressive appearance at the yacht club's Christmas Eve dinner. It was Bunty's first new suit in over thirty years. A thankful audience listened intently to the descriptions of this globetrotter, who droned on with such verbosity that he almost missed the last train to Stoke-on-Trent.

Like clockwork, a lovely guest arrived at Rock Cottage on Christmas morning, after two weeks' absence: Rodney, the doll's house collector. In Bunty and Averil's absence, he had occupied the house to such an extent that his hosts barely had room to move. Rodney had also purchased two old pianos, which he had decided to restore at the family home. He played a Christmas jingle on one. The copious punch available made it easier to stomach. Though Bunty had nothing to give, he was presented with a little gift from everybody. He made note of each and every gift in his diary, in order to thank his loved ones properly later.

This was the final Christmas which Humphrey's girlfriend Mareijke attended. She and three friends suffered a fatal accident on the motorway just four weeks later. Another motorist, under the influence of alcohol, collided head first with their vehicle. Humphrey was in Paris at the time with friends, including the husband of one of the girls.

"It was only too well that Bunty happened to be abroad at the time," said Hazel later. "When such horrible things occur, you're simply better off without him. His presence just makes everything worse. It was a terrible time. Humphrey was inconsolable for a month."

In Arles, Bunty, with the assistance of the trusted Eddie, devoted himself to a thorough spring cleaning of the ark, or at least, whatever the two understood of the term. All there is to tell from this is that Bunty's best pair of shoes sunk to the bottom of the Rhône, later joined there by his dark blue suit jacket to boot. At last, the journey continued leisurely down the Rhône again, complete with all-night parties on board. Bunty extended an open invitation to join him at Rock Cottage any time to every one of his guests. One particularly eye-catching guest was a gorgeous, young French girl, to whom Bunty offered the chance to come back to England for au pair employment, promising to look after her personally … fortunately, she didn't take this offer too seriously.

However, Bunty and Eddie decided against braving the Mediterranean without a professional skipper, but still planned to visit Greece and Turkey via an alternative route. So, they returned to Arles to moor, and this time it was Averil who went down to collect Bunty and Eddie in the Citroën and bring them back to England.

A little border incident

BUNTY HAD BARELY BEEN home a month or so before he became restless and wanted to return to his ship. On this occasion, he found no one willing to accompany him, so Averil had to sacrifice herself.

They took the ark up the Rhône for two weeks, passing the Saône and the Rhine-Rhône canal until they reached Mulhouse in Alsace. Averil proved once more that she was a sublime navigator, and that the ship was in considerably safer hands with her at the helm than Captain Bunty.

The next inland leg brought about the coincidence (or perhaps it was fate?) that Bunty & Co and I crossed paths. Unplanned, unannounced and unexpected; pure chance, and in a place that nobody would ever have guessed.

First of all, it should be reported that Bunty's next maritime leg took him from Mulhouse across the Rhine and then up to Mannheim. The special thing about this enterprise was that they reached their destination on land as well as on water. Bunty and Eddie had driven down to Mulhouse in the Vauxhall 30/98; Averil, Hazel and her son Peter in the Citroën. Bunty intended to use the ark as a floating fixed quarters of sorts, sometimes here, sometimes there, employing the Vauxhall for occasional sorties to potential vintage car meetings, whilst the Citroën would be used as a courier for the less important jobs.

One of their excursions from their mooring place in Mannheim was to Austria. Hazel and Peter took care of the ark, whilst Bunty and Eddie thundered on to Graz, Averil in pursuit with the baggage in the DS23 – which had English plates at the time. Bunty considered the rally in Styria to be rather tedious, mostly because he failed to find anyone who was interested in his never-ending stories. So, the decision was made to return home early to Mannheim, before the event had finished.

A change of scenery: a gloriously hot Sunday in August, at the border between Austria and Germany. I am stood, alongside hundreds of tourists, in a traffic jam at the Schwarzenberg customs control point at 5 o'clock in the afternoon. This is a place that demands patience; Austrian border officials have always revelled in their 'call of duty,' checking the chassis number of every individual car, telephoning directories across Europe to check the legitimacy of identification numbers, rummaging through the luggage of lone female travellers. Four or five cars ahead of me stood a dark grey vintage tourer, waiting in the queue. Since the convoy in front remained almost stationary, I got out of my family Volkswagen and wandered over to get a closer look – recognising it as a Vauxhall from the early twenties. Sat behind the wheel was a very familiar face, with his assistant Eddie in the passenger seat. A coincidence?

We wanted to wait until we reached a car park on the other side of the border before enjoying the ceremonial greetings, but this would mean successfully navigating the tollgate and passport control first. The car in front of the Vauxhall began to move; as Bunty went to follow, his mind presumably still distracted by my appearance, he unexpectedly stalled the car.

It wouldn't restart. Eddie hopped out of the cockpit, and he and I attempted to push and bump-start the Methuselah into life again … the car was facing uphill, it was very hot out, and we were getting nowhere … when we finally shoved our way to the crossing point, covered in sweat, all set to leave beautiful Austria in the most inglorious fashion, it was the guardians of German law who intervened.

"You are on the motorway, gentlemen," began our lecture from the man with the service cap. "Here, a vehicle has to be able to move of its own accord. Or you can use a breakdown service. If you require repairs, then please head over there – he pointed in the direction that we had come from, back into the country whose border patrol had let us through with a knowing wink just moments before.

Would it not be possible to stop just on the other side of the crossing point at that car park …? The problem was surely only something minor …

Our pleas were met with disapproving head-shaking. "Please turn back!" The Vauxhall's immobility brought the queue of impatient Bavarians heading home to Munich to a standstill once more, this time for even longer. Manoeuvring and turning in the narrow toll gate passage at the border was as good as impossible. My offer of towing the vintage car with my Volkswagen bus for a few metres until the engine restarted was dismissed with strict damnation. "Of its own accord, as stated in the regulations!"

Applying his best knowledge of the German language, Bunty explained that he was a famous personality, that the officer must please refer to his passport, which bore many visa stamps, and that he also had – what a threat! – very good contacts to the press. Nothing helped. "Then we'll just have to try and repair the damage now," declared Bunty, getting out of the car at the same time and attempting to open the bonnet. Eddie was waiting, tools in hand.

"That is absolutely not permitted!" screamed the border official, and he angrily instructed us to push the car across to the car park for official customs vehicles … exactly where we had suggested moving in the first instance: onto German soil. There, no sooner had Eddie cleaned out the filter of the fuel pump, which lasted barely seven or eight minutes, than the engine began to roar like it had half a century ago. After much admonition and advice, we finally received our passports back. Mila, my wife, who had taken control of the Volkswagen and was unaware of all the drama that had ensued, collected me once more, and we met up with Averil in the Citroën after five miles at the motorway service station in Bad Reichenhall. She had been waiting for Bunty and Eddie there and was somewhat astonished to see us following in pursuit. Over coffee and cake (it was my round, that was made very clear), we exchanged our stories of border crossings the world over.

It was quite late by the time we left. Our encounter wasn't over, however, until Bunty had the chance to explain once more about his plan to reach the Danube via inland waterways. "You'll see, my nephew is correct. I'll get in touch when we reach Vienna. Please be my guests on board, you two …"

Before this, Bunty meandered his way along the Rhine, the Main and the Neckar, and I received numerous letters from romantic stopping points en route. Since the summer was shorter than expected once again, winter accommodation needed to be found for the ark. Thomas and Gerhard van Ackeren were more than happy to organise this.

No Rolls-Royce on the South Pacific atoll

THE WINTER MONTHS IN dark Europe had never suited Bunty, so it was quite common for him to swindle a few weeks away in warmer climes, whenever the day-to-day temperature in northern Europe dropped near freezing point. However, during this year's winter, Bunty set his escape in motion with particular consequence: he booked a journey to the South Pacific. The only issue was that this journey wouldn't be offset as a business excursion by the Scott-Moncrieff company, in contrast to almost every previous journey that Bunty had undertaken, carried out as 'representative' of the Ltd., not least in order to visit existing customers or acquire new ones. But on the South Pacific atoll, according to the company's financial advisor, it was highly improbable that Bunty would succeed in selling someone a Rolls-Royce: the finance department thus refused to acknowledge his trip as worthy of the necessary company expenses.

Given that he'd known Bunty a long time, the financial advisor must have been aware that Mr Scott-Moncrieff made it his mission to convince anyone of the contrary. He rented a hotel room on the smallest Fijian isle and managed to talk the hotel director into wanting to buy a Rolls-Royce Silver Cloud – to such an extent that he made a commitment to purchase without seeing the vehicle and even offered to cover the delivery costs! In a collect call to his loved ones back home, Bunty shared the news of his remarkable success and outlined his instructions for commission. Using this money, he intended to finance additional flights to Australia and New Zealand. However, Humphrey made the transfer dependent on a down payment on the Silver Cloud, which unfortunately never arrived.

Despite this setback, Bunty had enough pocket money on him to enjoy a flight around the islands and a ferry across to Ai Sokula and Savusavu. "It's very beautiful here, just the planes and ships are overcrowded to bursting point, it's incredibly uncomfortable," he wrote to Averil. "The people here have a wonderful way of welcoming foreigners. One who made me feel particularly at home was a young girl, whose name escapes me, but who is really lovely and will accompany me on the flight back home to England. The little darling will help you with the housework and help ease your workload, my dear Averil. I'll apply for an exit permit here and make sure that the youngster gets a visa for Great Britain. The consul general, who has invited me for dinner tonight, will sort that out."

Bunty returned home without the Pacific Islander. Not without first stopping off in Australia and New Zealand, however, though he did so without receiving additional funds.

Travelling Australia in a gullwing

THEN, IT WAS MY turn to receive a long letter from Bunty. "With Jumbo Goddard, my old friend in Sydney, I have undertaken wonderful trips in a Mercedes Gullwing. We visited George Brooks in Adelaide, who doesn't just own a marvellous collection of classic Rolls-Royces, but also an impressive collection of old whiskies. But above all, my dear, I met with Bob Chamberlain, whose guest I am at the time of writing. He is a specialist for Benz cars and is currently restoring a model from 1908, a large chain drive car which he found here in Busch … I will write a full report up and send it over to you. I had to cut some time off of the New Zealand leg of the trip, as I was offered the chance to spend a week with good friends by invitation."

The report reached me later on. Operating under the title 'Weit von der Heimat' (Far From Home), he had described every last detail of this old vehicle, whose heritage Mr Chamberlain had thoroughly researched. Bunty loved this car, certainly no less than the Mercedes Gullwing. Getting into the cockpit of this mighty beast must have proven just as arduous for him as having to get out again.

Ten weeks of adventure holidaying in the Antipodean region of the globe is enough to satisfy the wanderlust of any passionate globetrotter for a while and justify a breather. Bunty, however, had barely arrived home when he found himself packing his bags once more, with a freshly renewed desire to travel. He drove down to Bad Hönnigen, Germany, in the OM and took the ark back out on water with Gerhard van Ackeren and two further friends. The previous year's pattern of land and river parties continued; the gentlemen enjoyed themselves profusely.

At long last, Bunty's ark reached Wuerzburg. Accompanying him on land was one of his minions in the OM, and they occasionally swapped places. Bunty was taking his turn chauffeuring the sports car when he was invited to a vintage car rally at a grassy estate on the banks of the river Main by Helmut Feierabend. Such parties are renowned for being particularly festive, just the way Bunty preferred. When he failed to get his car to the ark's mooring spot that night (it's questionable whether he would even have found it), Bunty blamed the lavish consumption of delicious Franconian wine … Only Helmut Feierabend and his companions knew the truth. They had slightly jacked up the rear axle of the OM, so that the wheels spun freely when gears were engaged. Some compassionate souls had witnessed Bunty's failings and offered to drive him to the ark, where he slept. When morning came, it was Gerhard's turn to take control of the car once more, he could find no evidence of any issue: what was the problem again, Bunty? Of course, the moment Bunty disappeared, the wheels on his OM had been lowered back down to ground level once more ...

For anyone who isn't familiar with Helmut Feierabend: his garage, established in 1962 from a converted locksmiths' and specialised in the restoration of historical vehicles in Wuerzburg, led to widespread acclaim. Feierabend was the first to establish such a workshop with very high standards in Germany, and word spread quickly of his prowess; leading him to take on more assignments than he could cope with. After he passed away in 2007, his son Thomas took over the firm.

Engine-knocking knockers

A FEW DAYS LATER, a message reached the ark's owner – passed on through yours truly – that he should head to Baden-Baden post-haste. In the Suedwestfunk television studio there, Bunty was to give an interview. As the backdrop for his performance, the channel's editor had unfortunately not prepared a Rolls-Royce or a Mercedes, but rather a 1904 Gladiator racing car, an exotic breed, belonging to the late collector Uwe Hucke. Bunty shone with excellent German, and what had dumbfounded the interviewer most of all: the old gent knew so much about the French brand Gladiator, with no preparation beforehand, that one could easily have assumed he'd spent his entire life working with this make alone.

"Had there been a Mercedes in the studio, I would've had a great deal more amusing stories to tell," he said to me, as I accompanied him back to Wuerzburg. "For example, that I was once the owner of an SSK model, which I was only able to acquire so cheaply because it belonged to a lady who had enormous difficulty driving the car. You know that in the middle of the steering wheel hub there are two levers to adjust the throttle and the ignition, which require great experience and a gentle touch to change the settings for particular circumstances. Well, the lady from whom I purchased the car was none other than Dorothy Paget, who had such enormous breasts that they always came into contact with the levers whilst driving, thus obstructing her repeatedly. I would have liked a vivid explanation as to how she started the car with those melons, because I mean, it's a really interesting story, isn't it? All because of the biggest bosom in the world ..."

I was familiar with the story already, and knew the Mercedes in question. Whether she was really so busty would have to be confirmed by Tim Birkin, whose project she financed, but he sadly passed away as long ago as 1933. Dorothy died in 1960, just 55 years of age. The lady with the most expensive cars and supposedly the biggest breasts in the world also owned the priciest racehorse in the world.

At long last, it was finally time for Bunty to learn that his cousin at the Royal Geographic Society was the victim of an error regarding the Rhine-Main-Danube canal. But before a decision was made about how to successfully navigate a 30-feet long and ten feet wide ship from Wuerzburg-on-the-Main to Passau-on-the-Danube, winter fell once more. With it came the need for Bunty to choose a new destination in the southern hemisphere for his next trip.

At that time, he received a letter from the very hotel manager in Fiji, whose Silver Cloud deal had unfortunately fallen through. The good man had taken on a new position in Bangkok, and invited Bunty to visit him in Thailand.

There's no fool like an old fool

THAILAND! ADMITTEDLY, BUNTY'S LEFT foot had flared up again and left the old gentleman in a hospital bed for two weeks, so he used this time to study maps. Unfortunately, there weren't as many addresses in Thailand for him to tap into. After several delays, Bunty began his journey to Bangkok, spending four weeks there and returning home on Christmas Eve with mountains of souvenirs. For Averil, he brought another cuckoo clock, a Black Forest model of Asian manufacture, while Hazel received a vinyl of Thai opera music. As a gift for himself, Bunty had bought a bright yellow summer jacket, the luminosity of which was incredibly striking in the English December fog. There's no fool like an old fool ...

Bunty even wore the canary-yellow jacket to Christmas dinner, which brought severe criticism. A pink shirt and a violet tie completed his burlesque outfit. Unfortunately, he garnished his new jacket first with gravy and then finally with a little chocolate pudding, adding further colourful nuances. Averil's suggestion of immediately taking the textile to the dry cleaner's was batted away vehemently by Bunty: he considered this a complete waste of money – the stains would certainly just fade out over time. Of course, this process happened just as slowly as with every other tie in his collection, not one of which had been afforded the luxury of dry cleaning.

Bunty's foot had worsened since his return from Thailand. No sooner were the Christmas celebrations through than Bunty went back to hospital. This frustrated the old chap terribly, none more so than when the doctors ordered him to rest for eight weeks and lectured him against driving. After this period was over, Bunty's first excursion in the Vauxhall took him to partake in the Oulton Park race. Bunty wore sandals and kept pace admirably, considering he was now 76 years old; the most senior participant by a distance. He manoeuvred his Vauxhall as in years gone by, with daring and courage; performing power slides much to the terror of the competition and the racing committee. When he collected a prize at the end, it was a recognition of his intrepidity as much as it was compassion for his handicap.

There's no fool like an old fool ...

It wasn't just his dodgy foot which Bunty had to manage; he also had to undergo cataract surgery. In the circumstances, his traditional birthday festivities were put on hold. Bunty used this peace and quiet to dictate letters and make telephone calls – hour upon hour upon hour. And during this time, he finally came to the decision that he would mobilise his big supercharged Mercedes, which had been patiently awaiting his refurbishment (this one wasn't previously belonging to Mrs Paget, however).

It was soon time again for Humphrey to be presented with another fait accompli. He returned from a three-day excursion, on which Hazel had accompanied him, and couldn't believe his eyes when he saw the entire garage team working on the fragments of that Mercedes, which sat peacefully tucked away for the past twenty years. Bunty had issued the command and the workforce had followed his directions ... The car, a 1929-30 Tourist Trophy competitor, in those days driven by Rudolf Caracciola, would surely have been recognised as a particularly valuable piece by Humphrey too – enough to be worth the restoration costs – but, at the same time, this work threatened to destroy the company's entire daily routine. Bunty had acquired the car in 1951 for a laughable scrap price of £250. The story of the car's previous ownership by Caracciola, or at least his steering of it in 1930, had been officially confirmed, according to Bunty, along with the knowledge that the vehicle was subsequently owned by Lord Howe (the fifth Earl Howe, to be precise; Edward Richard Francis Asheton, though Viscount Curzon didn't use the car in competitions. His Le Mans victory in 1931 was completed in his Alfa Romeo). Bunty had no information regarding the whereabouts of the car in the period of 1932 to 1951.

A girl named Rosemary

WINTER OF 1982-83 BROUGHT with it several surprises. Bunty discovered that the vicar, who had tripped over his garden chair and subsequently almost plunged head-first into the goldfish pond, was moving parish. By his own admission, Bunty had little time for church folk, but he regretted the departure of this vicar, because he had been hoping that he would one day marry Humphrey and Judy. Humphrey seemed at the time to want nothing to do with wedlock. Another surprise came in the form of a young lady by the name of Rosemary.

In contrast to the call girl Rosemarie who was murdered in October 1957 in Frankfurt, this lady didn't own a Mercedes SL. The only remote connection between the two was that Bunty was driving a 230 SL when he picked her up. A charming old man in an open-top, two-seater Mercedes could hardly fail. Bunty didn't just invite her for a ride, which then became tea with the family at Rock Cottage, but also offered her the chance to accompany him on a flight to Manila.

Rosemary "is taking wonderful care of me and my foot," Averil had the pleasure to read via a postcard from the Philippines. She retaliated by selling his 230 SL during her husband's absence.

Surprise number three: Humphrey finally agreed publicly to marry Judy. It was a long and festive wedding (without a Rolls-Royce cavalcade, Humphrey had outlawed this), and even Rosemary was invited as a guest. She never made another appearance, not without good reason. Bunty, for whom the tension of the occasion during the long ceremony had grown unbearable, suddenly let go when his son breathed the words "Yes I do," expelling a particularly evil-smelling gas behind him while shouting: "Thank the Lord, I'm so happy!"

Incidentally, it was indeed the old vicar who conducted the wedding ceremony. Bunty took care of this.

Judy and Humphrey set off on a long holiday less than 24 hours later. Humphrey intended to start a new life in Spain long-term – a safe distance away from his father. Outsiders couldn't see just how severe the feud between father and son had become, which was particularly difficult for Averil and Hazel. On the one hand, they loved and adored the eccentric old gentleman unconditionally, and tried to respect him, but, on the other hand, Humphrey had the best arguments on his side, when he felt compelled to put Daddy in his place – which was required with increasing regularity. In Humphrey's eyes, the senior's purchases and behaviour were no longer funny quirks: they were damaging the company.

To India for permanent care?

WHENEVER HUMPHREY WAS ABSENT, Bunty continued to instruct the entire team to work on the Mercedes – as long as the car was still in the Scott-Moncrieff premises. Eventually, Humphrey was left with no choice but to retrospectively sanction the work, though he was very reluctant to do this. His father would then set off in a hurry on another trip of his own; so as to avoid the risk of further conflict. He and Eddie (the poor chap had to use his entire annual leave) travelled to Regensburg this time in the Vauxhall, in order to set about translocating the ark over the Danube – by land, of course.

I was tasked with organising transport with the railway authorities. Bunty had decided to do this by train, an operation which was about half the price of the use of a low-loader by road. Coordinating all the logistical details and bookings took several weeks. Finally, the ark could swim the current of the Danube: from Regensburg, Bunty could at long last continue his European voyage. Surprisingly, he was no longer in a hurry to reach the Black Sea; he was quite sure about this and instead travelled confidently home to celebrate the birthday of his goddaughter, Fiona. Keeping in touch with her was a concern of Bunty's for one particular reason: Fiona's boyfriend was a man to Bunty's taste. The young man was a very good driver and owned a power boating license to boot. In future, he would be an ideal replacement for Eddie as Bunty's primary companion on continental excursions. Eddie was already set to be decommissioned, because he intended to marry and his bride-to-be Margaret wanted her lover at home rather than abroad. Eddie's leaving party involved a marvellous dinner at one of the best restaurants in the Cheshire countryside. Humphrey had made his attendance conditional on Bunty buying a new suit after the loss of his expensive suit jacket. The old gentleman was not allowed to show up wearing the yellow, gravy-stain-spotted model.

However, nobody wanted to risk allowing him to go shopping alone. This responsibility fell to Hazel, who was expected to accompany the Senior Manager to the clothiers, where she was not to simply help with selection, but was also given full power of attorney to buy the suit.

Bunty knew exactly how to capitalise on this in his typical fashion. "The lady will be paying for me," he explained loudly and clearly to the girl at the till, so that everybody in the shop could hear. "As she owes me a few small favours, in return for helping out with a single woman's needs … if you know what I mean!"

It was one of numerous shops which Hazel refused to enter for a second time, with or without Bunty. It also spared her from taking part in Eddie's leaving do. Humphrey explained: "It was agreed that my father should pay the bill, as a gesture for the years of service of our dear Eddie. So, after dessert, Father requested the bill. Then he rummaged with such striking theatrics through the pockets of his new suit that everyone could guess what was coming next. 'Kids,' he said, 'I have actually forgotten to take my wallet out of the old jacket. Humphrey, good boy, would you be a dear and lend me enough to cover this? I knew full well that I would never receive the expenses back. He'd managed to pull it off again. I was fuming."

Bunty had to put back his next planned European trip, organised in connection with Eddie's leaving party, for a few days, because he received an offer for a television interview with the BBC. To Bunty's disappointment, however, none of his favourite topics were being debated. Instead, he was expected to comment on modern car design. He took this opportunity to blasphemously badmouth all new models, berating their engineers and reprehending their lack of originality – he employed every swear word that came to mind to express his aversion to modern cars.

"They'll never broadcast that!" he claimed in reference to the interview, though he sat in watching the BBC every night for several days. The interview was indeed broadcast, unabridged, without as much as a single sentence edited out … Bunty was astonished.

It appeared as though Bunty had grown tired of inland waterway traffic, because, to the surprise of his family, he suddenly confronted them for a change with a plan, which involved a voyage to India. He had booked a journey to New Delhi, Benares and Madras with 'Happy Tours,' a coach travel company whose passengers were predominantly students. You slept in tents and ate tinned food for the duration; Bunty was the only senior on the trip. Two young English girls took him under their wing, which carried a great deal of responsibility. The old gentleman was in need of practically permanent care, because his foot injury had flared up again and he also had nutritional problems.

Any sane person in Bunty's position would have cut the trip off in Kabul at the absolute latest. The extremely hot temperatures were giving him great discomfort, the steady rocking aboard the omnibus made him seasick. In Peshawar, the bus suffered an unrepairable breakdown – the group had to alight and board another bus, already packed with locals and their belongings – including goats, chickens and lambs. At one of the many pauses for photos, Bunty took his shoes off in order to photograph a holy pond; and in doing so, he contracted a rather serious illness. He collapsed in New Delhi, and his two Samaritans rushed him to a hospital. They organised a plank bed so that the old chap could continue the bus journey.

Bunty's health gradually improved, he also refused to miss out on anything from the holiday, which he had paid for in advance. And so, the tour continued, to Daund, Manmad, Ajanta and Agra. After visiting the Taj Mahal, Bunty followed part of the group who were heading to Kathmandu: he wasn't missing this opportunity. Here, his wallet was stolen – fortunately on this occasion, his passport wasn't inside it. After this stop, he finally conceded and flew back home; the pain in his foot had become unbearable. Once he was back home, Bunty's condition improved very quickly. Just a few weeks later, he felt fit enough once more to continue his boating trip and finally reach the Black Sea.

He was accompanied for the journey along the Danube through Hungary and Romania by Tim, Fiona's boyfriend. Tim proved himself to be a perfect navigator and guided the ark to the Bosphorus without a hitch. Here, Bunty took control of the rudder, past the beautiful Dardanelles, with their many cliffs. The two seamen were filled with particular pride when they received a dipping of the flag from a Soviet destroyer.

This was followed by a tranquil island cruise, permeated by numerous retsina parties, through the Aegean, ending rather abruptly in Lemnos, when Bunty woke in his bunk to discover himself alone: Tim had said goodbye in French! In a note left for the skipper, he made clear that he had had enough of the trip and wanted to return home.

Bunty decided (correctly) against venturing on alone. "I must have asked the entire population of the island in my attempts to find a navigator to steer my ship back to Rhodes," he later wrote in a travelogue. "Nobody was interested. They all came to inspect the ark, stayed for a drink or two and then left. At long last, I made the acquaintance of Dorothy and George, two tourists who were spending their holiday on the island and had grown bored. George was familiar with the basics of navigation, and he trusted himself to get us back to Rhodes … However, once we got there the pair of them left me alone once more. Luckily, I bumped into my old friend Dimitrios on the pink island, who has wanted to buy my OM from me for years … he was the one who organised a mooring spot for the ark, so that I could at last calm down and fly home."

Right: Bunty took every possible opportunity to take guests on board the ark for celebrations. This photo depicts Bunty giving an address on the front deck. The extensive network of inland waterways in Europe meant endless possibilities for route planning (which were always subject to change). The 'operations' were left to Averil and Eddie.

Above: Mooring on the banks of the Rhône. The team spent a lot in fees trying to find a yacht harbour, let alone the lock charges, which were due almost daily.

Right: Sometimes repairs were required in emergencies. The life raft had made way for a little dinghy, which was much more use on journeys.

25.9.73   Motor Yacht "Bunty's Ark"
in Yachthafen Wiesbaden-Schierstein.

My dear Helewart,

This is a quick note to tell you that the worst part of the journey to Nuremberg is, I hope, over.

From Vitry le François to Toul was full of problems. The French government spends an absolute minimum on the maintenance of the Rhine-Marne canal, so naturally they are always closing sections of it for emergency repairs. It took us one week to do 100km. At last, at Frouard, we got onto the Mosel, and things were easier.

The Rhine was, as ever, dull, dirty and dangerous, but, thank goodness, apart from the last 5 km between this excellent harbour and the Main, it is behind us.

We leave here early tomorrow (26ᵗʰ) morning and hope to arrive at Würzburg 1ˢᵗ or 2ⁿᵈ October. I shall stay there a few days as I want to see something of that lovely city. Here we face another problem – on 4ᵗʰ October my crew leave me permanently and go to Munich on their way home. However, I hope that I have a friend coming who will crew me for the last 64 k.m. to Nürnberg. So I should be there in very good time for our appointment on 22ⁿᵈ with Munich Broadcasting.

So those are the plans up to date. If you want to write to me about anything, c/o Poste Restante, Hauptpostamt Würzburg, to reach them not later than October 4ᵗʰ. If you like to join me on the Würzburg-Nuremberg trip, you will be most welcome – but come on October 4ᵗʰ and sleep the night on board, so that we can start early on 5ᵗʰ. Hope you can make it

Yours, Bunty

Left: A photo taken in 1975. A beaming Bunty in the cockpit of a 4.5-litre Blower Bentley, once driven by Tim Birkin. Bunty described his driving impressions in the car magazine 'Automobil Chronik'.

Above: In the mid-1970s, Bunty remained an active driver on the circuit, participating in his vintage Vauxhall as seen here, although the RAC did threaten to revoke his license. Later, the beautiful car was acquired by well-known collector Gregor Fisken.

WEIT von DER HEIMAT

by David Scott-Moncrieff

The late Fritz Erle, who even as an old man had a wonderful memory said, categorically, that only ten of the extremely successful 1910 Prinz Heinrich Benz cars were ever built. Although quite a few were sold which looked like Prinz Heinrich cars, but had very ordinary touring engines. The 1910 cars were developed from the chain driven Benz which did so well in the 1908 Prinz Heinrich trial. The 1910 cars have shaft drive with separate close ratio four speed gearboxes. The 1910 engines have langer water jackets and also more water around the ports and exhaust valve guides. The 1908 engines were 115 x 175mm whereas the ten 1910 engines comprised four 115 x 175mm and six 105 x 165. All were geared for the Prinz Heinrich rally to give around 85 m.p.h. at peak revolutions of 2300 r.p.m. The engines of these two cars were tremendously advanced for their time. Each cylinder had two overhead inlet valves and two overhead exhaust valves. Dual ignition was by two Bosch magnetos. Valve push rods and rocker gear was exposed, but all other engine moving parts were neatly enclosed. Lubrication was affected by a group of pumps in a separate housing, set for different oil delivery rates, and driven from the exhaust camshafts. Virtually every moving part and the cylinder walls are all lubricated from this. The H connecting rod carried a tube up the side as did the early Rolls-Royce, to lubricate the gudgeon pins.

Of these ten highly interesting car, two are in U.S.A. one in France and one in Germany. During my recent visit to Australia, a friend of a friend of mine said casually at lunch "If you can come to my house this afternoon I can show you something that will interest you". And there, to my amazement, were two more survivors of the original ten Prinz Heinrich Benz! And what is more he was able to tell me virtually the whole history of both cars and how they came to be so far away from their birthplace in Mannheim.

Three quarters of a century ago there lived, on the south coast of Australia, a wealthy importer named A. T. Craig. Several of his friends had new fangled motorcars, which, in spite of the Australian dirt roads, enabled them to drive longer distances faster than their horse-carriages. So Mr. Craig on his next visit to London bought a motorcar and advertised for a chauffeur. Several chauffeurs went for interview to the Savoy Hotel, where he was staying, and he engaged one called Wilkinson. He had picked an excellent chauffeur, but a motorcar that was slow on a flat road and would only drag itself up hills at walking pace.

Wherever there are two or more Englishmen, there is a club, and Australia, having been founded by the English, was no exception. Soon Mr. Craig was the laughing stock of his club, for it was immediately apparent that he owned by far the slowest car in town. One man particularly irritated him. They both lived in the same area, up some some very steep hills. He would stop at a pub and be waiting outside with the tankard of beer in his hand to watch Craig crawling up the hill at walking pace. Then he would race past him and again be waiting outside a pub on the next hill to watch poor Craig crawling past.

It was less the use of costly spare parts which bothered junior manager Humphrey, but rather the employment of the entire workforce onto this project, which Bunty ordered in his son's absence. This was the reason why Humphrey gave Eddie custody of the Mercedes without further ado — Bunty would have to finance it out of his own pocket.

Right: Bunty's text on the photo: "Monday, 3rd December 1984. Finally, I was able to have a first trial sitting in my Mercedes…" The restoration of the SSK, known in England as a 38/250 hp, was dragged out over many years, because it was constantly interrupted. While Bunty was out of town, Humphrey ensured that the car was left in Eddie's private garage.

TELEPHONES – LEEK 380300
LEEK 384300 SHOWROOMS, AND LEEK 384020 WORKS
CABLES: BUNTYCARS, LEEK, STAFFS
TELEX 36440

DAVID SCOTT-MONCRIEFF & SON LTD.

D. W. H. SCOTT-MONCRIEFF,   A. M. A. SCOTT-MONCRIEFF,   H. D. SCOTT-MONCRIEFF,   H. M. ROBINSON

Purveyors of Horseless Carriages to the Nobility and Gentry since 1927

ROLLS-ROYCE & BENTLEY CAR SPECIALISTS

V.A.T. REG. NO. 279 1212 55

| Showrooms:
2 MACCLESFIELD ROAD
LEEK, STAFFS
ST13 8LA | Workshops:
BRITANNIA WORKS
WEST STREET
LEEK, STAFFS | When Closed:
ROCK COTTAGE
BASFORD HALL
LEEK, STAFFS | Reg. Office:
Les House, High Road
Wembley, Middx
Reg No. 806200
All Correspondence to Showrooms |

<u>Ein Alte Treue Freund</u>

I was delighted to see a picture, in your article on Bentleys, of my much loved "Charlotte", a four seater convertible with coachwork by Vanden Plas. Your photograph was taken on the FIVA Rally in Ireland, in, I think, 1965.

When I bought "Charlotte" around twenty years ago, she was in very poor shape. She had belonged for a long time to a schoolmaster, who on schoolmaster's wages, could not afford to spend on anything more than putting petrol in the tank. The poor car had, frankly, been run into the ground. She was rebuilt by that ace mechanic Eddie Berrisford. Since then I have driven her on rallies all over Europe between Greece and Schlosweg-Holstein, and indeed several on the less usual side of the iron curtain, the last one in which we competed was in Poland. I don't suppose that "Charlotte" will rally much in 1982, because this years rallies, starting with the Norwegian rally at the end of May will have to be a proving ground for the 1938 "Super eight" Packard convertible, completely rebuilt for the Peking-Paris. I have never driven in China, so I can only guess. But my guess is that the most suitable car for this sort of terrain would be soft sprung American with an engine that gives plenty of power without being highly stressed and what better than the best American — a Packard? Also, it gives "Charlotte" some respite for much needed bodywork attention. The English Van den Plas firm must not be confused with Belgian Van den Plas. The latter were of the finest coachbuilders in Europe, ranking with Barker and Erdmann and Ross. The English firm was started by a branch of that family, in a shed next door to the one in which W.O. Bentley was building his first 3 litre. They built very pretty bodies, but they were all built down to a price. They economised on the quality of the wood used for the body frame, and for the last twenty years poor "Charlotte's" frame has been steadily deteriorating. So at present she is off the road having virtually all her timbers replaced with seasoned ash. Seasoned ash is not very easy to find, and the whole operation is horribly costly, but she is worth every penny of it. So let us hope that after the Peking-Paris she will be seen again in the Deutsch Allgemeiner-Schnauferl Club Rallies, and others all over Europe.

Bunty Scott-Moncrieff

Left: Every now and then I would receive manuscripts (with headings in German) from Bunty, which he had dictated to Hazel, with the request that I translate and publish it.

*Above: "Mercedes: Bunty's favourite cars"
wrote Hazel on the back of this photo. She was
spot on with this assessment, and Bunty even
wrote a book about the history of this marque.
He would also have written just as good a
book about Rolls-Royce; given his unrivalled
competence, experience and knowledge, it
would have surely found many buyers.*

*Right: Lord Montagu of Beaulieu and Bunty
with some veteran cars at the Old Rhinebeck
airfield, upstate New York. I met the
gentlemen at the occasion of an international
FIVA rally which took place in the USA during
October, 1985, in which several German
teams were also participating. Meeting Bunty
wasn't planned, coincidence had struck once
more, as it so often seemed to.*

ROCK COTTAGE,
BASFORD HALL,
LEEK,
STAFFS.

10th June, 1974

Dear Halwart,

    I am working now on an article for you on one of the Birkin-Pagett blown Bentley team, photograph herewith. The owner has been very kind in letting me drive it so I shall be able to give you my impression straight from the horse's mouth as well as the history of the car which includes several Le Mans, Brooklands 500 mile race and the French Grad Prix that year that they held it at Pau. I shall also be sending you some very very good professional photographs of the car one of which I am hoping you will be able to use for the cover.

    I still don't know the date of the Nurburgring race meeting and I am told that the following weekend there is a race meeting for old cars at Salzburg. I will be most grateful if you could let me have exact dates soonest possible and even better, entry forms.

    All the best,

Yours,

Halwart Schrader Esq.,
8 München 90
Menterschwaigstr. 11.

Left: This letter sent to me accompanied the photo displayed on page 195, which shows Bunty at the wheel of a 4.5-litre Blower Bentley.

Right: A final photo of Bunty at the wheel of his beloved vintage Vauxhall sports car, before he had to give up driving. The 30/98 survives in best care-taking hands.

The Horseless Carriage

Issue No 2   *Quarterly journal for collectors and restorers*   **Autumn 1990**

I AM delighted with the response to our first issue of THE HORSELESS CARRIAGE. Already our second issue has doubled in size.

Our aim is to keep our friends and customers up to date with the restoration business.

In this issue you will find items on restoration, insurance, originality and a few anecdotes of our trade.

Being involved for so many years with 'old' cars, I am often asked questions and told snippets of news.

Your comments and opinions on the vast subject of classic car ownership are always welcome.

So, do drop me a line and we'll put your views down in print.

Hazel Robinson, Editor in chief "Our aim is to keep our friends and customers up to date"

This summer has seen many of England's classic car events.

Scott-Moncrieff put in an appearance at the Rolls-Royce Enthusiasts Club annual rally at Castle Ashby in June.

It was nice to meet our old friends and customers from all over the world.

As ever, there were some lovely examples of Rolls-Royce and Bentley cars on display. (See page 6)

By the way, did you go to the Bentley Drivers Club event in Kensington? I am sure our readers would love to share your personal account of the event in the next issue of THE HORSELESS CARRIAGE - due out at Christmas.

Investment brings a total service

AS WE go to press, Scott-Moncrieff are about to sign the lease on 5000 square feet of new premises, which are within minutes of their existing workshops.

"We are ready to provide a wider range of services to our clients and we needed to expand our facilities to do this," says the firm's owner Duncan Dickson.

By mid October they expect to have transferred their paint shop to the new site.

"We have invested in a new spray booth," says Duncan Dickson. "With this, plus the additional space, our paint spraying projects can be conducted more quickly, more efficiently and, as a result more cost-effectively from the client's point of view."

Back at the West Street headquarters where staffing levels have doubled in the last twelve months a more spacious layout is emerging

"We are now able to incorporate a dedicated clean area for reassembly of cars," says Duncan Dickson. "This is all part of our reorganisation process which will put us in a leading position to provide our customers with a 'total service'."

Left: At long last, his Mercedes-Benz SSK was finished, finally Bunty could take it with him to the 1986 international rally – it was to be his last. The route took him as far as Stuttgart. It was with a heavy heart that he accepted he was no longer in a position to drive himself, and so this task was delegated to a friend of the house.

Bad eyes, bad circulation, bad memory ...

AFTER ANOTHER PERIOD IN hospital as a result of his foot, a letter from Rhodes betrayed a secret Bunty had been trying to conceal. The ark's transmission needed to be changed; it had given up the ghost. The new transmission would cost a princely sum.

"This didn't appear to unsettle Bunty in the slightest," Hazel said later. He had, in his words, a quite brilliant idea for how to raise the funds for this expensive replacement: Lady Lyrintosh would pay for it, an immensely well-off woman, whom Bunty had gotten to know (we never discovered the occasion of their meet) and whose great desire in life was to journey along the Nile in a little boat. She promised Bunty a contract amounting to the exact cost of the replacement transmission, provided he made this voyage possible.

Two months later, Bunty was heading to Rhodes to accompany an acquaintance of Lady Lyrintosh, introduced to us as 'Mark' (via letter). Mark transported the ark, with its new transmission, to Cairo.

However, it soon transpired that travelling up the Nile is not readily sanctioned; a special permit is required ... Entangled in the thicket of Egyptian bureaucracy, poorly versed in the art of baksheesh, and above all abandoned by Lady Lyrintosh, who was yet to show up in Cairo and thus hadn't delivered the corresponding cheque to her skipper, Bunty and Mark saw no alternative but to return to Rhodes. Not without first stopping off at Aswan and Luxor, however.

The climate in Africa had given Bunty circulatory problems, while his eyesight was continuing to worsen. He ignored these of course, just as he did his bad foot. The doctors had ordered him a strict period of rest, but he continued to run around like a headless chicken. In the meantime, Bunty began to experience blackouts. He had received an invitation to attend a wedding; the groom even wanted him to be a guest speaker. Bunty was delighted to accept this. He organised a lovely gift for the couple and headed to the local registry office in the town hall in the Citroën, as was agreed. Bizarrely, not a person in sight was familiar to Bunty. The reason for this was that he had arrived a full week too early, having forgotten the date. Upon discovery of his error, Bunty decided against standing around like a lost lemon – dressed in his Sunday best – at the registry office, and so he sauntered into another wedding ceremony taking place, giving the lucky couple his gift and promptly receiving an invitation to the ceremonial luncheon. For Bunty, the day had been saved.

"We would have been fools to have believed that Bunty would have stopped driving because of his injury," remembered Hazel. "He was willing to have a cataract operation, but he refused to wear glasses and despite his broken foot, he refused to take stock … or his daily insulin injection …"

The old man even had bad luck with his 'good foot': he tripped and broke his ankle – irreparably. He had to put up with a steel plate and an orthopaedic ankle brace, since he didn't want to be bound to a wheelchair. Bunty handled the news in a composed manner, and soon after he was forging new plans. Averil was to drive him across Europe.

However, one thing he did have to come to terms with was selling the ark. One of his friends in Greece carried this out on Bunty's behalf. The proceeds were more than modest, even though the boat required a refurbished engine after having got that new transmission.

Bunty started driving again. The following Easter Sunday, he meandered tentatively through the neighbourhood in his Vauxhall, relieved to find that – in his eyes – he was still master of the situation. At least he was able to convince himself of this, while every other driver swerved to avoid him and mothers grabbed their children tightly and yanked them out of harm's way.

Peking-Paris at last?

AROUND THIS TIME, THE wheels were in motion for a repeat of the historical race from Peking to Paris, held in 1907. Bunty was thrilled by the thought of participating in the rally behind the wheel of a 1938 Packard, which he had acquired "insanely cheaply," and now sought a sponsor to finance his entry. With the help of several friends, he found a company who were willing to pay for the famous Mr Scott-Moncrieff to race. Since Bunty ceased to speak of anything other than the second Peking-Paris challenge, assumptions were made in certain circles that he was actually one of the event organisers.

Word spread, and soon Hazel was handling calls daily, ranging from prospective participants enquiring about registration to nosy newspapers seeking out the inside scoop. Nobody seemed to have considered that the war in Afghanistan and other military conflicts in Asia would foil the plan. Presumably, Bunty would have nominated himself as peacemaker given the chance. The race would have to be postponed – for the time being at least …

Learning that the Peking-Paris rally was on hold, Bunty registered for more club races. Averil was powerless: she would've had to shackle her husband to the bed to stop him. But she too was a restless spirit. She'd given up remonstrating with Bunty long ago; everyone knew he was a child at heart and that he had to be left to do as he pleased. He also undertook a monstrous and immensely challenging journey through southern USA and Central America, to which he was invited by an acquaintance with a Jeep, before later completing a rally to Poland.

In June 1982, he wrote to me on his personalised, light blue paper, outlining his intentions to partake in a rally in Russia – the first such event ever to be held in the USSR – in place of the failed Peking-Paris competition. Of course, at the same time, he complained about the conditions to which foreign participants were subjected: "My Packard can't arrive via land, it has to come in using the sea route (Riga), while I should arrive by plane. But I certainly won't be sending my treasured Packard unaccompanied to Russia, a country where they are known to steal all the tyres and even the headlight bulbs from parked cars in no time at all. But please don't tell anyone else what I think of the Russians, because I am still trying to acquire permission to arrive via land."

Unfortunately, Bunty didn't succeed in his attempts.

New schemes had to be prepared. And Judy was taken very much by surprise, when her father-in-law began chatting up Penny, a friend of hers who occasionally visited Rock Cottage. Rosemary had been replaced.

Penny was a very cute, lovely girl, who had finished her medical studies and who, over a cup of tea, happened to mention in passing that she would one day like to travel to the Far East. Voicing such a thing in Bunty's presence could only end one way; the old philanderer immediately and spontaneously invited her to fly with him to Thailand.

In Penny, Bunty had not only an attractive and intelligent travel companion, but also a trained medical supervisor! Even Averil was on board. The odd couple flew to Bangkok, from there onto Rangoon and other destinations in South Asia. For the first three weeks, nobody received any mail – leading to anxiety as to the whereabouts of the pair. Then, two or three postcards arrived at once.

It was only after their return that Penny revealed her records to Hazel. The young doctor had noted: "October 23: Bangkok, lost voice. October 28: Poo-Guang, tried to find insulin all day. November 5: Laphong, intestinal disorder. November 13: Kuala-Lumpur, treated boil on knee. November 16: Malacca City, caught infection. December 2: Yogyakarta, foot treated in hospital. December 5: retreatment …" No entries in Penang, Samui or Singapore.

Back in England, Bunty was advised to undergo another eye operation. He wanted to think about this in Brazil … his answer was to book a flight to Rio de Janeiro. Without Penny.

When asked about the trip, he responded: "Yeah pretty good, only that I couldn't see anything at all for several days. But my vision came back again with time. Really strange."

Bunty had planned it perfectly to make sure he was in Rio during the carnival. His postcards heralded the festivities, whilst their motifs proved beyond all doubt that he could see once more. They depicted very scantily-clad beach beauties, without bananas in their hands this time. "What we only came to discover later was that he lay unconscious in his hotel room for 24 hours at one point. We only found this out indirectly. Perhaps Bunty didn't even realise himself …"

Averil managed to convince Bunty to undergo the second cataract operation. This was successful in restoring his eyesight to half-capacity.

No help from
the helpful dragon

THE RESTORATION OF THE supercharged Mercedes was still no nearer completion. It was simply a question of funding. The one-time biggest second-hand Rolls-Royce dealer in the world admittedly presided over a sufficient apanage and could have made at least some of this available for the restoration budget but, instead, he continued to spend it on trips abroad in charming company ...

But was he not also a successful author? Granted, his sailing stories had found no acceptance, but giving up on such matters wasn't in Bunty's DNA. He decided to write a children's book and use the proceeds to finance further work on the Mercedes. It's possible that he received inspiration for this from his little granddaughter Chloe. The publishing house in London, to whom he sent the manuscript, declined interest, but there seemed to be a chance in America. The connection to a US publisher was established by June, the former secretary of the Royal Thames Yacht Club. She offered to edit and retype Bunty's novel. She would come regularly to Rock Cottage, slowly but surely bringing the *Story of the Helpful Dragon* to paper.

June also arranged an extended stay at Rock Cottage for married couple and publishing duo Ed and Conny Wachs, from America. In order to ensure that he could give them a finished copy of the manuscript, Bunty would get up at six-thirty every morning, finishing the book with June's help. Ed Wachs, also an owner of a Packard V12 convertible, took the script back to America with him and promised to examine it in-depth.

The book was never published. Despite that, Ed and Bunty remained friends. Bunty's various literary efforts had been remarkably different in their levels of success. Some prompted a frantic scramble to secure his commitment and collaboration, while others saw the manuscripts returned with negative, even derisive remarks. His book on veteran cars in 1955, contemporaneous with the release of his book on Mercedes, experienced two further editions, and in 1963 Batsford published Bunty's (aforementioned) legendary work on the classics of the thirties. It wasn't tailored for a big readership, but anyone who has a copy on their bookshelf today owns a treasure that demonstrates wonderfully Bunty's unique approach to life.

There was even a vinyl recording of him. To a background of engine noise, Bunty commentates: a feast for the ears. Not for everyone, however.

Bunty's actively professed love for Bugatti and Mercedes cars was viewed by some of his Rolls-Royce customers as treachery, but he never saw it quite as black and white. He was able to admire a beautiful Alfa Romeo just as deeply as he would a Packard, a Bentley, an Isotta-Fraschini or a Frazer-Nash. At this time, Bunty presided over a sizeable collection of the finest classics, and if he wanted to continue his Mercedes restoration project, he would have to sell two or three of them. Until such a time as he was finally able to sit behind the steering wheel of this treasure for the first time in decades, Bunty continued to chauffeur himself around with pleasure in his OM or the Vauxhall. To his delight, a television team approached him with the offer of a big show and even a payment fee of considerably more than Bunty had ever received.

"The fee had been paid to him in cash, we knew nothing about it," explained Hazel. "The money was nearly enough to finish off the Mercedes. Instead, he rang me a few days later from somewhere and said: Sweetie, I have just this moment bought myself a steam car ..."

Hazel was tasked with informing Averil. He had supposedly yearned for a steam car since his childhood ... the car was a magnificent monstrosity, built in 1905, and Bunty had bought it from a friend in Germany. Months passed before the car was deemed operational; when Bunty finally set off on his first drive, it transpired that the handling was a little too complicated for the old gentleman. Bunty never exercised his childhood dream again. Not all dreams are meant to be pursued. Everyone was relieved when Bunty eventually decided to dispose of the rarity.

Further excursions followed – one to Majorca with Averil, one with Penny to Oberammergau, one with Gottfried to America. In October 1985, America hosted the FIVA World Rally, and Ed Wachs had committed to trusting Bunty and Gottfried with his Packard twelve-cylinder. I happened to be in the same corner of Upstate New York at the same time, albeit on a different mission entirely, and bumping into Bunty there was a great pleasure. And not just him, incidentally: Ulrich Springer and Dieter Röhll in a 1925 Minerva, along with other party guests Max Rauck, Heidi Hetzer, Edward Lord Montagu ... Bunty was in good company. He also met with Peter Helck, the renowned American automotive artist, who – despite being almost blind – wanted to portray Bunty at the wheel of a Mercedes; the artwork was to decorate the cover of a new book. Helck, already in his nineties, died soon after. Neither the painting, nor the accompanying book were realised.

No advertisements for David Scott-Moncrieff & Son, Ltd had appeared in the British motor presses for a long time, and stock lists had ceased to be sent in since May 1982. "No stock, no stock lists," read Bunty's commentary. "The recession has immobilised our car trade. Sales have dropped off so far that we are now only able to operate the workshop. If you know someone whose car we should fix up, please recommend our service!" he wrote to me.

Humphrey had left the daily business and was now active on the international stage as an estate agent. He had meanwhile moved to Andorra with Judy and daughter Chloe. They soon brought a sweet set of twins into the world. Bunty wanted to visit them more than anything, but was hindered by the sad passing of his Auntie May. She left behind a sizeable inheritance for the Scott-Moncrieffs: the Mercedes restoration was back on the cards once more!

As his last official act in Leek, Humphrey had arranged a nasty surprise for his father, returning from his USA trip. The Mercedes was gone. The car was now in Eddie's garage. Eddie had likewise left the firm and had begun working as an independent restorer. But since he almost never saw any money for it, Eddie was in no rush to do more than was necessary to his former employer's car.

As Bunty's precious Mercedes remained off the road, he continued to drive the grey Vauxhall AOA2 with daring and style, despite his 77 years and numerous bodily handicaps. The coffee-brown Charlotte was also commonly employed, and Averil, likewise in her seventies, continued to take part in club rallies as often as time allowed, either in 'La Folie' or in a stunning Frazer-Nash. She eventually purchased a Bugatti type 57, a blue roadster with the registration number OPJ2, which she acquired from Twink Wincop. One weekly newspaper even named this racing driver 'Pensioner of the Year.' Averil didn't like the title one bit.

One final dream is fulfilled

BUNTY APPEARED MORE AND more often at Eddie's, badgering him to recommence work on the Mercedes. Eddie drew up a cost estimate. And Bunty did something that shocked and outraged his entire family: he sold Charlotte. Humphrey was particularly indignant and screamed down the telephone: "You don't just sell such a reliable car! Besides, it belongs to the family, not you alone …"

Humphrey, despite residing in Andorra, remained a partner in the company and demanded to see the details of Eddie's quote.

This damned Mercedes … Was the car really worth the rigmarole …? Shortly before everything was finished, a crack was discovered in a cylinder head. The reproduction of the head cost as much as a Mini. But as hard as it was to believe, the day finally came when the car was finished. It was the end of April, 1986, and Bunty was understandably excited to take this beige giant out for its first journey: a journey he had waited so very long for.

The trip was to Germany and represented yet another high point in Bunty's life – perhaps the most significant. Admittedly, he didn't consider himself able to drive the two-tonne supercharged beast himself, but that had no discernible impact on his joy. The large star on the radiator cap, which I had marvelled at years before on the mantlepiece in Bunty's living room, was experiencing its first venture onto German soil after many decades.

Bunty took an acquaintance by the name of Faiud with him on the journey, a man who seemed reasonably proficient behind the wheel. Averil didn't have the confidence, Humphrey refused to partake in any such expeditions anyway, and everyone else that Bunty trusted were sat behind the wheel of their own respective classics, partaking in this rally to celebrate the 100th birthday of the automobile. Averil sent her husband off with a little, two-level stepladder, to help relieve him when embarking and disembarking.

The rally was superbly organised, and the author of *Three-Pointed Star* received all the attention he had hoped for. This supercharged Mercedes with the British registration MSV584 wasn't the only one of its kind in the throng of veteran cars, but it was certainly one of the most beautiful models on show.

I had the pleasure of partaking in a (borrowed) 1938 BMW 328 sports. Our meeting after such a long time meant, for Bunty, the opportunity to introduce me to his table – in German.

Several of the ladies and gentlemen knew me already, but those who heard the introduction for the first time were just as stunned as I was: Bunty asserted that I had been his "Literary agent for Germany" for the past twenty years; that I was about to bring an important book of his to market. He did so very mysteriously, and I am quite sure that he was serious about writing another book. Perhaps his memoirs?

With astounding sprightliness, Bunty presented dozens of amusing stories, not with the full smoothness to which we were accustomed, but just as ornate and digressive as ever; he was his old self. And he loved the Baden wine.

When he clambered into the passenger seat of his Mercedes the following morning and disappeared off onto the Black Forest High Road with his driver Faud, his light leather cap was the last I ever saw of Bunty. The sound of his rumbling, 7-litre OHC engine must have been long-lost music to his ears.

Bunty's 79th birthday, which followed shortly after, was celebrated as merrily as ever. He accounted all the details to me: the best part was receiving a mobile phone – state-of-the-art technology back then. Everywhere he went, he would take this around and make endlessly long phone calls from the garage, the toilet, the garden, the kitchen.

Soon after, Lord Montagu was hosting a 60th birthday party, and although the party wasn't for Bunty, he became the centre of attention: he wore his canary-yellow jacket once more. For those who knew Bunty well, this registered as an indication that he was planning another trip to the Orient. As a matter of fact, this was indeed exactly what Bunty was scheming. Would he manage to persuade Penny into accompanying him once more …? No, she was unavailable. Rosemary likewise, and Hazel had to stay at home in order to lead the company.

In early 1987, Hazel celebrated her 25th year of service. The team organised a wonderful dinner party for her, which unfortunately came to a distressing conclusion: Bunty collapsed after a bilious attack and was rushed to hospital via ambulance.

Barely free of the gallstones, Bunty boarded a flight to Bombay (Mumbai today) – alone. Old friends were waiting for him upon arrival. A uniformed chauffeur drove him around for two weeks, wherever he pleased. If only he had been stopped from bathing in the Sal River at Benaulim. He promptly contracted an infection and returned immediately to England in shivers. He was taken from Heathrow directly to hospital …

Bunty's chatter was just as limitless as before. He entertained the staff and fellow patients with the most unbelievable stories. Indeed, it was in the middle of a particularly exciting tale about temple dancers from Udaipur that he suddenly lost consciousness. The doctors rang Averil immediately. She came running with Hazel to find a winking Bunty, who simply said: " … Now, where was I exactly?"

Five days later, he returned to Rock Cottage. His eightieth birthday was fast approaching; he wanted to celebrate it at home, rather than in a hospital.

"We never close"

IT WASN'T JUST BECAUSE of his birthday that Bunty wanted to escape hospital as quickly as possible. The local elections were taking place, and he didn't want a postal vote, he intended to show his support for the Tories on ballot paper. Every day, a nurse would visit him, care for his feet and listen patiently to all the stories that he would tell. The scene played out like a feuilleton, to which the nurse would listen as she bandaged her patient's legs.

Bunty professed to feeling better and better each day, and soon he was forging new travel plans. He fished out books about Polynesia from the bookcase and asked Hazel to enquire about flight prices to Tahiti. Before this, however, he wanted to celebrate his eightieth birthday party in spectacular fashion for two reasons; the year also marked the sixtieth anniversary of his company's inauguration.

"I can still picture him in front of me now, sat in pyjamas on the veranda," Hazel said. "He had the list of invited guests in his hand and the list of drinks to organise. We booked a jazz band, as we had at several birthday parties in times gone by." It became as hectic as ever, and Bunty was delighted that more guests than ever before were being invited, including several new friends that he had recently made in India.

For the first time in his life, Bunty appeared to exercise rationality of his own accord: "I ought not to get too excited," his wise words went, "I have to save my strength."

On Saturday morning, he called Hazel on his mobile phone. "Please come over here and speak to the people that are putting up the party tent. I think they're planning to put it up in the wrong place!" Hazel said she would just quickly tidy the kitchen and then be there in ten minutes.

Neville & Hillary were the company tasked with erecting the tent, an experienced caterer's, from whom Bunty had ordered his wine for decades. Hazel called the people and discovered that they were following Bunty's instructions precisely; the old gentleman needed reassuring. He had been strutting around in his pyjamas through the garden, giving constant and contradictory new instructions. Thereafter, Hazel rang Bunty back once more: "Bunty, you really have nothing to worry about …" before jokingly adding: "Perhaps it was a mistake, getting you that mobile phone last year? You're confounding all of us …"

He let out a dry 'hohoho' and hung up.

"It was the last time that I heard Bunty's voice. The next call I received came from Averil the following morning. She revealed to me that Bunty had passed away overnight.

"Averil was completely calm and composed. I also experienced no initial panic. The usual sadness, pain and yearning for the beloved oddball came later. Averil experienced the same. Bunty had raised the subject of death and burial so often in recent times that we knew exactly what to do …

"Humphrey and Judy had visited Rock Cottage just a couple of days before, deciding not to attend the big birthday party, and were already on their way back to Andorra. The very moment that Humphrey unlocked the front door, he received my telephone call; without even opening their suitcases, he and Judith turned around and took the first flight back. Ambrose and Claudia also travelled immediately to Rock Cottage."

Hazel found herself in the uncomfortable position of having to contact well over 200 birthday party invitees and inform them of the news – in 1987, there was no email, nor did most people have access to mobile phones. Many of those travelling from far and wide were already en route to the party destination. The party was due to take place on Wednesday; on Monday and Tuesday, Hazel worked her fingers to the bone on the telephone dial, sharing the sad news over and over. There were many, including the jazz band, whom she simply couldn't reach in time.

The events that unfolded on Wednesday July 1, 1987 at Rock Cottage are difficult to put into words. Excited and upbeat guests arrived, beeping and hooting, dressed for a garden party, with costly-wrapped presents under their arms, to be welcomed by others, wearing dark clothing, standing in the garden looking bleakly at the ground. Confusion was widespread, for those guests arriving abound with laughter and subsequent clamour were, of course, guests that Hazel had been unable to reach. It took a while for the realisation to sink in that this wasn't just another of Bunty's typical large-scale jokes.

Then, the roles changed. The sudden insecurity and helplessness of the uninformed caused the bereaved to offer their condolences and encouragement. And before long, it was a festive party once more. The longer the day went on, the more guests of both faculty arrived, neighbours and relatives in dark clothing and unassuming, excitable birthday well-wishers.

The popping of champagne proved a salvation, and the rather baffled Dixieland band eventually started to play. Bunty threw his final, great party. And it went ahead precisely as he would have wanted, whether he was alive and present or not. As far as his friends and guests were concerned, he was sitting in the corner, just out of sight, giggling with pleasure and twirling his moustache.

"We never close" was a figure of speech which Bunty loved to employ when his customers would show up outside of the company's listed opening hours. It seemed the perfect motto for this celebration too, at which nobody was supposed to be sad, on instruction of the deceased. Just as in life, Bunty was the centre of attention, everyone had a contribution to make which could only apply to him. The old man couldn't have wished for a more beautiful conclusion to such a fulfilling life. The old vicar who married Humphrey and Judy, Hermann Scott and Gerhard van Ackeren knew exactly what to say to everyone whom Bunty had held dear.

"This day should be celebrated with nothing more than happiness and rosé champagne," Gerhard concluded. "This is exactly what he would have asked, and we owe it to him to make this wish come true. After all, Bunty has given us all such extraordinary pleasure throughout his life!"

Epilogue

TO MY REGRET, I was unable to accept the invitation to the birthday party, because it fell while I was enjoying a trip through the USA, planned for a long time. When I returned to the news of Bunty's passing, I began to collect together everything I owned from him in the form of letters, fragments of manuscripts and photos. I had already published several articles about him during his lifetime. I spent weeks rummaging through my documents. Suddenly, an idea came to me, which Hazel had also thought of and suggested to me: to write a book about Bunty's life.

It lies before you now.

H S

> There was a young lady from Wantage
> of whom the town clerk took advantage.
> Said the borough surveyor:
> Of course you must pay her,
> You've altered the line of her frontage!
>
> D S M

Raymond Mays'
Magnificent Obsession

Bryan Apps – Foreword by Raymond Mays

This biography of Raymond Mays includes complete histories of ERA and
BRM, including race summaries, a foreword by Mays himself. Personal letters
addressed to the author from Alfred Owen, David Brown, Tony Rudd, Rivers
Fletcher, Bob Gerard, Ken Richardson, Juan Fangio, and many others add
intimacy to the story. Illustrated with over 100 of the author`s colour paintings.

ISBN: 978-1-845847-86-9
Hardback • 25x20.7cm • 208 pages • 243 pictures

For more information and price details, visit our website at www.veloce.co.uk
• email: info@veloce.co.uk • Tel: +44(0)1305 260068

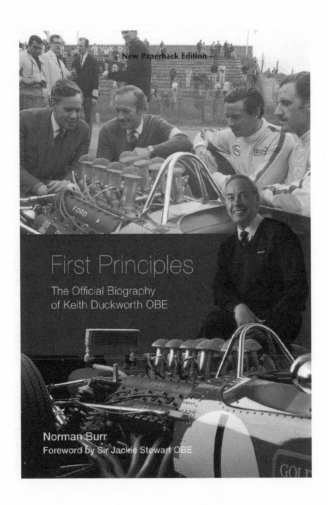

A chronicle of the life of Keith Duckworth OBE, the remarkable engineer, co-founder of Cosworth Engineering and creator of the most successful F1 engine of all time, the DFV. This is a rounded look at the life and work of the man – work which included significant contributions to aviation, motorcycling, and powerboating.

ISBN: 978-1-787111-03-5
Paperback • 23.2x15.5cm • 352 pages • 200 pictures

For more information and price details, visit our website at www.veloce.co.uk
• email: info@veloce.co.uk • Tel: +44(0)1305 260068

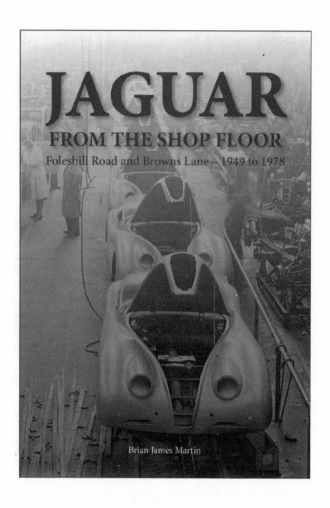

Part auto-biographical, and part historical, this book details life at the Jaguar company from the perspective of a long-time employee and enthusiast. Brian Martin's story tells of his experiences both on the production line and in the elite experimental department.

ISBN: 978-1-787112-79-7
Hardback • 23.2x15.5cm • 192 pages • 99 colour and b&w pictures

For more information and price details, visit our website at www.veloce.co.uk
• email: info@veloce.co.uk • Tel: +44(0)1305 260068